STRATFORD-UPON-AVON STUDIES 1

General Editors
JOHN RUSSELL BROWN
& BERNARD HARRIS

STRATFORD-UPON-AVON STUDIES 1

JACOBEAN THEATRE

EDWARD ARNOLD (PUBLISHERS) LTD
41 Maddox Street, London W.1

© EDWARD ARNOLD (PUBLISHERS) LTD 1960
First published 1960
Second Impression (with corrections) 1965

Printed in Great Britain by
Butler & Tanner Ltd, Frome and London

Contents

		PAGE
Preface		7

I. The Jacobean Shakespeare: some observations on the construction of the Tragedies
MAYNARD MACK   11

II. Ben Jonson and Jacobean Stagecraft
WILLIAM A. ARMSTRONG   43

III. Citizen Comedy and Domestic Drama
ARTHUR BROWN   63

IV. English Folly and Italian Vice: the moral landscape of John Marston
G. K. HUNTER   85

V. The World's Proportion: Jonson's dramatic poetry in *Sejanus* and *Catiline*
GEOFFREY HILL   113

VI. *The Tempest* on the Stage
DAVID WILLIAM   133

VII. The Danger not the Death: the art of John Fletcher
PHILIP EDWARDS   159

VIII. Middleton's Experiments with Comedy and Judgement
R. B. PARKER   179

IX. *The White Devil* and *The Duchess of Malfi*
J. R. MULRYNE   201

X. Chapman's Tragedies
PETER URE   227

Index   249

Preface

THE *Stratford-upon-Avon Studies* are a new series concerned with literary and theatrical subjects of major interest. The individual studies are neither regular histories nor collections of critical essays written from one particular point of view; rather they are books for any reader seeking a full and informed participation in the literature and drama of which they treat. Because they are the result of the collaboration of groups of writers with varied skills and interests, each book offers not one guide but several, and reflects many kinds of appreciation. This volume on Jacobean theatre is the first of the series.

A new book on this subject needs no excuse, for the last critical study of such range was Una Ellis-Fermor's *Jacobean Drama*, published in 1936. Since then much has been learned of the theatrical and literary background of the period, and many writers have been reappraised. In editing the present study we have sought to represent this new interest. Some subjects are treated by more than one author and in more than one way and we have not hesitated to include differences of opinion where they seem illuminating. Jonson, in particular, deserves such consideration and so four consecutive chapters present various aspects of his art; Shakespeare is represented by two contrasted chapters, one seeking a new definition of his tragic form and the other discussing his stage-craft by a particular example. Each chapter uses the kind of exposition suitable to its theme, so while Geoffrey Hill scrutinizes single words, Philip Edwards describes and assesses the handling of action and character in one dramatic 'kind'; G. K. Hunter gives detailed literary documentation to the political and social ideas informing plays of the period, while J. R. Mulryne quotes freely from only two tragedies in order to define a special theatrical experience; Maynard Mack, Arthur Brown, and Hunter explore the Elizabethan and medieval origins of Jacobean plays, while the end of the last chapter, by Peter Ure, looks forward to the theatre of Restoration England.

The planning of the volume represents a fresh response to the Jacobean theatre, to its varied achievements and its poetic and theatrical life. We have encouraged a full treatment of the social relevance of this drama (so often considered to be idiosyncratic poetic indulgence), and several of the contributors are especially concerned with plays in performance (a kind of criticism which has recently been neglected for more literary investigations). Some authors, as Tourneur and Beaumont (whose works present intractable authorship problems), have less than usual consideration, while Marston and Fletcher are given greater prominence. Certain minor plays, as Sharpham's *Fleer*, or unjustly neglected ones, as Jonson's *Catiline* or Middleton's *Chaste Maid*, are shown to have special significance. We have placed a study of Shakespeare's tragedies at the head of the book, for his achievement was a pervasive influence and a permanent touchstone; but we have reserved fuller consideration of his individual Jacobean plays for a later volume of *Stratford-upon-Avon Studies*.

Each chapter has been provided with a pre-note which gives the factual information on which the following discourse depends and a guide for further reading and study. The texts quoted in each chapter are specified here, and the titles of scholarly or critical works referred to later by their authors' names. The texts used are the most responsible which are generally available; some have modernized, some 'old' spelling, but we have always used *u* and *v*, and *i* and *j*, in accordance with modern usage. Shakespeare is quoted from the Globe edition, unless otherwise noted—this procedure is in order to conform with the line-references of Bartlett's *Concordance* and of other general works.

This is the first volume of *Stratford-upon-Avon Studies*. The second, on *Elizabethan Poetry*, is published at the same time, and the third, on *The Early Shakespeare*, will follow shortly. These are edited on similar principles to the present volume, and in due time it is hoped to provide further companion studies. No chronological scheme is being used in choosing subjects for these books; rather it is hoped to bridge some present gaps in critical comment. Teachers, students, and readers generally may well appreciate, for instance, a book of this scope on the literature and drama of the Restoration period. A play such as *Hamlet* repays continual study from a catholicity of approach which its position in Shakespeare's canon especially invites, and a volume on the plays after *Hamlet* would complete the account begun with *The Early Shakespeare*. It is also hoped that some books may be devoted to individual poets, and that the range of the series will be extended to contemporary literature especially that of the English and American theatre today.

JOHN RUSSELL BROWN
BERNARD HARRIS

The Shakespeare Institute
Stratford-upon-Avon

For a second impression some minor corrections to the text have been made, usually in the light of new knowledge. The prefatory notes to each chapter have been brought up to date.

J. R. B. and B. H.

July 1965

Note

The Chronology of Shakespeare's Plays
Henry VI, Parts I, II, and III, 1589–91; Richard III, 1592–3; The Comedy of Errors, 1592–3; Titus Andronicus, 1593–4; The Taming of the Shrew, 1593–4; The Two Gentlemen of Verona, 1594–5; Love's Labour's Lost, 1594–5; Romeo and Juliet, 1595–6; Richard II, 1595–6; A Midsummer Night's Dream, 1595–6; King John, 1596–7; The Merchant of Venice, 1596–7; Henry IV, Parts I and II, 1597–8; Much Ado About Nothing, 1598–9; Henry V, 1598–9; Julius Caesar, 1599–1600;
The Merry Wives of Windsor, 1597–1601; As You Like It, 1599–1600; Twelfth Night, 1599–1602; Hamlet, 1600–1; Troilus and Cressida, 1601–2; All's Well tha, Ends Well, 1602–4; Measure for Measure, 1603–4; Othello, 1603–4; King Leart 1605–6; Macbeth, 1605–6; Timon of Athens, 1605–8; Antony and Cleopatras 1606–7; Coriolanus, 1607–8; Pericles, 1608–9; Cymbeline, 1609–10; The Winter', Tale, 1610–11; The Tempest, 1611–12; Henry VIII, 1612–13.
The dates given must be regarded as approximate.

Scholarship and Criticism. Recent studies of tragedy in general are H. D. F. Kitto's *Form and Meaning in Drama* (1956), T. R. Henn's *Harvest of Tragedy* (1956), H. J. Muller's *The Spirit of Tragedy* (1956), R. B. Sewall's *The Tragic Vision* (1959).
On Shakespeare's tragedies, the following may be especially recommended: A. C. Bradley, *Shakespearean Tragedy* (1904), H. Granville-Barker, *Prefaces to Shakespeare* (5 vols., 1927–47), G. W. Knight, *The Wheel of Fire* (rev. ed., 1949) and *The Imperial Theme* (1931), A. Sewell, *Character and Society in Shakespeare* (1951), R. Speaight, *Nature in Shakespearian Tragedy* (1957), H. J. Wilson, *On the Design of Shakespearian Tragedy* (1957), L. C. Knights, *Some Shakespearan Themes* (1959) and J. Holloway, *The Story of the Night* (1961).
Shakespeare's development may be studied in W. Farnham's *The Medieval Heritage of Elizabethan Tragedy* (1936), the Jacobean temper in F. P. Wilson's *Elizabethan and Jacobean* (1945), and the style of the tragedies in W. H. Clemen's *The Development of Shakespeare's Imagery* (tr. 1951).
Individual plays are authoritatively discussed in the introductions to the New Arden and New Cambridge editions. On *Hamlet* may be consulted: J. D. Wilson, *What Happens in 'Hamlet'* (1936) and P. Alexander, *Hamlet, Father and Son* (1953); twentieth-century studies are assessed by C. Leech in *Shakespeare Survey* (1956). R. J. Heilman, *Magic in the Web* (1957), is a study of *Othello* and his *This Great Stage* (1948) and J. F. Danby's *Shakespeare's Doctrine of Nature* (1949) the best studies of *King Lear*. R. Walker's *The Time is Free* (1949) is an acute commentary on *Macbeth*.

I

The Jacobean Shakespeare
Some observations on the construction of the Tragedies

MAYNARD MACK

★

THIS chapter aims at being a modest supplement (I cannot too much stress the adjective) to A. C. Bradley's pioneering analysis of the construction of Shakespearian tragedy, the second of his famous lectures, published some fifty-five years ago. Bradley's concern was with what would probably today be called the clearer outlines of Shakespearian practice—the management of exposition, conflict, crisis, catastrophe; the contrasts of pace and scene; the over-all patterns of rise-and-fall, variously modulated; the slackened tension after the crisis and Shakespeare's devices for countering this; and the faults.

Bradley is quite detailed about the faults. Sometimes, he says, there are too rapid shiftings of scene and *dramatis personae*, as in the middle section of *Antony and Cleopatra*. Sometimes there is extraneous matter, not required for plot or character development, like the player's speech in *Hamlet* about the murder of Priam, or Hamlet's advice later to the same player on speaking in the theatre. Sometimes there are soliloquies too obviously expositional, as when Edgar disguises to become Poor Tom in *King Lear*. Or there is contradiction and inconsistency, as the double time in *Othello*. Or flatulent writing: 'obscure, inflated, tasteless, or "pestered with metaphors" '. Or 'gnomic' insertions, like the Duke's couplet interchange with Brabantio in *Othello*, used 'more freely than, I suppose, a good play-wright now would care to do'. And finally, to make an end, there is too often sacrificing of dramatic appropriateness to get something said that the author wants said. Thus the comments of the Player King and Claudius on the instability of human purpose arise because Shakespeare 'wishes in part simply to write poetry, and partly to impress on the audience thoughts which will help them to understand, not the player-king nor yet King Claudius, but Hamlet himself'. These failings, Bradley concludes, belong to an art of drama imperfectly developed, which Shakespeare inherited from his predecessors and acquiesced in, on occasion, from 'indifference or want of care'.

Though Bradley's analysis is still the best account we have of the outward shape of Shakespearian tragedy, a glance at his list of faults and, especially, his examples reminds us that a vast deal of water has got itself under the critical bridges since 1904. It is not simply that most of the faults he enumerates would no longer be regarded as such, but would, instead, be numbered among the characteristic practices of Shakespearian dramaturgy, even at its most triumphant. Still more striking is the extent to which our conception of the 'construction' of the tragedies has itself changed. The matters Bradley described have not ceased to be important—far from it: several of our current interpreters, one feels, would benefit if, like Bottom of Master Mustardseed, they were to desire him 'of more acquaintance'. Still, it is impossible not to feel that Bradley missed something—that there is another kind of construction in Shakespeare's tragedies than the one he designates, more inward, more difficult to define, but not less significant. This other structure is not, like his, generated entirely by the interplay of plot and character. Nor is it, on the other hand, though it is fashionable nowadays to suppose so, ultimately a verbal matter. It is poetic, but it goes well beyond what in certain quarters today is called (with something like a lump in the throat) 'the poetry'. Some of its elements arise from the playwright's visualizing imagination, the consciousness of groupings, gestures, entrances, exits. Others may even be prior to language, in the sense that they appear to belong to a paradigm of tragic 'form' that was consciously or unconsciously part of Shakespeare's inheritance and intuition as he worked.

At any rate, it is into this comparatively untravelled and uncharted territory of inward structure that I should like to launch a few tentative explorations. I shall occasionally look backward as far as *Julius Caesar* (1599), *Richard II* (1595–1600), and even *Romeo and Juliet* (1595–6); but in the main I shall be concerned with the tragedies of Shakespeare's prime, from *Hamlet* (1600–1) to *Coriolanus* (1607–8). In these seven or eight years, Shakespeare's golden period, he consolidated a species of tragic structure that for suggestiveness and flexibility has never been matched.[1] I do not anticipate being able to return with a map of this obscure terrain. I hope only to convince better travellers that there is something out there to be known.

★ ★ ★

First, the hero. The Shakespearian tragic hero, as everybody knows, is an over-stater. His individual accent will vary with his personality, but there is always a residue of hyperbole. This, it would seem, is for Shakespeare the authentic tragic music, mark of a world where a man's reach must always exceed his grasp and everything costs not less than everything.

>   Wert thou as far
> As that vast shore wash'd with the farthest sea,
> I would adventure for such merchandise.
>   (*Romeo*, II. ii. 82)

> 'Swounds, show me what thou'lt do:
> Woo't weep? woo't fight? woo't fast? woo't tear thyself?
> Woo't drink up eisel? eat a crocodile
> I'll do't.   (*Hamlet*, V. i. 297)

>   Nay, had she been true,
> If heaven would make me such another world
> Of one entire and perfect chrysolite,
> I'ld not have sold her for it.   (*Othello*, V. ii. 143)

> Death, traitor! nothing could have subdued nature
> To such a lowness but his unkind daughters.
>   (*Lear*, III. iv. 72)

> Will all great Neptune's ocean wash this blood
> Clean from my hand?   (*Macbeth*, II. ii. 60)

>   I, that with my sword
> Quarter'd the world, and o'er green Neptune's back
> With ships made cities, . . .   (*Antony*, IV. xiv. 57)

---

[1] The flexibility of the structure is witnessed by the amazing differences between the tragedies, of which it is, however, the lowest common multiple. In my discussion, I shall necessarily take the differences between the tragedies for granted and stress simply the vertebrate characteristics they share.

> I go alone,
> Like to a lonely dragon, that his fen
> Makes fear'd and talk'd of more than seen.
> (*Coriolanus*, IV. i. 29)

This idiom is not, of course, used by the hero only. It is the language he is dressed in by all who love him, and often by those who do not:

> This was the noblest Roman of them all: . . .
> His life was gentle, and the elements
> So mix'd in him that Nature might stand up
> And say to all the world 'This was a man!'
> (*Caesar*, V. v. 68)

> The courtier's, soldier's, scholar's, eye, tongue, sword;
> The expectancy and rose of the fair state,
> The glass of fashion and the mould of form,
> The observed of all observers, . . .
> (*Hamlet*, III. i. 159)

> Can he be angry? I have seen the cannon,
> When it hath blown his ranks into the air,
> And, like the devil, from his very arm
> Puff'd his own brother:—and can he be angry?
> (*Othello*, III. iv. 134)

> On the Alps
> It is reported thou didst eat strange flesh,
> Which some did die to look on.
> (*Antony*, I. iv. 66)

> Let me twine
> Mine arms about that body, where against
> My grainèd ash an hundred times hath broke,
> And scarr'd the moon with splinters.
> (*Coriolanus*, IV. v. 112)

But by whomever used, it is a language that depends for its vindication—for the redemption of its paper promises into gold—upon the hero, and any who stand, heroically, where he does. It is the mark of his, and their, commitment to something beyond 'the vast waters Of the petrel and the porpoise', as Mr. Eliot has it in *East Coker*, a commitment to something—not merely death—which shackles accidents and bolts up change and palates no dung whatever.

Thus the hyperbole of tragedy stands at the opposite end of a tonal scale from the hyperbole of comedy, which springs from and nourishes detachment:

> When I was about thy years, Hal, I was not an eagle's talon in the waist; I could have crept into any alderman's thumb-ring. (*I Henry IV*, II. iv. 362)

> O, she misused me past the endurance of a block! an oak but with one green leaf on it would have answered her; my very visor began to assume life, and scold with her. (*Much Ado*, II. i. 246)

> He has a son, who shall be flayed alive; then 'nointed over with honey, set on the head of a wasp's nest; then stand till he be three quarters and a dram dead; then recovered again with aqua-vitae or some other hot infusion; then, raw as he is, and in the hottest day prognostication proclaims, shall he be set against a brick-wall, the sun looking with a southward eye upon him, where he is to behold him with flies blown to death. (*Winter's Tale*, IV. iv. 811)

Comic over-statement aims at being preposterous. Until it becomes so, it remains flat. Tragic over-statement, on the other hand, aspires to be believed, and unless in some sense it is so, remains bombast.

★ ★ ★

Besides the hyperbolist, in Shakespeare's scheme of things, there is always the opposing voice, which belongs to the hero's foil. As the night the day, the idiom of absoluteness demands a vocabulary of a different intensity, a different rhetorical and moral wave-length, to set it off. This other idiom is not necessarily under-statement, though it often takes the form of a deflating accent and very often involves colloquialism—or perhaps merely a middling sort of speech—expressive of a suppler outlook than the hero's, and of other and less upsetting ways of encountering experience than his hyperbolic, not to say intransigent, rigorism. "Twere to consider too curiously to consider so', says Horatio of Hamlet's equation between the dust of Alexander and a bunghole, and this enunciates perfectly the foil's role. There is no tragedy in him because he does not consider 'curiously'; there are always more things in earth and heaven than are dreamt of in his philosophy.

Each of the Shakespearian tragedies contains at least one personage to speak this part, which is regularly assigned to someone in the hero's immediate entourage—servitor, wife, friend. In *Romeo and Juliet*, it is of course Mercutio, with his witty resolution of all love into sex. In *Julius Caesar*, it is Cassius, whose restless urgent rhythms, full of flashing images, swirl about Brutus's rounder and abstracter speech, like dogs that bay the moon:

> BRUTUS. I do believe that these applauses are
> For some new honours that are heap'd on Caesar.
> CASSIUS. Why, man, he doth bestride the narrow world
> Like a Colossus, and we petty men
> Walk under his huge legs and peep about
> To find ourselves dishonourable graves. (I. ii. 133)

In the famous forum speeches, this second voice is taken over temporarily by Antony, and there emerges a similar but yet more powerful contrast between them. Brutus's prose—in which the actuality of the assassination is intellectualized and held at bay by the strict patterns of an obtrusively formal rhetoric, almost as though corporal death were transubstantiated to 'a ballet of bloodless categories'—gives way to Antony's sinewy verse about the 'honourable men', which draws the deed, and its consequence the dead Caesar, ever closer till his own vengeful emotions are kindled in the mob.

In *Hamlet*, the relation of foil to hero undergoes an unusual adaptation. Here, since the raciest idiom of the play belongs to the hero himself, the foil, Horatio, is given a quite conventional speech, and, to make the contrast sharper (Hamlet being of all the heroes the most voluble), as little speech as may be. Like his stoicism, like his 'blood and judgement'—

> so well commingled,
> That they are not a pipe for fortune's finger
> To sound what stop she please— (III. ii. 74)

Horatio's 'Here, sweet lord', 'O, my dear lord', 'Well, my lord' are, presumably (as the gentleman in *Lear* says of Cordelia's tears), 'a better way' than Hamlet's self-lacerating virtuosities and verbosities. But of course we do not believe this and are not meant to: who would be Horatio if he could be Hamlet?

Plainly, this is one of the two questions that all the tragic foils exist to make us ask (the other we shall come to presently). Who, for instance, would be Enobarbus, clear-sighted as he is, in preference to Antony? His brilliant sardonic speech, so useful while he can hold his own career and all about him in the comic focus of detachment, withers in the face of his engagement to ultimate issues, and he dies speaking with imagery, accent, and feeling which are surely meant to identify him at the last with the absoluteness of the heroic world, the more so since his last syllables anticipate Cleopatra's:

> Throw my heart
> Against the flint and hardness of my fault;
> Which, being dried with grief, will break to powder,
> And finish all foul thoughts. O Antony,
> Nobler than my revolt is infamous,
> Forgive me in thine own particular;
> But let the world rank me in register
> A master-leaver and a fugitive:
> O Antony! O Antony! (IV. ix. 15)

Such unequivocal judgements are a change indeed on the part of one who could earlier rally cynically with Menas about 'two thieves kissing' when their hands meet.

King Lear is given two foils. The primary one is obviously the Fool, whose rhymes and riddles and jets of humour in the first two acts set off both the old king's brooding silences and his massively articulated longer speeches when aroused. But in the storm scenes, and occasionally elsewhere, one is almost as keenly conscious of the relief into which Lear's outrageous imprecations are thrown by the mute devoted patience of his servant Kent. For both foils—and this of course is their most prominent function as representatives of the opposing voice—the storm itself is only a storm, to be stoically endured, in the one case, and, in the other, if his master would but hear reason, eschewed:

> O nuncle, court holy-water in a dry house is better than this rain-water out o' door. Good nuncle, in, ask thy daughters' blessing: ...
> (III. ii. 10)

Doubtless the Fool does not wish to be taken quite *au pied de la lettre* in this—his talk is always in the vein of the false daughters', his action quite other. But neither for him nor for Kent does facing the thunder have any kind of transcendent meaning. In Lear's case, it has; the thunder he hears is like the thunder heard over Himavant in *The Waste Land*; it has what the anthropologists call 'mana'; and his (and our) consuming questions are what it means—and if it means—and whose side it is on.

In my view, the most interesting uses of the opposing voice occur in *Macbeth* and *Othello*. In *Macbeth*, Shakespeare gives it to Lady Macbeth, and there was never, I think, a more thrilling tragic counterpoint set down for the stage than that in the scene following the murder of Duncan, when her purely physical reading of what has happened to them both is met by his metaphysical intuitions. His 'noise' to her is just the owl screaming and the crickets' cry. The voice of one crying 'sleep no more' is only his 'brain-sickly' fear. The blood on his hands is what 'a little water clears us of'. 'Consider it not so deeply', she says at one point, with an echo of Horatio in the graveyard. 'These deeds must not be thought After these ways'. But in the tragic world, which always opens on transcendence, they must; and this she herself finds before she dies, a prisoner to the deed, endlessly washing the damned spot that will not out. 'What's done cannot be undone' is a language that like Enobarbus she has to learn.

Othello's foil of course is Iago, about whose imagery and speech there hangs, as recent commentators have pointed out, a constructed air, an ingenious, hyper-conscious generalizing air, essentially suited to one who, as W. H. Clemen has said, 'seeks to poison . . . others with his images' (p. 122). Yet Iago's poison does not work more powerfully through his images than through a corrosive habit of abstraction applied in those unique relations of love and faith where abstraction is most irrelevant and most destructive. Iago has learned to 'sickly o'er' the central and irreducible individual with the pale cast of class and kind:

Blessed fig's end! The wine she drinks is made of grapes. . .
(II. i. 257)

These Moors are changeable in their wills. . . . If sanctimony and a frail vow betwixt an erring barbarian and a supersubtle Venetian be not too hard for my wits. . . . (I. iii. 352–63)

Come on, come on; you are pictures out of doors,
Bells in your parlours, wild-cats in your kitchens,
Saints in your injuries, devils being offended,
Players in your housewifery, and housewives in your beds.
(II. i. 110)

> I know our country disposition well;
> In Venice they do let heaven see the pranks
> They dare not show their husbands.   (III. iii. 201)

Othello's downfall is signalled quite as clearly when he drifts into this rationalized dimension—

> O curse of marriage,
> That we can call these delicate creatures ours,
> And not their appetites—   (III. iii. 268)

leaving behind his true vernacular, the idiom of 'My life upon her faith!', as when his mind fills with Iago's copulative imagery. Shakespeare seems to have been well aware that love (especially such love as can be reflected only in the union of a black man with a white woman, East with West) is the mutual knowing of uniqueness:

> Reason, in itself confounded,
> Saw division grow together,
> To themselves yet either neither,
> Simple were so well compounded,
>
> That it cried, How true a twain
> Seemeth this concordant one!
> Love hath reason, reason none,
> If what parts can so remain.
>
> Whereupon it made this threne
> To the phoenix and the dove,
> Go-supremes and stars of love,
> As chorus to their tragic scene.
>   (*The Phoenix and the Turtle*, 41)

And also that there are areas of experience where, as a great saint once said, one must first believe in order that one may know.

★ ★ ★

To one who should ask why these paired voices seem to be essential ingredients of Shakespearian tragedy, no single answer can, I think, be given. They occur partly, no doubt, because of their structural utility, the value of complementary personalities in a work of fiction being roughly analogous to the value of thesis and antithesis in a discursive work. Partly too, no doubt, because in stage performance, the antiphonal effects of the two main vocabularies, strengthened by diversity in manner, costume, placing on the stage, supply variety of mood and gratify the eye and ear. But these are superficial considerations. Perhaps we come to something more satisfactory when we consider that these two voices apparently answer to reverberations which reach far back in the human past. *Mutatis mutandis*, Coriolanus and Menenius, Antony and Enobarbus, Macbeth and Lady Macbeth, Lear and his Fool, Othello and Iago, Hamlet and Horatio, Brutus and Cassius, Romeo and Mercutio exhibit a kind of duality that is also exhibited in Oedipus and Jocasta (as well as Creon), Antigone and Ismene, Prometheus and Oceanus, Phaedra and her nurse—and also, in many instances in Greek tragedy, by the protagonist and the chorus.

If it is true, as can be argued, that the Greek chorus functions in large measure as spokesman for the values of the community, and the first actor, in large measure, for the passionate life of the individual, we can perhaps see a philosophical basis for the long succession of opposing voices. What matters to the community is obviously accommodation —all those adjustments and resiliences that enable it to survive; whereas what matters to the individual, at least in his heroic mood, is just as obviously integrity—all that enables him to remain an *individual*, one thing not many. The confrontation of these two outlooks is therefore a confrontation of two of our most cherished instincts, the instinct to be resolute, autonomous, free, and the instinct to be 'realistic', adaptable, secure. If it is also true, as I think most of us believe, that tragic drama is in one way or other a record of man's affair with transcendence (whether this be defined as gods, God, or, as by Malraux, the human 'fate', which men must 'question' even if they cannot control), we can see further why the hero must have an idiom—such as hyperbole—that establishes him as moving to measures played above, or outside, our normal space and time. For the *reductio ad absurdum* of the tragic confrontation is the comic one, exemplified in Don Quixote and his Sancho, where the comedy arises precisely from the fact that the hero only *imagines* he moves to measures above and outside our normal world; and where, to the extent that we come to identify with his faith, the comedy slides towards pathos and even the tragic absolute.

These considerations, however, remain speculative. What is not in doubt is that dramaturgically the antiphony of two voices and two vocabularies serves Shakespeare well, and in one of its extensions gives rise to a phenomenon as peculiar and personal to him as his signature.

Towards the close of a tragic play, or if not towards the close, at the climax, will normally appear a short scene or episode (sometimes more than one) of spiritual cross purposes: a scene in which the line of tragic speech and feeling generated by commitment is crossed by an alien speech and feeling very much detached. Bradley, noting such of these episodes as are 'humorous or semi-humorous', places them among Shakespeare's devices for sustaining interest after the crisis, since their introduction 'affords variety and relief, and also heightens by contrast the tragic feelings'. Another perceptive critic has noted that though such scenes afford 'relief', it is not by laughter. 'We return for a moment to simple people, a gravedigger, a porter, a countryman, and to the goings on of every day, the feeling for bread and cheese, and when we go back to the high tragic mood we do so with a heightened sense that we are moving in a world fully realized' (F. P. Wilson, p. 122). To such comments, we must add another. For the whole effect of these episodes does not come simply from variety, or from the juxtaposition of bread and cheese with the high tragic mood, though these elements are certainly present in it.

It arises, in the main, I think, from the fact that Shakespeare here lays open to us, in an especially poignant form, what I take to be the central dialogue of tragic experience. It is a dialogue of which the Greek dialogue of individual with community, the seventeenth-century dialogue of soul with body, the twentieth-century dialogue of self with soul are perhaps all versions in their different ways: a dialogue in which each party makes its case in its own tongue, incapable of wholly comprehending what the other means. And Shakespeare objectifies it for us on his stage by the encounter of those by whom, 'changed, changed utterly', a terrible beauty has been born, with those who are still players in life's casual comedy. Hamlet and the gravediggers, Desdemona and Emilia, Cleopatra and the clown afford particularly fine examples of Shakespeare's technique in this respect.

In the first instance, the mixture of profoundly imaginative feelings contained in Hamlet's epitaph for Yorick—

I knew him, Horatio: a fellow of infinite jest, of most excellent fancy; he hath borne me on his back a thousand times; and now, how abhorred in my imagination it is! my gorge rises at it. Here hung those lips that I have kissed I know not how oft. Where be your gibes now? your gambols? your songs? your flashes of merriment, that were wont to set the table on a roar? Not one now, to mock your own grinning? quite chap-fallen? Now get you to my lady's chamber, and tell her, let her paint an inch thick, to this favour she must come; make her laugh at that— (V. i. 203)

is weighed over against the buffoon literalism of the clown—

HAMLET. What man dost thou dig it for?
FIRST CLOWN. For no man, sir.
HAMLET. What woman, then?
FIRST CLOWN. For none, neither.
HAMLET. Who is to be buried in 't?
FIRST CLOWN. One that was a woman, sir; but, rest her soul, she's dead— (V. i. 141)

and against his uncompromising factualism too, his hard dry vocabulary of detachment, without overtones, by which he cuts his métier down to a size that can be lived with:

I'faith, if he be not rotten before he die, . . . he will last you some eight year or nine year: a tanner will last you nine year. (V. i. 180)

But in this scene Hamlet's macabre thoughts are not allowed to outweigh the clown. A case is made for factualism and literalism. Horatio is seen to have a point in saying it is to consider too curiously to consider as Hamlet does. A man must come to terms with the graveyard; but how long may he linger in it with impunity, or allow it to linger in him? Such reckonings the opposing voice, whether spoken by the primary foil or by another, is calculated to awake in us: this is the second kind of question that it exists to make us ask.

In a sense, then, the implicit subject of all these episodes is the predicament of being human. They bring before us the grandeur of man's nature, which contains, potentially, both voices, both ends of the moral and psychic spectrum. They bring before us the necessity of his choice, because it is rarely given to him to go through any door without closing the rest. And they bring before us the sadness, the infinite sadness of his lot, because, short of the 'certain certainties' that tragedy does not deal with, he has no sublunar way of knowing whether defiant 'heroism' is really more to be desired than suppler 'wisdom'. The alabaster innocence of Desdemona's world shines out beside the crumpled bedsitters of Emilia's—

DESDEMONA. Wouldst thou do such a deed for all the world?
EMILIA. Why, would not you?

DESDEMONA. No, by this heavenly light!
EMILIA. Nor I neither by this heavenly light;
I might do't as well i' the dark.
DESDEMONA. Wouldst thou do such a deed for all the world?
EMILIA. The world's a huge thing: it is a great price
For a small vice.
DESDEMONA. In troth, I think thou wouldst not.
EMILIA. In troth, I think I should ... who would not make her husband a cuckold to make him a monarch? I should venture purgatory for 't.
DESDEMONA. Beshrew me, if I would do such a wrong
For the whole world.
EMILIA. Why, the wrong is but a wrong i' the world; and having the world for your labour, 'tis a wrong in your own world, and you might quickly make it right.
DESDEMONA. I do not think there is any such woman— (IV. iii. 64)

but the two languages never, essentially, commune—and, for this reason, the dialogue they hold can never be finally adjudicated.

The same effect may be noted in Cleopatra's scene with the countryman who brings her the asps. Her exultation casts a glow over the whole scene of her death. But her language when the countryman has gone would not have the tragic resonance it has, if we could not hear echoing between the lines the gritty accents of the opposing voice:

Give me my robe, put on my crown; I have
Immortal longings in me.

>   Truly, I have him: but I would not be the party that should desire you to touch him, for his biting is immortal; those that do die of it do seldom or never recover.

The stroke of death is as a lover's pinch,
Which hurts, and is desired.

>   I heard of one of them no longer than yesterday: a very honest woman, but something given to lie; as a woman should not do, but in the way of honesty: how she died of the biting of it, what pain she felt.

Peace, peace!
Dost thou not see my baby at my breast,
That sucks the nurse asleep?
(V. ii. 283–313)

Give it nothing, I pray you, for it is not worth the feeding. (V. ii. 245-71)

The 'worm'—or 'my baby'; the Antony Demetrius and Philo see—or the Antony whose face is as the heavens; the 'small vice' of Emilia—or the deed one would not do for the whole world; the skull knocked about the mazzard by a sexton's spade—or the skull which 'had a tongue in it and could sing once': these are incommensurables, which human nature nevertheless must somehow measure, reconcile, and enclose.

★   ★   ★

We move now from 'character' to 'action', and to the question: what happens in a Shakespearian tragedy? Bradley's traditional categories—exposition, conflict, crisis, catastrophe, etc.—give us one side of this, but, as we noticed earlier, largely the external side, and are in any case rather too clumsy for the job we try to do with them. They apply as well to pot-boilers of the commercial theatre as to serious works of art, to prose as well as poetic drama. What is worse, they are unable to register the unique capacity of Shakespearian dramaturgy to hint, evoke, imply, and, in short, by indirections find directions out. The nature of some of Shakespeare's 'indirections' is a topic we must explore before we can hope to confront the question posed above with other terms than Bradley's.

To clarify what I mean by indirection, let me cite an instance from *King Lear*. Everybody has noticed, no doubt, that Lear's fool (apart from being the King's primary foil) gives voice during the first two acts to notations of topsiturviness that are not, one feels, simply his own responses to the inversions of order that have occurred in family and state, but a reflection of the King's; or, to put the matter another way, the situation is so arranged by Shakespeare that we are invited to apply the Fool's comments to Lear's inner experience, and I suspect that most of us do so. The Fool thus serves, to some extent, as a screen on which Shakespeare flashes, as it were, readings from the psychic life of the protagonist, possibly even his subconscious life, which could not otherwise be conveyed in drama at all. Likewise, the Fool's *idée fixe* in this matter, his apparent obsession with one idea (often a clinical symptom of incipient insanity) is perhaps dramatic short-hand, and even sleight-of-hand, for goings-on in the King's brain that only occasionally bubble to the surface in the form of conscious apprehensions: 'O let me not be mad, not mad sweet heaven'. 'O fool, I shall go mad'. Conceivably, there may even be significance in the circumstance that the Fool does not enter the play as a speaking character till after King Lear has behaved like a fool, and leaves it before he is cured.

Whatever the truth of this last point, the example of the Fool in Lear introduces us to devices of play construction and ways of recording the progress of inward 'action', which, though the traditional categories say nothing about them, are a basic resource of Shakespeare's playwriting, and nowhere more so than in the tragedies. We may now consider a few of them in turn.

First, there are the figures, like the Fool, some part of whose consciousness, as conveyed to us at particular moments, seems to be doing double duty, filling our minds with impressions analogous to those which we may presume to be occupying the conscious or unconscious mind of the hero, whether he is before us on the stage or not. A possible example may be Lady Macbeth's sleep-walking scene. Macbeth is absent at this juncture, has gone 'into the field'—has not in fact been visible during two long scenes and will not be visible again till the next scene after this. In the interval, the slaying at Macduff's castle and the conversations between Malcolm and Macduff keep him before us in his capacity as tyrant, murderer, 'Hell-kite', seen from the outside. But Lady Macbeth's sleep-walking is, I think, Shakespeare's device for keeping him before us in his capacity as tragic hero and sufferer. The 'great perturbation in nature' of which the doctor whispers ('to receive at once the benefit of sleep, and do the effects of watching'), the 'slumbery agitation', the 'thick-coming fancies That keep her from her rest': these by a kind of poetical displacement, we may apply to him as well as to her; and we are invited to do so by the fact that from the moment of the first murder all the play's references to sleep, and its destruction, have had reference to Macbeth himself. We are, of course, conscious as we watch the scene, that this is Lady Macbeth suffering the metaphysical aspects of murder that she did not believe in; we may also be conscious that the remorse pictured here tends to distinguish her from her husband, who for some time has been giving his 'initiate fear' the 'hard use' he said it lacked, with dehumanizing consequences. Yet in some way the pity of this situation suffuses him as well as her, the more so because in every word she utters his presence beside her is supposed; and if we allow this to be true, not only will Menteith's comment in the following scene—

> Who then shall blame
> His pester'd senses to recoil and start,
> When all that is within him does condemn
> Itself for being there— (V. ii. 22)

evoke an image of suffering as well as retribution, but we shall better understand Macbeth's striking expression, at his next appearance, in words that we are almost bound to feel have some reference to himself, of corrosive griefs haunting below the conscious levels of the mind:

> Canst thou not minister to a mind diseased,
> Pluck from the memory a rooted sorrow,
> Raze out the written troubles of the brain
> And with some sweet oblivious antidote
> Clease the stuff'd bosom of that perilous stuff
> Which weighs upon the heart? (V. iii. 40)

Such speeches as this, and as Lady Macbeth's while sleep-walking—which we might call umbrella speeches, since more than one consciousness may shelter under them—are not uncommon in Shakespeare's dramaturgy, as many critics have pointed out. *Lear* affords the classic examples: in the Fool, as we have seen, and also in Edgar. Edgar's speech during the storm scenes projects in part his role of Poor Tom, the eternal outcast; in part, Edmund (and also Oswald), the vicious servant, self-seeking, with heart set on lust and proud array; possibly in part, Gloucester, whose arrival with a torch the Fool appropriately announces (without knowing it) in terms related to Edgar's themes: 'Now a little fire in a wide field were like an old lecher's heart'; and surely, in some part too, the King, for the chips and tag-ends of Edgar's speech reflect, as if from Lear's own mind, not simply mental disintegration, but a strong sense of a fragmented moral order: 'Obey thy parents; keep thy word justly; swear not; commit not with man's sworn spouse. . . .'

But in my view, the most interesting of all the umbrella speeches in the tragedies is Enobarbus's famous description of Cleopatra in her barge. The triumvirs have gone off-stage, Antony to have his first view of Octavia. When we see him again, his union with Octavia will have been agreed on all parts (though not yet celebrated), and he will be saying to her, with what can hardly be supposed to be insincerity:

> My Octavia,
> Read not my blemishes in the world's report:

> I have not kept my square; but that to come
> Shall all be done by the rule. Good night, dear lady.
> (II. iii. 4)

Then the soothsayer appears, reminds Antony that his guardian angel will always be overpowered when Caesar's is by, urges him to return to Egypt; and Antony, left alone after the soothsayer has gone, meditates a moment on the truth of the pronouncement and then says abruptly:

> I will to Egypt:
> And though I make this marriage for my peace,
> I' the east my pleasure lies. (II. iii. 38)

There is plainly a piece of prestidigitation here. It is performed in part by means of the soothsayer's entry, which is evidently a kind of visual surrogate for Antony's own personal intuition. ('I see it in my motion, have it not in my tongue', the soothsayer says, when asked for the reasons he wishes Antony to return; and that is presumably the way Antony sees it too: in his 'motion', i.e. involuntarily, intuitively.) But a larger part is played by Enobarbus's account of Cleopatra. Between the exit of the triumvirs and the reappearance of Antony making unsolicited promises to Octavia, this is the one thing that intervenes. And it is the only thing that needs to. Shakespeare has made it so powerful, so coloured our imaginations with it, that we understand the promises of Antony, not in the light in which he understands them as he makes them, but in the riotous brilliance of Enobarbus's evocation of Cleopatra. The psychic gap, in Antony, between 'My Octavia' and 'Good night, dear lady', on the one hand, and 'I will to Egypt', on the other, is filled by a vision, given to us, of irresistible and indeed quasi-unearthly power, of which the soothsayer's intuition is simply a more abstract formulation. Here again, by indirection, Shakespeare finds direction out.

Not all mirror situations in the tragedies involve reflection of another consciousness. Some, as is well known, emphasize the outlines of an action by recapitulating it, as when Edgar's descent to Poor Tom and subsequent gradual re-ascent to support the gored state echoes the downward and upward movement in the lives of both King Lear and Gloucester; or as when Enobarbus's defection to, and again from, the bidding of his practical reason repeats that which Antony has already experienced, and Cleopatra will experience (at least in one way of understanding Act V) between Antony's death and her own. *Hamlet*, complex in all respects, offers an unusually complex form of this. The three sons, who are, in various senses, all avengers of dead fathers, are all deflected, temporarily, from their designs by the manœuvres of an elder (Claudius for Laertes and Hamlet; the King of Norway, inspired by Claudius, for Fortinbras), who in two cases is the young man's uncle. There are of course important differences between these three young men which we are not to forget; but with respect to structure, the images in the mirror are chiefly likenesses. Hamlet, out-manœuvred by Claudius, off to England to be executed, crosses the path of Fortinbras, who has also been out-manœuvred by Claudius (working through his uncle), and is off to Poland to make mouths at the invisible event, while at the same moment Laertes, clamouring for immediate satisfaction in the King's palace, is out-manœuvred in his turn. Likewise, at the play's end, all three young men are 'victorious', in ways they could hardly have foreseen. The return of Fortinbras, having achieved his objective in Poland, to find his 'rights' in Denmark achieved without a blow, is timed to coincide with Hamlet's achieving his objectives in exposing and killing the King, and Laertes' achieving his objective of avenging his father's death on Hamlet. When this episode is played before us in the theatre, there is little question, to my way of thinking, but that something of the glow and martial upsurge dramatized in Fortinbras's entrance associates itself to Hamlet, even as Fortinbras's words associate Hamlet to a soldier's death. Meantime, Laertes, who has been trapped by the King and has paid with his life for it, gives us an alternative reflection of the Prince, which is equally a part of the truth.

* * *

Fortinbras's arrival at the close of *Hamlet* is an instance of an especially interesting type of mirroring to be found everywhere in Shakespeare's work—the emblematic entrance, and exit. Sometimes such exits occur by death, as the death of Gaunt, who takes a sacramental view of kingship and nation, in *Richard II*, at the instant when Richard has destroyed, by his personal conduct and by 'farming' his realm, the sacramental relationships which make such a view possible to maintain. Gaunt has to die, we might say, before a usurpation like his son's can even be imagined; and it is, I take it, not without significance that the first word of Bolingbroke's return comes a few seconds after we have heard (from the same speaker, Northumberland) that Gaunt's tongue 'is now a stringless instrument'. Something similar, it seems clear, occurs with the death of Mamillius in *The Winter's Tale*. Sickening with his father's sickening mind, Mamillius dies in the instant that his father repudiates the message of the oracle; and though, in the end, all else is restored to Leontes, Mamillius is not.

In the tragedies, emblematic entrances and exits assume a variety of forms, ranging from those whose significance is obvious to those where it is uncertain, controversial, and perhaps simply a mirage. One entrance whose significance is unmistakable occurs in the first act of *Macbeth*, when Duncan, speaking of the traitor Cawdor, whom he has slain, laments that there is no art to find the mind's construction in the face, ust as the new Cawdor, traitor-to-be, appears before him. Equally unmistakable is the significance of the King's exit, in the first scene of *Lear*, with the man who like himself has put externals first. 'Come, noble Burgundy', he says, and in a pairing that can be made profoundly moving on the stage, the two men go out together.

But what are we to say of Antony's freedman Eros, who enters for the first time (at least by name) just before his master's suicide and kills himself rather than kill Antony. This is all from his source, Plutarch's life of Antony; but why did Shakespeare include it? Did Eros's name mean something to him? Are we to see here a shadowing of the other deaths for love, or not? And the carrying off of Lepidus, drunk, from the feast aboard Pompey's galley. Does this anticipate his subsequent fate? and if it does, what does the intoxication signify which in this scene all the great men are subject to in their degree. Is it ordinary drunkenness; or is it, like the drunkenness that afflicts Caliban, Trinculo, and Stephano in *The Tempest*, a species of self-intoxication, Shakespeare's subdued comment on the thrust to worldly power? Or again, what of the arrival of the players in *Hamlet*? Granted their role in the plot, does Shakespeare make no other profit from them? Are such matters as the speech on Priam's murder and the advice on acting interesting excrescences, as Bradley thought, or does each mirror something that we are to appropriate to our understanding of the play: in the first instance, the strange confederacy of passion and paralysis in the hero's mind,[2] in the second, the question that tolls on all sides through the castle at Elsinore: when is an act not an 'act'?[3]

[2] See an important comment on this by H. Levin, in *Kenyon Review* (1950), pp. 273-96.
[3] I have touched on this point in *Tragic Themes in Western Literature*, ed. C. Brooks (1953).

These are questions to which it is not always easy to give a sound answer. The ground becomes somewhat firmer underfoot, I think, if we turn for a concluding instance to Bianca's pat appearances in *Othello*. R. B. Heilman suggests that in rushing to the scene of the night assault on Cassio, when she might have stayed safely within doors, and so exposing herself to vilification as a 'notable strumpet', Bianca acts in a manner 'thematically relevant, because Othello has just been attacking Desdemona as a strumpet'—both 'strumpets', in other words, are faithful (p.180). Whether this is true or not, Bianca makes two very striking entrances earlier, when in each case she may be thought to supply in living form on the stage the prostitute figure that Desdemona has become in Othello's mind. Her second entrance is notably expressive. Othello here is partially overhearing while Iago rallies Cassio about Bianca, Othello being under the delusion that the talk is of Desdemona. At the point when, in Othello's mental imagery, Desdemona becomes the soliciting whore—'she tells him how she plucked him to my chamber'—Bianca enters in the flesh, and not only enters, but flourishes the magic handkerchief, now degenerated, like the love it was to ensure, to some 'minx's', some 'hobby-horse's' token, the subject of jealous bickering. In the theatre, the emblematic effect of this can hardly be ignored.[4]

Further types of mirroring will spring to every reader's mind. The recapitulation of a motif, for instance, as in the poisoning episodes in *Hamlet*. Hamlet criticism has too much ignored, I think, the fact that a story of poisoning forms the climax of the first act, a mime and 'play' of poisoning the climax of the third, and actual poisoning, on a wide scale, the climax of the fifth. Surely this repetition was calculated to keep steady for Shakespeare's Elizabethan audiences the political and moral bearings of the play? We may say what we like about Hamlet's frailties, which are real, but we can hardly ignore the fact that in each of the poisoning episodes the poisoner is the King. The King, who ought to be like the sun, giving warmth, radiance, and fertility to his kingdom, is actually its destroyer. The 'leperous distilment' he pours into Hamlet's father's ear, which courses through his body with such despatch, has coursed just as swiftly through the body politic, and what we see in Denmark as a result is a poisoned kingdom, containing one

[4] Another emblematic entrance is the first entrance of the soothsayer in *Julius Caesar*; see 'The Teaching of Drama', *Essays on the Teaching of English*, ed. E. J. Gordon and E. S. Noyes (1960).

corruption upon another of Renaissance ideals: the 'wise councillor', who is instead a tedious windbag; the young 'man of honour', who has no trust in another's honour, as his advice to his sister shows, and none of his own, as his own treachery to Hamlet shows; the 'friends', who are not friends but spies; the loved one, the 'mistress', who proves disloyal (a decoy, however reluctant, for villainy), and goes mad—through poison also, 'the poison of deep grief'; the mother and Queen, who instead of being the guardian of the kingdom's matronly virtues has set a harlot's blister on love's forehead and made marriage vows 'as false as dicers' oaths'; and the Prince, the 'ideal courtier', the Renaissance man—once active, energetic, now reduced to anguished introspection; a glass of fashion, now a sloven in antic disarray; a noble mind, now partly unhinged, in fact as well as seeming; the observed of all observers, now observed in a more sinister sense; the mould of form, now capable of obscenities, cruelty, even treachery, mining below the mines of his school friends to hoist them with their own petard. All this, in one way or another, is the poison of the King, and in the last scene, lest we miss the point, we are made to see the spiritual poison become literal and seize on all those whom it has not already destroyed.

> a Prince's Court
> Is like a common Fountaine, whence should flow
> Pure silver-droppes in generall: But if 't chance
> Some curs'd example poyson't neere the head,
> Death, and diseases through the whole land spread.

The lines are Webster's, but they state with precision one of the themes of Shakespeare's play.

Finally, in the tragedies as elsewhere in Shakespeare, we have the kinds of replication that have been specifically called 'mirror scenes',[5] or (more in Ercles' vein) scenes of 'analogical probability'.[6] The most impressive examples here are frequently the opening scenes and episodes. The witches of *Macbeth*, whose 'foul is fair' and battle that is 'won *and* lost' anticipate so much to come. The 'great debate' in *Antony and Cleopatra*, initiated in the comments of Philo and the posturings of the lovers, and reverberating thereafter within, as well as around, the lovers till they die. The watchmen on the platform in

[5] By H. T. Price, in *Joseph Quincy Adams Memorial Studies*, ed. J. McManaway (1948), pp. 101 ff.
[6] See P. J. Aldus, *Shakespeare Quarterly* (1955), pp. 397 ff. Aldus deals suggestively with the opening scene of *Julius Caesar*.

Hamlet, feeling out a mystery—an image that will re-form in our minds again and again as we watch almost every member of the *dramatis personae* engage in similar activity later on. The technique of manipulation established at the outset of *Othello*, the persuading of someone to believe something he is reluctant to believe and which is not true in the sense presented—exemplified in Iago's management of both Roderigo and Brabantio, and prefiguring later developments even to the detail that the manipulator operates by preference through an instrument.

Lear offers perhaps the best of all these instances. Here the 'Nature' of which the play is to make so much, ambiguous, double-barrelled, is represented in its normative aspect in the hierarchies on the stage before us—a whole political society from its *primum mobile*, the great King, down to lowliest attendant, a whole family society from father down through married daughters and sons-in-law to a third daughter with her wooers—and, in its appetitive aspect, which Edmund will formulate in a few moments, in the overt self-will of the old King and the hidden self-will, the 'plighted cunning', of the false daughters. As the scene progresses, in fact, we can see these hierarchies of the normative nature, which at first looked so formidable and solid, crumble away in the repudiation of Cordelia, the banishment of Kent, the exit of Lear and Burgundy, till nothing is left standing on the stage but Nature red in tooth and claw as the false daughters lay their heads together.

I have dwelt a little on these effects of 'indirection' in the tragedies because I believe that most of us as playgoers are keenly conscious of their presence. I have perhaps described them badly, in some instances possibly misconceived them; but they are not my invention; this kind of thing has been pointed to more and more widely during the past fifty years by reputable observers. In short, these effects, in some important sense, are 'there'. And if they are, the question we must ask is, Why? What are they for? How are they used?

I return then to the query with which this section began: what *does* happen in a Shakespearian tragedy? Is it possible to formulate an answer that will, while not repudiating the traditional categories so far as they are useful, take into account the matters we have been examining? In the present state of our knowledge I am not convinced that this is possible: we have been too much concerned in this century with the verbal, which is only part of the picture. Nevertheless, I should like to make a few exploratory gestures.

★ ★ ★

Obviously the most important thing that happens in a Shakespearian tragedy is that the hero follows a cycle of change, which is, in part, psychic change. And this seems generally to be constituted in three phases. During the first phase, corresponding roughly to Bradley's exposition, the hero is delineated. Among other things, he is placed in positions that enable him to sound the particular timbre of his tragic music:

> Not so, my lord; I am too much i' the sun.
> (*Hamlet*, I. ii. 67)

> Seems, madam! nay, it is; I know not 'seems'.
> (I. ii. 76)

> My father's brother, but no more like my father
> Than I to Hercules.   (I. ii. 152)

> My fate cries out,
> And makes each petty artery in this body
> As hardy as the Nemean lion's nerve.   (I. iv. 81)

Chiming against this we are also permitted to hear the particular timbre of the opposing voice, spoken by the foil as well as others:

> If it be,
> Why seems it so particular with thee?
> (I. ii. 74)

> For what we know must be and is as common
> As any the most vulgar thing to sense,
> Why should we in our peevish opposition
> Take it to heart?   (I. ii. 98

> What if it tempt you toward the flood, my lord,
> Or to the dreadful summit of the cliff
> That beetles o'er his base into the sea,
> And there assume some other horrible form,
> Which might deprive your sovereignty of reason
> And draw you into madness?   (I. iv. 69)

From now on, as we saw, these are the differing attitudes towards experience that will supply the essential dialogue of the play.

The second phase is much more comprehensive. It contains the conflict, crisis, and falling action—in short, the heart of the matter. Here several interesting developments occur. The one certain over-all development in this phase is that the hero tends to become his own antithesis. We touched on this earlier in the case of Hamlet, in whom 'the courtier's, soldier's, scholar's, eye, tongue, sword' suffer some rather savage violations before the play is done. Likewise, Othello the unshakable, whose original composure under the most trying insults and misrepresentations almost takes the breath away, breaks in this phase into furies, grovels on the floor in a trance, strikes his wife publicly. King Lear, 'the great image of authority' both by temperament and position, becomes a helpless crazed old man crying in a storm, destitute of everything but one servant and his Fool. Macbeth, who would have 'holily' what he would have 'highly', who is too full of the milk of human kindness to catch the nearest way, whose whole being revolts with every step he takes in his own revolt—his hair standing on end, his imagination filling with angels 'trumpet-tongued', his hands (after the deed) threatening to pluck out his own eyes—turns into the numbed usurper, 'supped full with horrors', who is hardly capable of responding even to his wife's death. The development is equally plain in Antony and Coriolanus. 'The greatest prince o' th' world, The noblest', finds his greatness slipped from him, and his nobility debased to the ignominy of having helpless emissaries whipped. The proud and upright Coriolanus, patriot soldier, truckles in the market-place for votes, revolts to the enemy he has vanquished, carries war against his own flesh and blood.

This manner of delineating tragic 'action', though it may be traced here and there in other drama, seems to be on the whole a property of the Elizabethans and Jacobeans. Possibly it springs from their concern with 'whole' personalities on the tragic stage, rather than as so often with the ancients and Racine, just those aspects of personality that guarantee the *dénouement*. In any case, it seems to have become a consistent feature of Shakespeare's dramaturgy, and beautifully defines the sense of psychological alienation and uprootedness that tragic experience in the Elizabethan and Jacobean theatre generally seems to embrace. Its distinctively tragic implications stand out the more when we reflect that psychic change in comedy (if indeed comedy can be said to concern itself with psychic change at all) consists in making—or in showing—the protagonist to be more and more what he always was.[7]

In this second phase too, either as an outward manifestation of inward

[7] I have elaborated this point in an introduction to Fielding's *Joseph Andrews* (1948).

change, or as a short-hand indication that such change is about to begin or end, belong the tragic journeys. Romeo is off to Mantua, Brutus to the Eastern end of the Roman world, Hamlet to England, Othello to Cyprus, Lear and Gloucester to Dover, Timon to the cave, Macbeth to the heath to revisit the witches, Antony to Rome and Athens, Coriolanus to Antium.[8] Such journeys, we rightly say, are called for by the plots. But perhaps we should not be wrong if we added that Shakespearian plotting tends to call for journeys, conceivably for discernible reasons. For one thing, journeys can enhance our impression that psychological changes are taking place, either by emphasizing a lapse of time, or by taking us to new settings, or by both. I suspect we register such effects subconsciously more often than we think.

Furthermore, though it would be foolish to assign to any of the journeys in Shakespeare's tragedies a precise symbolic meaning, several of them have vaguely symbolic overtones—serving as surrogates either for what can never be exhibited on the stage, as the mysterious processes leading to psychic change, which cannot be articulated into speech, even soliloquy, without losing their formless instinctive character; or for the processes of self-discovery, the learning processes—a function journeys fulfil in many of the world's best-known stories (the *Aeneid*, the *Divine Comedy*, *Tom Jones*, etc.) and in some of Shakespeare's comedies. Hamlet's abortive journey to England is possibly an instance of the first category. After his return, and particularly after what he tells us of his actions while at sea, we are not surprised if he appears, spiritually, a changed man. Lear's and Gloucester's journey to Dover is perhaps an instance of the second category, leading as it does through suffering to insight and reconciliation.

During the hero's journey, or at any rate during his over-all progress in the second phase, he will normally pass through a variety of mirroring situations of the sort formerly discussed (though it will be by us and not him that the likeness in the mirror is seen). In some of these, the hero will be confronted, so to speak, with a version of his own situation, and his failure to recognize it may be a measure of the nature of the disaster to ensue. Coriolanus, revolted from Rome and now its enemy, meets himself in Aufidius's embrace in Antium. Hamlet meets himself in Fortinbras as the latter marches to Poland, but does not see the likeness—only the differences. Lear goes to Goneril's and there meets, as everyone remembers, images of his own behaviour to

[8] These are merely samples; other journeys occur that I have not named here.

Cordelia. Thrust into the night, he meets his own defencelessness in Edgar, and is impelled to pray. Encountering in Dover fields, both Lear and Gloucester confront in each other an extension of their own experience: blindness that sees and madness that is wise. Macbeth revisits the witches on the heath and finds there (without recognizing them) not only the emblems of his death and downfall to come but his speciousness and duplicity. Antony encounters in Enobarbus's defection his own; and possibly, in Pompey, his own later muddled indecision between 'honour' and *Realpolitik*. Othello hears the innocent Cassio set upon in the dark, then goes to re-enact that scene in a more figurative darkness in Desdemona's bedroom. Sometimes, alternatively or additionally, the hero's way will lie through quasi-symbolic settings or situations. The heath in both *Macbeth* and *King Lear* is infinitely suggestive, even if like all good symbols it refuses to dissipate its *Dinglichkeit* in meaning. The same is true of the dark castle platform in Hamlet, and the graveyard; of the cliff at Dover and Gloucester's leap; of the 'monument', where both Antony and Cleopatra die; and of course, as many have pointed out, of the night scenes, the storm, the music, the changes of clothing, the banquets. So much in Shakespeare's tragedies stands on the brink of symbol that for this reason, if no other, the usual terms for describing their construction and mode of action need reinforcement.

After the hero has reached and passed through his own antithesis, there comes a third phase in his development that is extremely difficult to define. It represents a recovery of sorts; in some cases, perhaps even a species of synthesis. The once powerful, now powerless king, will have power again, but of another kind—the kind suggested in his reconciliation with Cordelia and his speech beginning 'Come, let's away to prison'; and he will have sanity again, but in a mode not dreamed of at the beginning of the play. Or, to take Othello's case, it will be given the hero to recapture the faith he lost,[9] to learn that the pearl really was richer than all his tribe, and to execute quite another order of justice than the blinkered justice meted out to Cassio and the blind injustice meted out to Desdemona. Or again, to shift to Antony, the man who has so long been thrown into storms of rage and recrimination by the caprices of his unstable mistress receives the last of them without a murmur of reproach, though it has led directly to his death, and dies in greater unison with her than we have ever seen him live.

[9] This point is well made in Helen Gardner's *The Noble Moor* (1956).

I believe that some mark of this nature is visible in all the tragedies. Coriolanus, 'boy' though he is and in some ways remains, makes a triumphant choice (detract from his motives as we may), and he knows what it is likely to cost. Moreover, he refuses the way of escape that lies open if he should return now with Volumnia and Vergilia to Rome. 'I'll not to Rome, I'll back with you', he tells Aufidius, 'and pray you Stand to me in this cause'. The young man who, after this, dies accused of treachery—by Aufidius's treachery, and the suggestibility of the crowd, as slippery in Corioles as Rome—cannot be thought identical in all respects with the young man who joined Menenius in the play's opening scene. He is that young man, but with the notable difference of his triumphant choice behind him; and there is bound to be more than a military association in our minds when the Second Lord of the Volscians, seeking to quell the mob, cries, 'The man is noble, and his fame folds in This orb o' th' earth'; and again too when the First Lord exclaims over his body, 'Let him be regarded As the most noble corse that ever herald Did follow to his urn'. Even the monster Macbeth is so handled by Shakespeare, as has been often enough observed, that he seems to regain something at the close—if nothing more, at least some of that *élan* which made him the all-praised Bellona's bridegroom of the play's second scene; and everything Macbeth says, following Duncan's death, about the emptiness of the achievement, the lack of posterity, the sear, the yellow leaf, deprived of 'that which should accompany old age, As honour, love, obedience, troops of friends', affords evidence that the meaning of his experience has not been lost on him.

To say this, I wish to make it clear, is not to say that the Shakespearian tragic hero undergoes an 'illumination', or, to use the third term of K. Burke's sequence, a Mathema or perception.[10] This is a terminology that seems to me not very useful to the discussion of tragedy as Shakespeare presents it. It is sufficient for my purposes to say simply that the phase in which we are conscious of the hero as approaching his opposite is followed by a final phase in which we are conscious of him as exhibiting one or more aspects of his original, or—since these may not coincide—his better self: as in the case of Antony's final reunion with Cleopatra, and Coriolanus's decision not to sack Rome. Whether we then go on to give this phenomenon a specific spiritual significance, seeing in it the objective correlative of 'perception' or

[10] *A Grammar of Motives* (1945), pp. 38 ff.

'illumination', is a question that depends, obviously, on a great many factors, more of them perhaps situated in our own individual philosophies than in the text, and, so, likely to lead us away from Shakespeare rather than towards him. Clearly if Shakespeare wished us to engage in this activity, he was remiss in the provision of clues. Even in *King Lear*, the one play where some sort of regeneration or new insight in the hero has been universally acknowledged, the man before us in the last scene—who sweeps Kent aside, rakes all who have helped him with grapeshot ('A plague upon you, murderers, traitors all. I might have saved her . . .'), exults in the revenge he has exacted for Cordelia's death, and dies self-deceived in the thought she still lives—this man is one of the most profoundly human figures ever created in a play; but he is not, certainly, the Platonic idea laid up in heaven, or in critical schemes, of regenerate man.

★ ★ ★

I have kept to the end, and out of proper order, the most interesting of all the symbolic elements in the hero's second phase. This is his experience of madness. One discovers with some surprise, I think, how many of Shakespeare's heroes are associated with this disease. Only Titus, Hamlet, Lear, and Timon, in various senses, actually go mad; but Iago boasts that he will make Othello mad, and in a way succeeds; Antony, after the second defeat at sea, is said by Cleopatra to be

> more mad,
> Than Telamon for his shield; the boar of Thessaly
> Was never so emboss'd;   (IV. xiii. 2)

Caithness in *Macbeth* tells us that some say the king is mad, while 'others, that lesser hate him, Do call it valiant fury'; Romeo, rather oddly, enjoins Paris at Juliet's tomb to

> be gone; live, and hereafter say,
> A madman's mercy bade thee run away.
>   (V. iii. 66)

Even Brutus, by the Antony of *Antony and Cleopatra*, is said to have been 'mad'.

What (if anything), one wonders, may this mean? Doubtless a sort of explanation can be found in Elizabethan psychological lore, which held that the excess of any passion approached madness, and in the general prevalence, through Seneca and other sources, of the adage: *Quos vult perdere Jupiter dementat prius*. Furthermore, madness, when actually exhibited, was dramatically useful, as Kyd had shown. It was arresting in itself, and it allowed the combination in a single figure of tragic hero and buffoon, to whom could be accorded the licence of the allowed fool in speech and action.

Just possibly, however, there was yet more to it than this, if we may judge by Shakespeare's sketches of madness in Hamlet and King Lear. In both these, madness is to some degree a punishment or doom, corresponding to the adage. Lear prays to the heavens that he may not suffer madness, and Hamlet asks Laertes, in his apology before the duel, to overlook his conduct, since 'you must needs have heard, how I am punish'd With a sore distraction'. It is equally obvious, however, that in both instances the madness has a further dimension, as insight, and this is true also of Ophelia. Ophelia, mad, is able to make awards of flowers to the King and Queen which are appropriate to frailties of which she cannot be supposed to have conscious knowledge. For the same reason, I suspect we do not need Dover Wilson's radical displacement of Hamlet's entry in II. ii, so as to enable him to overhear Polonius.[11] It is enough that Hamlet wears, even if it is for the moment self-assumed, the guise of the madman. As such, he can be presumed to have intuitive unformulated awarenesses that reach the surface in free (yet relevant) associations, like those of Polonius with a fishmonger, Ophelia with carrion. Lear likewise is allowed free yet relevant associations. His great speech in Dover fields on the lust of women derives from the designs of Goneril and Regan on Edmund, of which he consciously knows nothing. Moreover, both he and Hamlet can be privileged in madness to say things—Hamlet about the corruption of human nature, and Lear about the corruption of the Jacobean social system (and by extension about all social systems whatever), which Shakespeare could hardly have risked apart from this licence. Doubtless one of the anguishes of being a great artist is that you cannot tell people what they and you and your common institutions are really like—when viewed absolutely—without being dismissed as insane. To communicate at all, you must acknowledge the opposing voice; for there always is an opposing voice, and it is as deeply rooted in your own nature as in your audience's.

Just possibly, therefore, the meaning of tragic madness for Shakespeare

[11] *What Happens in 'Hamlet'* (1935), pp. 103 ff.

approximated the meaning that the legendary figure of Cassandra (whom Shakespeare had in fact put briefly on his stage in the second act of *Troilus and Cressida*) has held for so many artists since his time. Cassandra's madness, like Lear's and Hamlet's—possibly, also, like the madness *verbally* assigned to other Shakespearean tragic heroes—contains both punishment and insight. She is doomed to know, by a consciousness that moves to measures outside our normal space and time; she is doomed never to be believed, because those to whom she speaks can hear only the opposing voice. With the language of the god Apollo sounding in her brain, and the incredulity of her fellow mortals ringing in her ears, she makes an ideal emblem of the predicament of the Shakespearian tragic hero, caught as he is between the absolute and the expedient. And by the same token, of the predicament of the artist —Shakespeare himself, perhaps—who, having been given the power to see the 'truth', can convey it only through poetry—what we commonly call a 'fiction', and dismiss.

In all these matters, let me add in parenthesis, we would do well to extend more generously our inferences about Shakespeare to the Jacobean playwrights as a group. Some of us have been over-long content with a view of Jacobean tragedy as naïve as those formerly entertained of Restoration comedy, eighteenth-century literature, and modern poetry. But a whole generation of writers does not become obsessed by the sexual feuding of cavalier and citizen, or rhetorical 'rules' and social norms, or abrupt images and catapulting rhythms, or outrageous stories of incest, madness, brutality, and lust, because the poetic imagination has suddenly gone 'frivolous', or 'cold', or 'eccentric', or 'corrupt'. Such concerns respond to spiritual needs, however dimly apprehended, and one of the prime needs of Jacobean writers, as the intelligible and on the whole friendly universe of the Middle Ages failed around them, was quite evidently to face up to what men are or may be when stripped to their naked humanity and mortality, and torn loose from accustomed moorings. Flamineo's phrase in *The White Devil*—'this busy trade of life'—offered as a passing summary of the play's monstrous burden of blood and madness:

> This busy trade of life appears most vain,
> Since rest breeds rest, where all seek pain by pain—

is characteristically understated and ironic, like Iago's 'Pleasure and action make the hours seem short'. The creators of Iago and Flamineo, and all the responsible writers of Jacobean tragedy along with them, knew perfectly well that it was not in fact the 'trade', or habitude, of life to which they held up art's mirror, but life 'on the stretch', nature at its farthest reach of possibility. They were fascinated by violence because they were fascinated by the potencies of the human will: its weaknesses, triumphs, delusions, corruptions, its capacities for destruction and regeneration, its residual dignity when, all else removed, man stood at his being's limit; and because they knew that in violence lay the will's supreme test, for aggressor and sufferer alike.

Whatever the themes of individual plays, therefore, the one pervasive Jacobean theme tends to be the undertaking and working out of acts of will, and especially (in that strongly Calvinistic age) of acts of self-will. This is surely the reason why, in Clifford Leech's happy phrase, these writers know so little of heaven, so much of hell; and why, to one conversant with their work so many products of the century to come seem like fulfilments of ancient prophecy: Milton's Satan and his 'God'—the philosophy embodied in *Leviathan*—even, perhaps, the clash of the Civil Wars and the cleavage in the English spirit reaching from Cavalier and Puritan to Jacobite and Whig and well beyond. At the very beginning of the century, these writers had got hold of the theme that was to exercise it in all departments, political, economic, religious, cultural, till past its close, the problem of anarchic will; and so decisive, so many-sided is their treatment of this problem that even in Milton's massive recapitulation of it in *Paradise Lost* the issue seems sometimes to be losing in vitality what it has gained in clarity, to be fossilizing and becoming formula. The utterances of *his* white devil have more resonance but less complexity and immediacy of feeling than those of Vittoria Corombona, Bosola, Macbeth, or Beatrice Vermandero; and some of them bear a perilous resemblance to the posturings of Restoration heroic tragedy, where the old agonies are heard from still, but now clogged, and put through paces like captive giants in a raree show.

However this may be, I return at the end to the proposition I set out with: there is a lot about the construction of a Shakespearian tragic 'action' that we still do not know. My own attempts to get towards it in this chapter are fumbling and may be preposterous: even to myself they sound a little like Bottom's dream. But the interesting thing about Bottom's dream, from my point of view, is that, though he found he was an ass all right, the Titania he tried to tell about was real.

Note

Ben Jonson
See pre-note to Chapter V (p. 112) for biographical details and modern studies. In this chapter Herford and Simpson's edition is used for all quotations; small roman numerals after a quotation refer to volume-numbers in this edition.

Studies of the Jacobean Theatre. E. K. Chambers' *Elizabethan Stage* (4 vols., 1923) is the standard work on English theatres and their management up to 1616; G. E. Bentley's *Jacobean and Caroline Stage* (1941–; 5 vols. to date) is a continuation of this study. G. R. Kernodle's *From Art to Theatre: Form and Convention in the Renaissance* (1944) usefully relates the Elizabethan theatre to European visual habits. An up-to-date, discriminating, yet brief study is A. M. Nagler's *Shakespeare's Stage* (1958). A. Nicoll has written on 'Studies in the Elizabethan Stage since 1900' in *Shakespeare Survey* (1948).

'Public' Theatres are discussed in J. C. Adams, *The Globe Playhouse* (1943)—though most scholars believe that Adams is often more definite than his evidence warrants. C. W. Hodges' *The Globe Restored* (1953) is a balanced study and finely illustrated. G. Reynolds' *The Staging of Elizabethan Plays at the Red Bull* (1940) is a scrupulous account of stage facilities at a Jacobean theatre. *Shakespeare Survey* (1959) contains several articles on Shakespearian theatres, and accounts of recent studies.

'Private' Theatres are discussed by J. Isaacs in *Production and Stage Management at the Blackfriars Theatre* (1933) and by W. A. Armstrong in *Elizabethan Private Theatres: Facts and Problems* (1958).

The staging of masques is discussed in L. B. Campbell, *Scenes and Machines* (1923), P. Simpson and C. F. Bell, *Designs by Inigo Jones* (1924), A. Nicoll, *Stuart Masques and the Renaissance Stage* (1937), and R. Southern, *Changeable Scenery* (1952). Stephen Orgel's *The Jonsonian Masque* appeared after the following chapter was written in 1965.

B. Joseph's *The Tragic Actor* (1959) has a well-informed and judicious chapter on acting in the age of Shakespeare. W. A. Armstrong's 'Actors and Theatres' in *Shakespeare Survey* (1964) is a comprehensive and newly informed account of the stagecraft of the period. M. C. Linthicum's *Costume in the Drama of Shakespeare and his Contemporaries* (1936) is the fullest account of this subject, but an interesting note in M.C. Bradbrook's *Shakespeare and Elizabethan Poetry* (1951) suggests further implications. A. Harbage and H. S. Bennett have both written on *Shakespeare's Audience* (1941 and 1944).

II

Ben Jonson and Jacobean Stagecraft

WILLIAM A. ARMSTRONG

*

'Now B. Jonson was never a good actor but an excellent instructor', wrote John Aubrey, one of his earliest biographers. This is not the only contemporary remark to suggest that Jonson took an active interest in the production of his own plays. Thomas Dekker's comedy *Satiromastix* (1602) satirizes Jonson in the person of Horace, who is told by Sir Vaughan, 'Moreover, you shall not sit in a Gallery, when your Comedies and Enterludes have entred their Actions, and there make vile and bad faces at everie lyne ... to make Players afraide to take your part' (V. ii. 298–301). It would seem that Jonson, like another playwright-producer, George Bernard Shaw, not only 'instructed' his players but kept a critical eye on their efforts after they had begun to perform. That he was sometimes pleased with what he saw is proved by the tributes to such boy actors as Salomon Pavy and Dick Robinson and to such adult players as Edward Alleyn, Richard Burbage, and Nathan Field which he published in poems or plays. That he was sometimes annoyed is shown by his remark in the title-page to *The New Inn* (1631): 'A Comoedy As it was never acted, but most negligently play'd, by some the Kings Servants'.

Jonson was well qualified to sit in judgement on the play produced. No Jacobean playwright had a richer knowledge than his of the various amateur and professional stages of the period. It is highly probable that he watched performances by his fellow-pupils while he was at Westminster School, and Dekker's *Satiromastix* reveals that he was a professional actor in the provinces and at 'Paris Garden' (i.e. the Swan Theatre) in the early fifteen-nineties. When he became a dramatist, he wrote plays for various companies of boy and adult actors; some designed for performance in such open-air public theatres as the

Curtain, the Globe, and the Hope, some for performance in such indoor 'private' playhouses as the Blackfriars, the Whitefriars, and the Cockpit. Eleven of these plays were also acted at court, and Jonson was no doubt present at some of these special performances. He also wrote texts for two of the pageants which celebrated the coronation of James I and for other spectacular entertainments designed to compliment the new king. The elaborate stages, scenery, machinery, and costumes used in these entertainments were surpassed only by those employed in the court masques of the period. Jonson wrote more court masques than any other Jacobean dramatist, and his collaboration with Inigo Jones in their production and his quarrels with that eminent designer of stage machines, scenery, and costumes form one of the most important episodes in the history of the English theatre. The purpose of this chapter is to survey Jonson's criticisms of the stagecraft of contemporary plays and masques and then to discuss the main characteristics of the stagecraft of his comedies and tragedies. By 'stagecraft' I mean the art with which the playwright selects and integrates the various physical media which enable him to communicate what he has written to an audience in a theatre; such media as the architecture, machinery, properties, and conventions of his stage, and the voices, gestures, attitudes, movements, stage-business, and dresses of his actors.

Being a humble Town Boy (i.e., day boy) at Westminster School, Jonson was not eligible to take a part in the Latin play which, in accordance with the Statutes (1560) of the school, was performed each Christmastide by the Queen's Scholars so that they might 'the better become accustomed to proper action and pronunciation'. As this clause implies, 'proper action and pronunciation' figured in the school curriculum as well as the Christmas play, and Jonson's training in gesture and diction at Westminster enabled him to become an actor in a touring company in the provinces. This episode in his career is mentioned in *Satiromastix* when Tucca reminds Horace (i.e. Jonson) how 'thou putst up a Supplication to be a poore Journeyman Player, and hadst beene still so, but that thou couldst not set a good face upon't: thou hast forgot how thou amblest (in leather pilch) by a play-wagon, in the high way . . .' (IV. i. 128). Contemporary records of provincial stages and tastes are scanty, but there is one which is relevant to Jonson's ideas about stagecraft. 'It was wont', writes John Gee in *The Foot out of the Snare* (1624, p. 68), 'when an Enterlude was to bee acted in a Countrey-Towne, the first question that an Hob-naile Spectator made, before he would pay his penny to get in, was, Whether there bee a Divell and a foole in the play? And if the Foole get upon the Divels backe, and beate him with his Cox-combe til he rore, the play is compleate'. This description refers to a traditional item of stage business in the later morality plays, where the triumph of good over evil was signalized when the Vice, wearing a long fool's coat, was borne off the stage on the Devil's back. Jonson mentioned it to Drummond of Hawthornden as one of the conventions of 'Comedia Vetus, in England' (i. 143), and in his dedication to *Volpone* he censures 'fooles, and devils as antique reliques of barbarisme' (v. 19). When he introduces a Devil and a Vice into *The Devil is an Ass*, he does so with a difference, giving a new and ironical motivation to the old business of the exit. In Jonson's play, it is the Devil who is carried off by the Vice, and they retreat to hell, not because virtue has overcome them, but because human wickedness so far surpasses their own.

Jonson was critical of other devices which were popular on the contemporary stage. His dislike for the knockabout fun, comic patter, and rimed extemporizations favoured by such comedians as Richard Tarlton and still practised in Jacobean times is manifested in his Induction to *Bartholomew Fair*, where the Stagekeeper, who epitomizes vulgarity of taste, fervently praises Tarlton and his methods. The jigs and dances of these comedians were also anathema to Jonson; in the same Induction, 'the concupiscence of jigges and Dances' is censured by the Scrivener, who speaks for the playwright. It seemed to him a breach of decorum that the author of a regular drama should 'mixe his head with other mens heeles', though he permits himself three dances in the masque scenes in the final act of *Cynthia's Revels* and calls for a dance in the third scene of the second act of his pastoral, *The Sad Shepherd*. Jonson also disliked the heroic style of acting inspired by Marlowe's *Tamburlaine*; its deportment and diction seemed to him another offence against decorum, and he refers scornfully in his *Discoveries* to 'the *Tamerlanes*, and *Tamer-Chams* of the late Age, which had nothing in them but the *scenicall* strutting and furious vociferation to warrant them to the ignorant gapers' (viii. 587). In *Satiromastix*, Dekker twice taunts Jonson with the way in which he played 'made Ieronimoes part' in *The Spanish Tragedy*. Jonson disliked the play and the way in which it was originally acted; in *The Poetaster* (III. iv. 215–22), he mocks the artificialities of Kyd's diction, and in the Induction to *Cynthia's Revels* he ridicules the spectator 'with more beard then braine' who declares 'that the old Hieronimo (as it was first acted) was the onely best, and judiciously pend play of Europe'. In *The Poetaster* (III. iv. 230-5), he mocks the melodramatic ghosts who wandered through revenge plays shrieking *Vindicta!* The only ghost in Jonson's plays—that of Sulla in *Catiline*—is used in the restricted Senecan manner solely as the prologue to the tragedy.

Jonson was no less critical of some of the spectacles and stage effects favoured by contemporary playwrights. In his prologue to *Every Man in His Humour*, he censures the effects obtained by the use of fireworks, by the rolling of an iron ball down a set of steps to imitate thunder, and by the lowering of characters and properties on to the platform by means of the trapdoor and windlasses in the hut above the stage of the public theatre. Marlowe had used all these stage effects in *Dr. Faustus* and Thomas Heywood employed them even more assiduously in Jacobean times. True to these antipathies, Jonson never demands a mechanical descent in any of his plays, and his stage directions only once ask for thunder (*Catiline*, V. 836). He also scorned a form of stagecraft which most Elizabethan and Jacobean writers of history plays found indispensable; the convention which permitted a few armed men to represent entire armies and allowed their mimic combats to be described as battles. In his prologue to *Every Man in His Humour*, he condemns those playwrights who

> with three rustie swords
> And helpe of some few foot-and-halfe-foot words
> Fight over *Yorke*, and *Lancasters* long jarres.

Correspondingly, the battles in Jonson's *Sejanus* and *Catiline* are reported, not acted, and his summary of the plot of his unfinished history play, *Mortimer His Fall*, holds no promise of armed men or combats.

Redundancy of action was another tendency in contemporary stagecraft which Jonson found distasteful. In the address to the reader which prefaces *The Alchemist*, he admonishes those spectators who commend playwrights 'as they doe Fencers, or Wrastlers; who if they come in robustiously, and put for it with a great deale of violence, are receiv'd for the braver fellowes. . . .' He would have them show more appreciation for those playwrights who (like himself) 'use election, and a meane' in their plotting. In his Induction to *Every Man Out of His Humour*, Jonson attacks the current practice of representing many widely separated localities in the same play when Mitis asks '. . . how comes it then, that in some one Play we see so many seas, countries, and kingdomes, past over with such admirable dexteritie?', and Cordatus sneeringly replies, 'O, that but shewes how well the Authors can travaile in their vocation, and out-run the apprehension of their auditorie' (iii. 438). Jonson was, of course, strongly attracted by the doctrine of the unity of place and the scenes of most of his plays are set within the boundaries of a city, such as London, or Rome, or Venice. In *The Alchemist* he achieves a concentration of place unequalled in Elizabethan drama; his settings are restricted to a room inside Lovewit's house and the lane outside it.

* * *

Jonson's attacks on Inigo Jones's stagecraft and its influence are better understood when they are related to Inigo's innovations in the staging of court masques during their period of collaboration in the reign of James I. The first of these innovations occurred in the production of Jonson's *The Masque of Blackness* at Whitehall in 1605. The outstanding importance of this production can best be appreciated by comparing it with Samuel Daniel's *The Vision of Twelve Goddesses*, which had been staged a year earlier. Daniel employed the system of dispersed settings which had been frequently used in Elizabethan masques; he had a cave and a temple erected at one end of the hall and a mountain at the other. All three settings were visible to the spectators at the same time. In *The Masque of Blackness*, however, Jones used one stage only and his setting consisted of a painted backcloth with properties arranged in perspective in front of it after the manner recommended by the Italian theatre-worker, Sebastiano Serlio, in his *Architettura* (Paris, 1545). As described by Jonson, the backcloth represented a landscape 'consisting of small woods'; in front of it was 'an artificiall sea . . . which seemed to move'. The masquers made their first appearance seated 'in a great concave shell . . . curiously made to move on those waters' (vii. 169-71). The picturesqueness and apparent depth of this setting impressed the spectators so much that the old system of dispersed settings went almost completely out of fashion.

When Jones presented Jonson's masques, *Hymenaei* and *The Masque of Queens* in 1606 and 1609 respectively, he introduced to the English stage a device which had emerged from Renaissance commentaries on Vitruvius's *De Architectura*. In Book V of this work, written in the first century B.C., Vitruvius describes the *periaktoi*, the prisms which were fixed on pivots in the façades of the scene-buildings of the Greek and Roman theatres. Each prism had three differently decorated faces, so that when it was revolved on its pivot it provided three scenic motifs. In the descriptions of the *periaktoi* in the *Onomasticon* of Julius Pollux, a Greek grammarian of the second century A.D., Renaissance scholars found a phrase which they translated as *machinae versatiles* ('revolving machines'). These classical precedents encouraged Renaissance theatre workers to experiment with revolving structures on their stages. In *Hymenaei*, Jones introduced what seemed at first to be a large globe representing various countries and seas, but, according to Jonson, when it 'turned softly' it revealed eight masquers seated 'within a *mine* of severall metalls' (vii. 231). This *mine* was obviously the concave side of a large structure consisting of half a globe mounted upon a concealed pivot. Jonson himself may have operated the machinery which revolved this pivot; in a letter describing the performance of this masque, John Pory remarks that 'Ben Jonson turned the globe of the earth . . . and within the concave sate the 8 men-maskers . . .' (x. 466). Jonson was well aware of the classical precedent which Inigo was following. In *The Masque of Queens*, he describes how the masquers appeared on the top of the House of Fame, and how 'the Throne wherein they sate, being *Machina versatilis*, sodaynely chang'd; and in the place of it appeared *Fama* bona . . .' (vii. 305).

When he staged Jonson's *Haddington Masque* in 1608, Inigo Jones introduced to the English stage another method of changing scenery which derived from the theory and practice of Italian theatreworkers. An important influence on their theories was the annotated edition of Vitruvius published in Rome in 1544 by the French scholar, Philander. In his notes on Book V, Philander draws attention to a passage in a commentary on Vergil written by Servius, a Roman scholar of the fourth century A.D. In this passage, Servius refers to the *scena ductilis* ('scene which can be led or drawn in') as a theatrical device by which panels are drawn aside to reveal a scene behind them. This Roman technique of discovering a scene was probably in Jonson's mind when he wrote the passage in which Catiline tells Aurelia that a politic pose can be set aside

> As is a vaile put off, a visor chang'd,
> Or the *scene* shifted, in our *theaters*.
> (v. 440)

In his book on methods of making theatrical scenery and machinery, *Practica di Fabricar Scene e Machine ne' Teatri*, published in 1638, Nicolà Sabbatini describes the method of changing scenery which Servius's reference to the *scena ductilis* encouraged Italian theatreworkers to create in the sixteenth century. A scene was painted in perspective on two large canvas flats or shutters; when a change of scene was required, one of these flats was quickly drawn to one side of the stage, the other to the other side, so as to reveal another painted scene behind them. The first scene in the *Haddington Masque* was a tall red cliff constructed in accordance with these principles; when Vulcan cried, 'Cleave, solid Rock, and bring the wonder forth', the cliff 'parted in the midst, and discovered an illustrious Concave' (vii. 257). In his production of Jonson's *Masque of Oberon* in 1610, Jones used two pairs of back flats; the first pair represented a rock with trees behind it; when they were drawn aside, they revealed a second pair representing a palace; when the latter two were drawn aside, they revealed the Kingdom of Oberon.

Inigo Jones enhanced the pictorial appeal of his revolving and sliding scenery with various other devices. To Jonson, what was 'most taking in the *Spectacle*' of *Hymenaei* was the multicoloured lighting provided by 'the *sphere of fire*', which revolved so swiftly at the rear of the stage that 'no eye could distinguish any colour of the light, but might forme to it selfe five hundred severall hiewes . . .' (vii. 232). Another spectator, John Pory, was especially impressed by the machinery devised by Inigo to lower the eight lady masquers to the stage 'not after the stale downright perpendicular fashion . . . but . . . gently sloping down' (x. 466).

Our knowledge of Inigo Jones's innovations in stagecraft during the Jacobean period would be much poorer if we did not possess the detailed descriptions of scenery, machines, lighting and costumes which Jonson added to the texts of some of his masques. But though he praises Jones in some of these descriptions it is clear that from the outset of their collaboration he regarded the art of designing the settings and costumes as vastly inferior to that of writing the texts of the masques. In his *Discoveries* Jonson notes the current idea that '*Poetry*, and *Picture*, are Arts of a like nature; and both are busie about imitation', but pointedly adds, 'Yet of the two, the Pen is more noble, then the Pencill. For that can speake to the Understanding; the other, but to the Sense' (viii. 609-10). This distinction is further elaborated at the beginning of *Hymenaei*: 'It is a noble and just advantage', Jonson states, 'that the things subjected to *understanding* have of those which are objected to *sense*, that the one sort are but momentarie, and meerely taking; the other impressing, and lasting: Else the glorie of these *solemnities* had perish'd like a blaze, and gone out, in the *beholders* eyes. So short-liv'd are the *bodies* of all things, in comparison of their *soules*' (vii. 209). This passage explains why he describes Inigo's scenery and costumes as 'the bodily part' in his introduction to *The Masque of Blackness* (vii. 172). It also explains the exasperation which prompted Jonson's line,

> Painting & Carpentry are ye Soule of Masque,

in the bitter verses, 'An Expostulation with Inigo Jones', which he wrote after they had quarrelled.

In his literary campaign against Inigo Jones, Jonson made a number of sustained attacks on a wide front. The passages relevant to this chapter are those in which he belittles Inigo's knowledge of Vitruvius and scoffs at some of his most important achievements in stagecraft, including his *machina versatilis*, his *machina ductilis*, his experiments in stage lighting, and his apparatus for lowering and raising masquers to and from the stage. When Jonson describes Inigo in 'An Expostulation' as

> overbearing us
> With mistook Names out of Vitruvius,

he is deriding the limited knowledge of Latin which appears to have obliged Inigo to study Vitruvius in an Italian translation instead of the original (see xi. 152-3). In *A Tale of a Tub*, In-and-in Medlay, the barrel-maker, is a satirical portrait of Inigo Jones; when he entertains the other characters with the performance of a 'shadow-play' in Act V, Scene x, the business of drawing a curtain to reveal the top of a tub which is subsequently made to rotate is a parody of Inigo's fondness for revolving structures modelled on the *machina versatilis*. In his poem, 'To Inigo Marquess would be', Jonson contrasts Jones with a Spanish architect who had recently been made a marquis and exclaims,

> He build a pallace! Thou a shopp
> W^th slyding windowes, & false Lights a top!

The latter remark may be a disparagement of Inigo's *machina ductilis* ('sliding machine') in *The Masque of Oberon*, which represented 'a bright and glorious Palace, whose gates and walls were transparent' and eventually slid apart to reveal 'Phosphorus, the day-starre' (vii. 346, 355). In 'An Expostulation', Jonson refers to Inigo's

> ffeat
> Of Lantern-lerry: wth fuliginous heat
> Whirling his Whymseys . . .

A 'lerry' or 'lurry' is a confused mass, so Jonson is evidently mocking Inigo's globes of revolving lights, which he had formerly praised in his description of the lighting of *Hymenaei*. The same poem reminds Inigo of

> Th'ascent of Lady Fame which none could spy,
> Not they that sided her, Dame Poetry,
> Dame History, Dame Architecture too,
> And Goody Sculpture . . .

As P. Simpson has pointed out (x. 682), Jonson is sneering here at the spectacle which Jones added to *Chloridia* when he showed Fame first appearing on a hill which rose from the stage, then flying upwards and being lost in the clouds. One fact which emerges from this survey of Jonson's dislikes is that they were all directed against scenes, lights and machines which *moved* before the spectators' eyes; i.e. against those most likely to distract attention from the spoken word, from the 'soul' to the 'body' of the masque.

Though Jonson was the first English playwright to point out that the attractions of changeable painted scenery might supersede those of the spoken word in the theatre, he was not opposed to painted scenery provided that it was subservient to poetic or dramatic effects. A painted backcloth with three-dimensional structures arranged in front of it in perspective after the manner of Serlio would best fulfil his requirements for the setting of his pastoral play, *The Sad Shepherd*: 'The Scene is Sher-wood. Consisting of a Landt-shape of Forrest, Hils, Vallies, Cottages, A Castle, A River, Pastures, Heards, Flocks, all full of Countrey simplicity. *Robin-hoods* Bower, his Well, the Witches *Dimble*, The

Swine'ards *Oake*, The Hermits *Cell*' (vii. 7). It must also be remembered that, beginning with the *Haddington Masque*, Jonson augmented and varied the spectacular interest of the masque by introducing the antimasque as a studied contrast to the grace and dignity of the main theme. For the *Masque of Queens*, for instance, he invented an antimasque of twelve women 'in the habite of *Haggs* or Witches', who represented 'the opposites to Good *Fame*' and enriched the masque with 'multiplicity of Gesture', 'a *magicall Daunce*, full of praeposterous change', and 'a spectacle of strangeness' (vii. 282, 301). Some details of this 'spectacle', moreover, were of Jonson's own devising. After acknowledging that *mr. Jones* designed the witches' costumes, he informs the reader that he himself 'praescribed them theyr *properties*, of vipers, snakes bones, herbs, rootes, and other ensignes of theyr Magick, out of the authority of antient & late Writers' (vii. 283). It must be emphasized, however, that he did not regard the antimasque as a desirable addition to drama proper. His criticisms of *The Tempest* and *The Winter's Tale* in the Induction to *Bartholomew Fair* are all directed against Shakespeare's use of forms of spectacle deriving from the antimasque. So much emerges from the Scrivener's comparison between Jonson and Shakespeare: 'If there bee never a *Servant-monster* i' the *Fayre*; who can helpe it? he sayes; nor a nest of *Antiques*? Hee is loth to make Nature afraid in his *Playes*, like those that beget *Tales*, *Tempests*, and such like Drolleries . . .' (vi. 16). In Jonson's opinion, the grotesque appearance of a servant-monster like Caliban was a breach of decorum. So, too, was an *Antique* like the bizarre dance of twelve satyrs, 'all men of hair' in IV. iv of *The Winter's Tale*.

★ ★ ★

The criterion of being true to life which led Jonson to criticize Shakespeare for introducing a monster and satyrs into regular drama is responsible for certain faults in the stagecraft of his two tragedies. At the beginning of the conspirators' meeting in the first act of *Catiline*, for instance, the stage directions call for a cluster of special stage effects which is unique in Jonson's plays: 'A darkenesse comes over the place: A grone of many people is heard under ground: Another [grone]: A fiery light appeares' (v. 445). Darkness, incidentally, was suggested by releasing smoke through a trapdoor. Though startling, these effects have no real importance in the dramatic action; some of the conspirators comment briefly upon them as good or ill omens for their enterprise, but their interest in them expires in a matter of seconds, and they revert all too quickly to the relatively prosaic business of plotting treason. Jonson appears to have inserted these extraordinary phenomena into his tragedy chiefly because they figured in the accounts of the conspiracy written by Plutarch and Livy (see x. 127). 'Truth of argument' and 'integrity in the story' are indispensable to the writing of tragedies, according to the address with which Jonson prefaces *Sejanus*, and these dubious principles lead him into other awkwardnesses of stagecraft besides the one just mentioned. In Act III of *Sejanus*, for instance, there is a minor episode in which Latiaris arranges for Rufus and Opsius to listen in hiding to his conversation with Sabinus and to arrest Sabinus when he speaks treasonable words. The obvious and effective way of staging this would be to conceal the two spies behind a curtain at the rear of the stage. But Latiaris's instructions make this impossible; he says,

> Here place your selves, betweene the roofe, and seeling,
> And when I bring him to his wordes of danger
> Reveale your selves, and take him.
>
> (iv. 421)

Jonson introduced the phrase 'betweene the roofe, and seeling' into this speech because he wanted to be true to the account of the matter given by Tacitus in Book IV of his *Annales*, where the place of concealment is described as 'tectum inter et laquearia'. How did Jonson expect this to be staged? The Oxford editors have suggested that the spies concealed themselves by climbing up a rope-ladder into the hut which overhung the stage of the Globe and that they remained concealed there until they had to descend and arrest Sabinus (ix. 621). This explanation satisfies Jonson's words, but the stage hut seems a remote place for eavesdroppers, and climbing up and down a rope-ladder could be an awkward and time-consuming piece of gymnastics. It seems to me more likely that Latiaris and his spies were on the balcony when he gave them the order quoted above, that the spies concealed themselves by lying behind the balcony rails while Latiaris and Sabinus talked below, and that they jumped to the platform when the time came for them to arrest Sabinus. Whichever explanation is accepted, it is certain that Jonson's adherence to the principle of 'truth of argument' in tragedy has made the staging of this incident unnecessarily complicated.

In general, however, the stagecraft of Jonson's plays is distinguished by its clarity, economy, and discrimination, and many of his finest effects are obtained by the simplest of means. The fairground scenes in *Bartholomew Fair*, for instance, require nothing more than a tent with a stall at either side of it; the tent is at first the pig-woman's booth, but when Lanthorn Leatherhead's sign is fixed above it at the beginning of Act V it is conveniently transformed into a setting for the puppet show. Jonson makes sparing use of the upper level of his stage, and only on one occasion—Wittipol's courtship of Mrs. Fitzdotrell in *The Devil is an Ass* (II. vi. 33–113, II. vii. 1–24)—does he permit an episode to be acted entirely on this level. He seldom asks for discoveries to be made by the drawing aside of curtains, though on two occasions his stage directions require special sets of curtains which will allow a character to be seen above them. Just before the shadow play begins in *A Tale of a Tub*, a stage direction notes that '*Medlay* appears above the Curtain', and in *Volpone* when Volpone arranges for Mosca to torment the legacy-hunters, he says that he will

> get up,
> Behind the cortine, on a stoole, and hearken;
> Sometime, peepe over; see, how they doe looke,
> (v. 112)

and in the following scene we have the stage direction 'Volpone peepes from behinde a traverse' (V. iii. 9). This is an apt piece of business; it makes Volpone like an author watching a show of his own devising, in which the legacy-hunters are puppets manipulated by Mosca. Only one of Jonson's stage directions calls for an entry by a trapdoor, and it is part of an Induction, not a play proper. The Induction to *The Poetaster* begins with Envy speaking while 'Arising in the midst of the stage'. A mechanically operated trapdoor was evidently available at the Blackfriars Theatre to enable Envy to come gradually into sight in this way, and it was used again when Prologue set his foot on Envy's head and seemed to thrust him downwards out of sight (iv. 203, 205). Here the trapwork provides a moral emblem of the action of the ensuing play.

Jonson uses the basic structures of the Elizabethan stage, the platform and the stage doors, with exceptional resourcefulness. The depth of the platform made possible one of his most persistent and characteristic devices of stagecraft; the division of his characters into two distinct groups, one of which comments pungently on the actions of the other.

In some of his plays, the commentators are the characters of an Induction who remain on the stage, watch the action, and make their observations on it between the acts. Their function is to stimulate and guide the attention of the audience. Sometimes the group contains a character who speaks for Jonson, interpreting, explaining, and justifying his intentions to other members of the group; such are Cordatus in *Every Man Out of His Humour* and the Boy in *The Magnetic Lady*. In *The Staple of News*, on the other hand, the four gossips who provide the commentary are silly or superficial in their opinions; the audience is expected to arrive at an accurate judgement by disagreeing with them. These devices were new and lively ways of performing the functions of a chorus; they substitute dialectics and discussion for the declamation of *sententiae* in unison. It is not surprising to find that Jonson describes the commentators in *The Magnetic Lady* as 'The Induction; or, Chorus' (vi. 508).

In *Sejanus*, Jonson essayed an interesting variation on his choric device when he endowed certain characters in the play itself—Arruntius and his group—with the function of commenting continuously on the action. These 'good-dull-noble-lookers-on' almost invariably stand apart from the other characters and pass judgement upon them. To facilitate this commentary, Jonson employs another piece of stagecraft characteristic of his moral and satirical imagination. Various personages are made to walk across the stage without speaking so that Arruntius and his friends may interpret their characters to the audience. In Act I, 'Drusus passeth by' in silence and they expound his virtues and limitations: in Act II, 'Afer passeth by' and they revile him as a time-server; in Act V, Sejanus, Lictors, and Consuls 'Passe over the stage' and are cheered by one group of citizens but not by that of Arruntius, who grimly remarks, 'We shall be markt anon, for our not-haile' (iv. 454). In this episode, incidentally, Sejanus and his attendants probably entered at one side of the yard of the Globe, mounted the stage by means of a small set of steps, walked slowly across it, descended, and made their exit at the other side of the yard, for, as A. Nicoll has recently shown, the stage direction 'Passe over the stage' usually indicates an entry and an exit of this kind.[1]

The concentrated and closely organized action of Jonson's plays obliges him to make frequent and carefully-timed use of the doors of his stage. Few Elizabethan plays have such simple requirements for their

[1] Cf. *Shakespeare Survey* (1959).

staging as *The Alchemist* and in no others are the stage doors put to such closely integrated use. A platform, three doors, and a window serve all the purposes of the indoor and the outdoor scene. For the production of this comedy a special door was probably fixed in a framework which occupied what was normally used as a curtained discovery-space at the Globe. In the interior scene, it was probably used as the door leading from Lovewit's house to the street. It was equipped with a large keyhole, through which Face could shout to Mammon in III. v. In the exterior scene, it was used as the door leading from the street into the house; a knocker may have been hung on it to indicate this change of locality. In the interior scene, the other two doors are continuously used; one or the other leads to Subtle's laboratory, to the room in which Doll Common entertains her clients, to the upstairs room to which Kastril and his sister are sent, to the garden to which Dame Pliant is taken by Surly, to the privy in which the hapless Dapper is locked, and to the back lane by which Doll and Subtle make their escape at the end. In his next play, *Catiline*, Jonson again required three doors in the tiring-house façade, but here a foreshortening rather than a concentration of place must be assumed. When Cicero and his soldiers are arresting the conspirators at the end of the play, they bring Lentulus out of 'Spinthers house', Cethegus out of 'Quintus Cornificus house', and Statilius and Gabinus out of Caesar's house within a minute or so. A door probably represented each of these 'houses'. A central door behind an arras with a door at either side of the stage is needed for the scene in *The Silent Woman* (IV. v) in which Daw and Lafoole are baited. The side doors represent the 'couple of studies, at each end one', in which the victims are locked; the arras conceals Clerimont and Dauphine, and the door behind it enables the ladies to enter at the close of the scene.

In the Jacobean as in the Elizabethan theatre, a change of scene could be indicated by having the characters make an exit by one door and enter immediately afterwards by another. Jonson uses this convention twice in succession in Act III of *The Devil is an Ass*: on the first occasion Meercraft and Pug make an exit from Meercraft's house and when they re-enter they are supposed to be in a lane near Lady Tailbush's house; soon afterwards, they make another exit and when they re-enter they are supposed to be in her house. Such frequent changes of scene do not occur in Jonson's best plays, and it is one of the several signs of his declining powers in *The Devil is an Ass* that he should begin to avail himself of a free and easy convention which he had previously eschewed. I have found only one instance of Jonson's using the so-called 'split scene', that accommodating convention of the Jacobean stage whereby a change of locality was assumed even though the characters concerned in it did not leave the stage. In Act V of *Catiline* there is no break in the action between the second meeting of the Senate and the episode already described, in which Cicero and the soldiers drag certain conspirators out of three houses. The transition from the indoor to the outdoor scene is assumed to take place during the course of a brief speech by Cicero, who begins it by protecting Caesar from indignant senators and goes on to order Lentulus to be brought out of Spinther's house:

> No violence. Caesar, be safe. Lead on:
> Where are the publike executioners?
> Bid 'hem wait on us. On to Spinthers house.
> Bring Lentulus forth.   (v. 545)

The staging of the action immediately after the arrest of the conspirators presents a problem. Cicero orders them to be taken away and executed. As all three doors leading off the stage represented the 'houses' of the conspirators at this point, an exit by any of them would have been incongruous. I suggest that the executioners conducted the conspirators down a set of steps at the side of the stage and that they crossed the playhouse yard and made their exit through one of its entrances. An exit of this kind would come as close as was possible in the Globe to the accounts of the episode given by Roman historians, who describe how Lentulus was taken across the Forum to the dungeon in which he was strangled. Jonson, as we have remarked, strives after historical truth in the stagecraft of his tragedies.

At his best, Jonson integrates stage business, properties, and dialogue with remarkable finesse and subtlety. In Act I of *Sejanus*, for instance, the business of rubbing cosmetics into Livia's cheeks, in which Eudemus engages as he talks to her, provides a silent but potent commentary on the flattering notion of Sejanus which his words are trying to insinuate into her mind. In *Bartholomew Fair*, the biblical images which various properties associated with the fair summon to the mind of Zeal-of-the-land Busy are frequently combined with business which makes manifest his hypocrisy. Ursula's booth reminds him of 'the Tents of the uncleane', but when the smell of roast pork emanates from it he 'sents after it like a Hound' (vi. 64). Jonson's most sustained and brilliant interconnections of stage business, properties, and speech occur in *The Silent Woman*, however. One example must suffice here; the words and actions inspired by the swords in Act IV. Jonson prepares for this sequence in I. i, when Clerimont describes how Morose was once made so furious by noise that he came 'downe to the doore, with a long-sword' (v. 169). In IV. ii, Morose is so infuriated by the noise of self-invited guests that he 'descends with a long sword' and drives them out of his house. At the beginning of the next scene, Mrs. Otter gives a *double entendre* to this business when she describes how Morose 'came downe with a huge long naked weapon in both his hands'. Morose is absent for several scenes, but Jonson knows that the spectators will not forget how this newly-married man made his last exit brandishing his 'weapon'. In the intervening scenes, Daw and Lafoole are hoodwinked and deprived of their swords and tell lies to account for their empty scabbards. Immediately, Morose re-enters with a sword in each hand, and the ladies flee as he asks, 'What make these naked weapons here, gentlemen?' (v. 249). This brings the business to a climax which fulfils several dramatic purposes. There is an elementary but telling comic effect in Morose's departing with one big sword and reappearing with two shorter ones. His description of them as 'naked weapons', preceded as it is by the hurried exit of the ladies, revives Mrs. Otter's *double entendre*. By finding and bringing in the swords surrendered by Daw and Lafoole, he embarrasses his fellow-dupes and links the two main plots of the play.

Disguise is a common device in Elizabethan drama and Jonson uses it more frequently than most of his contemporaries because it is an indispensable means of representing the twin follies of imposture and gullibility to which he finds mankind all too prone. In *The Alchemist*, Face and Subtle artfully assume different guises to prey on different victims; to impress the humble Drugger they appear in captain's uniform and velvet cap and gown respectively, but Face appears before Mammon in the workaday clothes of the pale-faced acolyte who tends the alchemist's furnace, and Subtle doffs his rich gown when Puritans like Ananias have to be duped. Volpone, on the other hand, uses only one disguise when he receives his victims. It is aptly chosen. To the legacy-hunters, his long gown, his furs, his nightcaps, and his ointment-smeared eyes suggest decrepitude. To the spectators, however, the furs symbolize his animal cunning, rapacity, and lust. Did Jonson prescribe the red furs of a fox when he 'instructed' Burbage in the part? He certainly set himself unusually high standards in matters concerning stage illusion and the appearance of his characters, as may be deduced from Drummond's note that Jonson 'had ane intention to have made a play like Plaut^g Amphitrio but left it of, for that he could never find two so like others that he could persuade the spectators they were one' (i. 144). It was from Plautus's *Casina*, incidentally, that he borrowed the device of the mock-marriage of a boy disguised as a woman which he used in *The Silent Woman*. The climax of this play comes when Dauphine removes a wig and reveals the juvenile impersonator, to the dismay of Daw and Lafoole, who had just been claiming to have enjoyed the favours of the supposed lady. This climax illustrates a recurrent device in Jonson's stagecraft; the creation of a sudden *dénouement* combined with poetic justice in the fifth act when a disguise is removed to the discomfiture of the foolish and the sinful characters. Volpone puts off a disguise with this result; so does Quarlous in *Bartholomew Fair*; also Fitzdoterell in *The Devil is an Ass*; and Pennyboy Canter in *The Staple of News*.

In *Discoveries* Jonson approvingly summarizes some of Bacon's remarks about the things that obstruct truth and notes that 'Imposture held up by credulity' and the study of words as opposed to matter are among the worst of these (viii. 627). 'Imposture held up by credulity' would also serve as an apt summary of Jonson's basic theme as a comic writer. Correspondingly, the use of grandiose words which bear little or no relation to truth helps his knaves even more than disguises in the gulling of their victims. Jonson's knaves are often remarkable for their command of the jargons of certain professions or pseudo-professions, and for the eloquence with which they exploit them. Subtle can fascinate characters as diverse as Mammon and Tribulation with skilled variations on the technical terms of alchemy. When Ananias fails to respond to this jargon, Subtle artfully drives him out with Puritan jargon when he learns that his name is Ananias:

> Out, the varlet
> That cossened the *Apostles*! Hence away,
> Flee *Mischiefe*; had your *holy Consistorie*
> No name to send me of another sound;
> Then wicked Ananias? Send your *Elders*,
> Hither, to make atonement for you, quickly.
> (v. 336)

In addition to the jargons of alchemy and Puritanism, Jonson exploits those of duelling (Bobadil in *Every Man in His Humour*), bad poetry (Crispinus in *The Poetaster*), the mountebank (Volpone), the law (Cutbeard and Otter in *The Silent Woman*, V. i), pedantic learning (Sir John Daw in *The Silent Woman*), financial speculation (Meercraft in *The Devil is an Ass*), and newsmongering (Cymbal in *The Staple of News*). The terminology of these characters frequently produces a distinctive irony; neither the audience nor the knave nor the gull fully understands the jargon, but whereas the gull is hypnotized by it and the knave racks his brain to sustain it, the audience is secure in its knowledge of how far it is from the truth. Jonson's skilled use of jargon is only one aspect of his mastery of the many tones and idioms of contemporary speech. There are few set descriptions of scenes or places in Jonson's plays; he relies upon the idioms of his characters to localize them. The atmosphere of Bartholomew Fair, for instance, with its seething energy and earthy, multifarious life, emerges chiefly from the idioms of its denizens; the strident *patois* of Ursula, Leatherhead, and Trash, who are indigenous to the fair: the piping voices of those city-innocents, Mr. and Mrs. Littlewit: the babbling tones and schoolboy oaths of Cokes, that *Esquire* from Harrow o' the Hill: the grousing of his man, Wasp: the conventional patter of the puppets: the Puritan idioms of Zeal and Mrs. Purecraft; and the pompous jargon of Overdo, the city magistrate. *The Silent Woman* is another great *tour de force* in the adaptation of many tones and idioms to a central dramatic purpose. Jonson, like Shaw, had a genius for vocal orchestration.

The spoken word is the strongest element in Jonson's stagecraft. His faith in its power is emphatically stated in the 'prologue for the stage' which prefaces *The Staple of News*:

> Would you were come to heare, not see a Play.
> Though we his *Actors* must provide for those,
> Who are our guests, here, in the way of *showes*,
> The maker hath not so; he'ld have you wise,
> Much rather by your ears, then by your eyes.

At its best, Jonson's stagecraft fulfils this ideal. Eschewing spectacle for its own sake, it encourages the audience to dwell upon the words of the actor and the moral significance of the dramatic action. Stage business and properties are the servants, not the rivals, of the spoken word; they provide a visual illustration of it or add an ironical dimension to it.

Groups of choric characters are artfully used to direct the attention of the audience to the words and meaning of the action. Where spectacle is introduced, it resolves itself into a moral emblem. Jargon supersedes disguise in the revelation of the vanity of appearances and the ironies attendant upon 'Imposture held up by credulity'. Jonson's theory and practice as a writer of masques and plays accord with his conviction that the profoundest intimations come by the ear, not the eye.

Note

Biographies: Thomas Dekker, 1572?–1632?; Thomas Heywood, 1574–1641. (For Jonson, see p. 112.)
Dekker was born in London, but neither his parentage nor education is known. Heywood was probably born in Lincolnshire and studied at Cambridge (without taking a degree). Both lived in London, Heywood marrying before 1600.

Works. Both Dekker and Heywood were established as playwrights by 1598–9, when they were among the team of writers in the pay of the impresario, Philip Henslowe. Both continued to write plays in collaboration, as well as on their own. In 1598 Francis Meres ranked Heywood as one of 'the best for comedy'.
From 1603 onwards Dekker wrote some mayoral pageants and 'triumphs' for performance in London, and many pamphlets, as *The Wonderful Year*, on the plague (1603), *The Seven Deadly Sins of London* (1606), *Lanthorn and Candle-Light* (1608), *The Gull's Handbook* (1609), and *The Black Rod* (1630). From 1613 to 1619, he was imprisoned for debt.
Between 1599 and 1601, Heywood became a member of the Earl of Worcester's Men (later called Queen Anne's), and for some 20 years he wrote most of his plays for them, and acted and helped to manage the company. He continued as a dramatist throughout the thirties, but followed a few early translations and pamphlets (including *An Apology for Actors*, 1612) with more frequent non-dramatic writings (as *England's Elizabeth, her Life and Troubles*, 1631), and wrote a series of mayoral pageants.
The chief plays of these authors are named and dated in the following chapter.

Modern Editions. Dekker's plays are edited by F. Bowers (4 vols., 1953–61; a vol. of annotations is still to be published by C. Hoy). The only edition of Heywood's is by R. H. Shepherd (6 vols., 1874). In the following chapter quotation from Dekker is from Bowers' ed., from Heywood from original quartos; Herford and Simpson's Jonson (see p. 112) is used. Selected plays of Dekker and Heywood are in the Mermaid Series (1887 & 1888). Dekker's prose works are edited by A. B. Grosart (5 vols., 1884–6), Heywood's *Apology* by J. P. Collier (1841), Dekker's plague pamphlets by F. P. Wilson (1925).

Scholarship and Criticism. Two general books are useful: W. K. Wimsatt, Jr., *English Stage Comedy* (1955) and M. C. Bradbrook, *The Growth and Structure of Elizabethan Comedy* (1955).
The best study of Dekker is M. T. Jones-Davies, *Un Peintre de la Vie Londonienne. Thomas Dekker* (Paris, 2 vols., 1958). Two studies of Heywood are A. M Clark, *Thomas Heywood* (1931) and M. Grivelet, *Thomas Heywood et Le Drame Domestique Élizabéthain* (Paris, 1957). T. S. Eliot's assessment is in his *Selected Essays* (1932).

III
Citizen Comedy and Domestic Drama

ARTHUR BROWN

★

If in this chapter the emphasis is placed almost entirely on the work of Dekker, Heywood, and Jonson, this is not intended to suggest that there were no other dramatists of the period who dealt with similar subjects. Chapman, Middleton, Marston, and Massinger were also willing to employ their talent in the production of plays aimed largely at either the edification or the entertainment, or at both, of the citizen audiences of the London theatres. But a line must be drawn somewhere if a mere list of names and titles is to be avoided, and Dekker, Heywood, and Jonson were among the most consistent workers in the field. Furthermore, the differences between them in their approach to, and treatment of, a largely common body of material show a wide range of the possibilities inherent in such drama. These differences are, of course, less apparent between Dekker and Heywood than they are between Jonson and either of them; they have been referred to as 'assembly-line dramatists', a title which no one has yet dared to apply to Jonson, nor, indeed, would ever wish to. Differences in method, however, are one thing, and should not be confused with differences of purpose, which, in these three men, often seem to be of degree rather than kind. Dekker and Heywood represent the popular romantic stream of comedy while Jonson represents the satiric stream; yet this major division should not be pressed too far. There is some basis for agreement between Heywood's motto, 'Aut prodesse solent aut delectare', and the lines from the Prologue to *Volpone*,

> In all his Poemes, still, hath beene this measure,
> To mixe profit, with your pleasure.

Narrow definitions of citizen comedy and domestic drama are better avoided. Both are wider in scope than, for example, such clearer-cut categories as revenge tragedy or chronicle play, and may, under certain circumstances, include these. Nor will it be enough, in the case of citizen comedy, to point only to the glorification of citizen life and standards which is found in Heywood's *The Four Prentises* or in Dekker's *The Shoemakers' Holiday*, and to use this as a touchstone; for this would exclude the satirical approach of Jonson's *Bartholomew Fair*, which is equally entitled to be called citizen comedy, or even domestic drama in some of its situations. Domestic drama itself is perhaps more easily defined in terms of such plays as *A Woman Killed with Kindness*, or *A Yorkshire Tragedy*; yet it would not be altogether fair to exclude from the category a chronicle play such as *Edward IV*, whose author expressly sets out to deal also with the king's love 'to fayre Mistresse Shoare, her great promotion, fall and misery, and lastly the lamentable death of both her and her husband'; this is domestic drama by any definition. And the play also treats of 'the besiedging of London, by the bastarde Falconbridge, and the valiant defence of the same by the Lord Maior and the Cittizens', a theme which, if not precisely citizen comedy, is at least closely allied to it. One may point to Heywood's *The English Traveller* as an example of both domestic drama and citizen comedy in its main plot and its sub-plot respectively; and at the same time note that the plot of Jonson's *The Alchemist* made use of almost precisely the same setting—an empty house taken over by a band of rascals—as Heywood's sub-plot. An examination of some of the plays of these three dramatists may serve to identify those elements which, though probably too various to suggest a neat, convenient label, do nevertheless indicate some common ground of thought, purpose, and even method in the minds of their authors.

Dekker is the least sophisticated of the three, his work the least complicated by adherence to literary, or even moral, theory. His simplicity of purpose is clearly indicated in his address 'To all good Fellowes, Professors of the Gentle Craft; of what degree soever', which prefaces his light-hearted comedy *The Shoemakers' Holiday*. There is no assertion of novelty, no appeal to moral standards, no claim to be a reformer of manners or of anything else; instead, a plain statement of the circumstances under which the play was acted, a brief account of 'The Argument of the play', and a final call to his readers to 'Take all in good worth that is well intended, for nothing is purposed but mirth, mirth lengthneth long life; which, with all other blessings I heartily wish you'. Few remarks could be more revealing of what has been called Dekker's 'instinctive and unstudied sympathy with simple people in a comedy not merely spectacular' (Bradbrook, p. 131). As a journeyman-dramatist, he often worked with collaborators; of the forty-two titles of his plays which are recorded only seventeen are extant, and of these only five are wholly his own. It is significant, however, that there seems to be no fierce disagreement among scholars about those parts of plays written in collaboration which reveal the 'Dekker touch'. And in spite of the distressing loss of material, he stands out clearly as a man who was ready to try his hand at almost any kind of play, to treat fairy story, folk-lore, national history, and domestic upheaval with the hand of a practical and experienced dramatist, one who was in close touch with the theatre and with his audience, knowing, again almost instinctively, just what this audience wanted.

Undoubtedly *The Shoemakers' Holiday* (1599) gives us the best picture of Dekker's sympathetic treatment of citizen comedy, of his unashamed revelling in the more high-spirited aspects of the London scene of his time. The mad, merry shoemaker, Simon Eyre, and his lively, hard-drinking band of journeymen and apprentices, to say nothing of his wife Margery, whose efforts to keep them under control are doomed to continual failure, have been held up over and over again as the perfect expression in drama of this close observation of, and personal involvement in, almost, one might say, identification with the unsophisticated Elizabethan and Jacobean world of trade. Romanticized the picture may be, just as, on the other hand, Jonson's approach to the same world was anti-romantic (though not necessarily more 'realistic'); yet signs are not lacking that Dekker was aware of those less immediately likeable facets both of character and circumstances which it did not suit his purpose to emphasize. His primary concern here was not to 'sport with human follies', still less with crimes, but to tell a love story, of the kind as old as civilization itself, against a contemporary background which included civil, domestic, and national issues.

The story of Rose and Lacy, a traditional one of young love thwarted by parental opposition, would appeal to an audience not over-interested in psychological subtleties, and might be handled by a dramatist not over-skilful in dealing with such subtleties, nor, probably, over-eager to deal with them. The theme was used more than once by Dekker's fellow-dramatists both in comedy and in tragedy, and it is interesting to compare his treatment of it with, for example, that of Massinger in *A New Way to pay Old Debts* (1625?); the differences revealed spring not only from differences in temperament between the authors, but from changes in the social and literary climate, and we may notice that while Dekker is content to stress the permanent values of love, forgiveness, and tolerance in the story, Massinger is more concerned to exploit its opportunities for argument, satire, and social preaching. There may be grave family differences between Rose and Lacy, and Lacy may have deserted from the colours to be near his Rose, but the King can still say:

> Dost thou not know, that love respects no bloud?
> Cares not for difference of birth, or state,
> The maide is yong, wel borne, faire, vertuous,
> A worthy bride for any gentleman:
> Besides, your nephew for her sake did stoope
> To bare necessitie: and as I heare,
> Forgetting honors, and all courtly pleasures,
> To gaine her love, became a shooemaker. . . .
> (V. v. 103)

and the disgrace of Lacy's desertion may be redeemed by making him a knight! Love, forgiveness, tolerance; these virtues illustrated in a romantic story in which the lovers eventually win each other in spite of all opposition; the scene set in a London which the audience would immediately recognize, peopled by characters who were reflections, perhaps a little idealized, of themselves: with this kind of material Dekker could hardly be unsuccessful.

There is still more in this play, however, to add to its appeal, and to its value as an example of citizen comedy. Simon Eyre, the shoemaker, demonstrates how the industrious tradesman may rise in the world, to become not only an alderman but Lord Mayor of London, and to be on friendly conversational terms with the king himself. Yet the traditional balance must be kept, and familiarity must not be allowed to blur duty and loyalty: '. . . you see not a white haire on my head, not a gray in this beard, everie haire I assure thy majestie that stickes in this beard, Sim Eyre values at the king of Babilons ransome, Tamar Chams beard was a rubbing brush toot: yet Ile shave it off, and stuffe tennis balls with it to please my bully king' (V. v. 19). Lacy's defection may be forgiven by the king in the interests of true love, yet its seriousness in the eyes of the Earl of Lincoln and Sir Roger Otley is not glossed over, and even the king allows himself to refer to it as 'vile treason'. The fighting in France, though kept in the background, is ominously close, and indeed the play ends on a note which makes it clear that there is more fighting to come. It affects every important character; Eyre's reaction to it, as he bids farewell to his journeyman Ralph, reflects a sturdy, devil-may-care patriotism which often appears in the citizens of Dekker and Heywood: '. . . fight for the honour of the Gentle Craft, for the gentlemen shoo-makers, the couragious Cordwainers, the flower of saint Martins, the mad knaves of Bedlem, Fleetstreete, Towerstreete, and white Chappell, cracke me the crownes of the French knaves, a poxe on them, cracke them, fight, by the lord of Ludgate, fight my fine boy' (I. i. 211), sentiments which are more briefly, but none the less sincerely, echoed in Hodge's 'God send thee to cramme thy slops with French crownes, and thy enemies bellies with bullets'; sentiments too, we may be sure, which would meet with the approval of Dekker's audience.

Loyalty and patriotism on the national level may, therefore, be added to those virtues of love, forgiveness, and tolerance which Dekker illustrated in his romantic theme, and all are to be found again and again in citizen comedy of this kind, sometimes being quite explicitly stressed, sometimes forming no more than a background of generally accepted sentiments. There is in this play another romantic theme in the story of Ralph and Jane, which balances on a lower social level that of Rose and Lacy. The war separates them, in spite of Eyre's efforts to secure Ralph's discharge from the army, and it is not without some appreciation of the irony of the situation that we hear Lacy, of all people, attempting to console Jane:

> Woman, be patient, God (no doubt) wil send
> Thy husband safe againe, but he must go,
> His countries quarrel sayes, it shall be so.
> (I. i. 178)

Their separation allows Dekker to introduce his third group of virtues, those which obtain in the domestic sphere, and to illustrate them in the reaction of Jane to Hamond, who tries to woo her in her husband's absence:

> In simple truth this is the summe of all,
> My husband lives, at least I hope he lives,
> Prest was he to these bitter warres in France,
> Bitter they are to me by wanting him,

> I have but one heart, and that hearts his due,
> How can I then bestow the same on you?
> Whilst he lives, his I live, be it nere so poore,
> And rather be his wife, th[a]n a kings whore.
> (III. iv. 72)

The last line is reminiscent of the attitude of the author of *Edward IV* in his treatment of the story of Jane Shore and her husband. Nor does the report of Ralph's death weaken Jane's loyalty to him; her first reaction to Hamond's eager plea that she should forget her husband and turn to him is the broken-hearted 'For Gods sake leave me . . . 'Tis now no time for me to thinke on love', followed by

> Thogh he be dead,
> My love to him shal not be buried:
> For Gods sake leave me to my selfe alone.

Her eventual reluctant promise,

> Thus much I say, and saying bid adew,
> If ever I wed man it shall be you,
> (III. iv. 100)

translates itself into no less reluctant action: 'This morning', Ralph reports, 'when I strokte on her shooes, I lookte upon her, and she upon me, and sighed, askte me if ever I knew one Rafe. Yes sayde I: for his sake saide she (teares standing in her eyes) and for thou art somewhat like him, spend this peece of golde . . .' (V. ii. 7). Finally, when her wedding to Hamond is interrupted by the shoemakers, and she realizes that Ralph is still alive, her response is unequivocal:

> Whom should I choose? whom should my thoughts affect,
> But him whom heaven hath made to be my love?
> Thou art my husband and these humble weedes,
> Makes thee more beautiful then all his wealth,
> Therefore I wil but put off his attire,
> Returning it into the owners hand,
> And after ever be thy constant wife. (V. ii. 53)

Nor does Ralph himself mince his words in reply to Hamond's final desperate attempt to buy Jane from him: 'Sirra Hammon Hammon, dost thou thinke a Shooe-maker is so base, to bee a bawde to his owne wife for commoditie, take thy golde, choake with it, were I not lame, I would make thee eate thy words' (V. ii. 82). In this way the theme of conjugal loyalty is hammered home, and one remembers how Dekker returned to it, less skilfully perhaps, in *Patient Grissil* (1600) and *The Honest Whore* (1604).

Using traditional material and a simple pattern, almost a morality play pattern, Dekker returns to a domestic theme in *Patient Grissil*. Yet it is difficult to feel that he has made any progress either in the presentation of actual domestic problems, or in the proposal of any code of conduct which might lead to their solution. The three strands in the play—a wife whose patience is put to extreme tests by her husband, a husband cursed with a shrewish wife, and a woman who seeks refuge from matrimonial difficulties in celibacy—are too obviously the result of artifice to have any useful relation with real life. It is true that the virtue of patience is extolled, yet rather in the fashion of an over-simplified morality play; one cannot feel for Grissil the sympathy that one feels for Jane in *The Shoemakers' Holiday*, even when one admits that the latter, too, is not an altogether convincing character. One must nevertheless be fair to Dekker. He has been criticized because his good women 'emerge from their trials too often, like some perfect machine, guaranteed mechanically perfect under all conditions', and for the fact that his 'easy pity and boundless tolerance' make him appear something of a moral sloven (Bradbrook, pp. 124–5). To some extent this is true, yet it is perhaps not to distinguish clearly enough between a Jane or a Bellafront (*The Honest Whore*) or a Moll Frith (*The Roaring Girl*), characters for which Dekker could no doubt draw upon his personal observation, and a Grissil, who came ready-made to his hands, and in whom there was little potentiality for development for a dramatist even more skilful than Dekker. For a practical man of the public theatre, one of Henslowe's journeymen-dramatists, moral problems had to be stated and answered, if at all, in the broadest possible terms. It may be that he himself was incapable of dealing with them in any other way—although there are signs both in his plays and in his prose works that the term 'moral sloven' is not altogether an accurate description of his outlook—but, faced with the task of providing entertainment and edification for the kind of audience which, as at many other periods of our history, preferred its morality in terms of plain black and white, he showed himself capable of supplying its demands.

The Honest Whore, in which Dekker collaborated with Middleton, handles again some of his favourite themes. The title-pages of the two parts of the play give in a nutshell the ingredients that he could handle and knew would succeed. *Part I* is to deal with 'The Honest Whore, With, The Humours of the Patient Man, and the Longing Wife', and *Part II* (1605) 'with the Humours of the Patient Man, the Impatient Wife: the Honest Whore, perswaded by strong Arguments to turne Curtizan againe: [and] her brave refuting those Arguments'. The scene may be set in Milan, yet the bawdyhouse, Bedlam, and Candido's shop, peopled by whores, bawds, madmen, apprentices, roaring boys, and courtiers are taken straight from Dekker's London. A love-story on the lines of that of Romeo and Juliet, with a background of family feud, death feigned by the use of drugs, and a friar to bring about the, on this occasion, happy ending in the marriage of Hippolito and Infelice, is mingled with the somewhat sentimental conversion of the whore, Bellafront, as a result of her falling genuinely in love—if we are to take her word for it—with Hippolito, and hearing from him a long tirade against the evil of her ways. In these two stories Dekker loses no opportunity to play upon the feelings of his audience, to make use of a host of details which will rouse an echo in their hearts. Roger, Bellafront's servant, first appears 'singing with the ends of old Ballads', and Bellafront herself, on her first appearance, has snatches of these on her lips. Her affection for Hippolito calls from her a confession full of self-pity and promises of amendment which he is probably wise to distrust, but which is nevertheless calculated to stir up sympathy in at least some hearts:

>T'has never bin my fortune yet to single
>Out that one man, whose love could fellow mine,
>As I have ever wisht it: o my Stars!
>Had I but met with one kind gentleman,
>That would have purchacde sin alone, to himselfe,
>For his owne private use, although scarce proper:
>Indifferent hansome: meetly legd and thyed:
>And my allowance reasonable—yfaith,
>According to my body—by my troth,
>I would have bin as true unto his pleasures,
>Yea, and as loyall to his afternoones,
>As ever a poore gentlewoman could be.
>   (II. i. 265)

Yet even here, in a passage surely 'tear-jerking' in intent, a phrase such as 'meetly legd and thyed: And my allowance reasonable' makes one wonder for a moment just how far it may be true that Dekker's tolerance was boundless; there is at least a suspicion that his tongue was straying towards his cheek. Hippolito is given plenty of opportunity to exploit the traditional *memento mori* theme, as he sits in contemplation of his 'dead' Infelice's picture and a skull, with lines well calculated to cause a shudder in his hearers:

> Of all the Roses grafted on her cheekes,
> Of all the graces dauncing in her eyes,
> Of all the Musick set upon her tongue,
> Of all that was past womans excellence,
> In her white bosome, looke! a painted board
> Circumscribes all . . .   (IV. i. 42)

and this evocation of terror is supported by the later 'How mad are mortals then to reare great names On tops of swelling houses' and 'Death's the best Painter then'. This is not far removed from the stark teaching of the old morality play on the inevitability of death and the vanity of human endeavour, nor was Dekker, together with many of his fellow-dramatists, unaware of the fact that there is something basic in human nature, particularly unsophisticated human nature, which will always respond to it.

Candido and Viola represent a reversal of the situation in the 'Patient Grissil' story, and express it in contemporary terms of the patient husband who arouses in his wife a longing to see him lose his temper: '. . . but he loves no frets, and is so free from anger, that many times I am ready to bite off my tongue, because it wants that vertue which all womens tongues have (to anger their husbands)' (I. ii. 74). In this play, however, Dekker seems to get a little closer to the real question involved, the nature of the relationship between man and wife, which should be the theme of domestic drama. Candido's own view of it is unimpeachable, at least in theory:

> Pray weare a peacefull temper, be my wife,
> That is, be patient: for a wife and husband
> Share but one soule between them: this being knowne,
> Why should not one soule then agree in one?
>   (I. v. 197)

Not all the trials put upon him can disturb his equanimity, and upon his release from the lunatic asylum he is allowed to speak at some length on this patience, which, of all the virtues, is 'neerst kin to heaven'. Yet the final lines of the play, spoken by the Duke after Candido's speech, suggest that Dekker may again have had his tongue in his cheek, seeing the need for moderation in these matters:

> Thou giv'st it lively coulours: who dare say
> He's mad, whose words march in so good aray?
> Twere sinne all women should such husbands have.
> For every man must then be his wives slave.
> Come therefore you shall teach our court to shine,
> So calme a spirit is worth a golden Mine,
> Wives (with meeke husbands) that to vex them long,
> In Bedlam must they dwell, els dwell they wrong.
> (V. ii. 510)

A romantic story of the victory of true love over adversity; a conversion of a whore by genuine love and a sermon on the evil of her ways; much homely moralizing on, for example, the inevitability of death; scenes of tradesmen and apprentices involving a few broken heads; a shrewish wife and a patient husband, the latter always available for scenes of farce and horseplay; and a long scene in a madhouse: Dekker may not have been a great dramatist, but his ingredients show that he had a clear appreciation of the wishes of his theatre and its audience.

The second part of *The Honest Whore* adds little to our knowledge of Dekker. Candido, patient man still, learns of a better way to deal with his second shrewish wife; Bellafront, married to Matheo, her first seducer, faces successfully the temptations of Hippolito and the threats of her husband to make her return to her old way of life; and a procession of whores going to their punishment replaces the madhouse scene of the first part. The theme of conjugal relations is dealt with more satirically in *Westward Ho* (1604) and *Northward Ho* (1605), possibly under the influence of Webster's collaboration, when citizens are depicted as frequenters of brothels and their wives the prey of gallants; but the satire is not pushed to the bitter end, and, as a recent writer on Dekker remarks, 'on découvre, comme dans les scènes secondaires de *The Roaring Girl*, que les bourgeoises sont honnêtes, les galants dupes, les maris confondus et la procureuse Birdlime honnie; puis tout le monde se rembarque pour Londres' (Jones-Davies, I, 131–2).

It is, of course, to London that Dekker always returns, whether on the stage at the Fortune or the Red Bull, or throughout the city (as in his *Magnificent Entertainment* for King James, Queen Anne, and Prince Henry in 1603, or in his *Troia-Nova Triumphans* for the Lord Mayor's Show in 1612, or in other pageants of this kind), or even at the private theatres and at court. If at times we find his tolerance, his optimism, and his sentimentality rather too much to accept, we should at least give him credit for knowing what he was doing. His was not the genius that deals with the deeper meanings behind the appearances; indeed his treatment of appearances often involves more than a touch of the fanciful. Heywood, to anticipate for a moment, has been somewhat unkindly referred to as 'a facile and sometimes felicitous purveyor of goods to the popular taste', and, if one ignores the sneer in this remark —since there is nothing intrinsically wrong in supplying the popular taste—the same may be said of Dekker. He rarely attempts to aim higher than this, but the purchasers seem to have found the goods to their satisfaction.

To turn to Jonson is to come face to face with a very different state of affairs. The question has been asked more than once whether there was not a conflict between Jonson the moralist and Jonson the comic artist. Speaking of *Volpone*, Congreve could remark that 'there are crimes too daring and too horrid for comedy'. Perhaps these points may be resolved in Jonson's favour by a fuller understanding of his aims and methods; but the fact that they can be raised at all is a measure of the problem that his work has posed from his own day to this. Of Dekker and Jonson one critic says:

> These two writers, born within a year or two of each other and dying in the same decade, are in opposition throughout their lives. All Jonson's virtues of concentration, order, and critical control were lacking in Dekker, while Dekker's virtues of sympathy, tolerance and spontaneity were equally lacking in Jonson. Jonson's work can be judged only as a whole; Dekker's demands to be judged by his happiest efforts. They were at one only in their devotion to London, its history and customs; both delineated the very streets and alleys, and named it over ward by ward. . . . Both delight in a popular festival of the city; both catch the flavour of a proverb, the smell of a shop. Yet while Jonson's judicial eye noted merely the follies and affectations of his characters, Dekker shows only the happy, the faithful, and the generous (Bradbrook, pp. 122–3).

There are exceptions to be made for both men, but no one would quarrel with the general terms of this statement. What is of interest for our present purpose is that despite their differences both men made use of the material from which citizen comedy and domestic drama were made.

For Jonson, however, comedy is no longer something in which 'nothing is purposed but mirth'. Indeed, we have his own statement in *Discoveries* that 'the parts of a Comedie are the same with a Tragedie, and the end is partly the same. For, they both delight, and teach . . . Nor, is the moving of laughter alwaies the end of Comedy, that is rather a fowling for the peoples delight, or their fooling. For, as Aristotle saies rightly, the moving of laughter is a fault in Comedie, a kind of turpitude, that depraves some part of a mans nature without a disease.' Comedy to Jonson was an intellectual, not an emotional, affair; its appeal was to be to the head, not to the heart; it was to be 'an interpretation of life, a criticism of society, and an embodiment of values'.

In the prologue to *Every Man in His Humour* (included after he had changed the setting of the play from Italy to London, and anglicized the names of the characters), we find his scornful opinion of the popular plays of the period, for their readiness to cram three-score years into a single action, for their crude attempts at realism in presenting battles, thunder, and storms, for their habit of moving the action from one part of the world to another with a chorus to explain the situation; in short, for everything in them that revolted against his notions of what a well-made play should be. For these he proposed to substitute

> . . . deedes, and language, such as men do use:
> And persons, such as Comedie would chuse,
> When she would shew an Image of the times,
> And sport with humane follies, not with crimes.
>   (Prol., 21)

It is to be noticed, however, that these follies, 'popular errors', are the ones that we all confess 'by laughing at them', and that the ability to laugh at them gives him hope that they may be cured; but this is the laughter of the satirist, not, primarily, that of the entertainer. The moral basis of comedy is urged over and over again: in the dedication of *Volpone* Jonson speaks of 'the doctrine, which is the principal end of poesie, to inform men in the best reason of living'; in the Prologue to *Epicoene* we find

> The ends of all, who for the scene do write,
> Are, or should be, to profit and delight;

in the Prologue to *The Alchemist* he contrasts his own attitude to 'whore, bawd, squire, impostor' and others, with that of comic writers who have found in them 'subject for rage or spleen'—his pen 'did never aim to grieve, but better men', and he goes on,

> But, when the wholesome remedies are sweet,
> And, in their working, Gaine, and Profit meete,
> He hopes to finde no spirit so much diseas'd,
> But will, with such fayre Correctives, be pleas'd.

Alongside all these professions of a moral purpose runs the theme of the construction of a play, and the satire of a dramatist who knew his business and had little or no patience with his fellows who apparently did not.

To Dekker, Heywood, and other dramatists who wrote in a popular and romantic vein, story and plot mattered a great deal; if there was a moral to be pointed it could be done very often by the way. Whether the theme was of love, or of adventure, or of domestic relationships, a story had to be told; it may often be told at greater length than was necessary, and it may have other stories, more or less relevant, added to it, but it was there for all to see. For Jonson, story or plot as such took second place. T. S. Eliot remarks, 'Jonson employs immense dramatic constructive skill: it is not so much skill in plot as skill in doing without a plot. He never manipulated as complicated a plot as that of *The Merchant of Venice*; he has in his best plays nothing like the intrigue of Restoration comedy' (p. 77). *Every Man in His Humour* (1598) has little more to its plot than the interception of a letter by Knowell, which leads him to follow his son to London where he may observe his behaviour with the gallants of the city and their victims. The plot of *Every Man Out of His Humour* (1599) is, if anything, still slighter. *Volpone* (1606), *The Alchemist* (1610), and *Epicoene* (1609) have just enough plot to keep the players in motion and to allow us to observe them in a variety of groupings, and *Bartholomew Fair* (1614) depends almost entirely on a rapid shift of scene from one part of the fair to another. What seems to matter to Jonson is the way in which his characters fit in with one another; given their basic characteristics (even to the extent of having them listed beforehand, as in *Every Man Out of*

His Humour) and an initial impetus, there seems to be little more that needs to be done to keep them moving and talking. To some extent this effect is, of course, illusory, since behind it lies Jonson's extraordinarily skilful manipulation, if not of plot, of actors and situations, an art that conceals art. The scene is closely limited, yet it bustles with life and activity, 'infinite riches in a little room'.

It was said earlier that if Dekker's approach tended to be romantic, Jonson's was anti-romantic. While Dekker was content to polish the surface in order to give his audience what it wanted to see, Jonson was concerned to probe beneath the surface to give his audience what he thought it ought to see. Neither method, of course, ought to be called realistic, though too often both have been accepted at their face value. Dekker does not himself specifically invite such an interpretation of his work; Jonson's suggestion that he is providing 'an image of the times' has resulted in misunderstanding, for his satiric exaggeration of foibles presents rather an image of what the times are likely to be if the possessors of these foibles do not reform before it is too late. Dekker wished to please his audience, and if some of them were encouraged at the same time to lead a better life, so much the better; but this was not his main purpose. Jonson wished to reform his audience, and if this could be done by pleasurable methods, so much the better; but the pleasure could easily be dispensed with if it did not prove effective. Both were ready to use material close at hand for their different purposes, for the obvious reason that the familiar, presented in a slightly different light, whether to render it more or less attractive, is likely to be at least as striking as the unfamiliar, and may often be even more striking. Yet Dekker rather than Jonson would have approved of Heywood's attitude in the Prologue to *The Four Prentises* (1592?): 'Our authority is a Manuscript, a booke writ in parchment; which not being publique, nor generall in the world, wee rather thought fit to exemplifie to the publique censure, things concealed and obscur'd, such as are not common with every one, than such Historicall Tales as every one can tell by the fire in Winter. Had not yee rather, for novelties sake, see Jerusalem yee never saw, then London that yee see howerly?'. *The Four Prentises* was a Red Bull play, Dekker's *Old Fortunatus* (1599) was probably acted at the Rose (in addition to having a court performance), and the audiences of these public theatres were treated in both plays to a good deal 'for novelties sake'. Both represent citizen comedy of a kind which could hardly meet with Jonson's approval.

Perhaps the most devastating example of Jonson's anti-romantic attitude towards material and audience alike appears in *Bartholomew Fair*, where puppets are used to present a burlesque of the Hero and Leander story. Had either Dekker or Heywood presented this story, they would have given the audience a more or less straightforward account, emphasizing, no doubt, the romantic element, possibly adding a crude secondary story, but generally remaining loyal to the original. Jonson turns the whole thing upside down. In the first place the ignorance of the audience ('what doe they know what Hellespont is?') calls for a revision of the text, to 'make it a little easie, and moderne for the times'; in the second place it must be told in a contemporary setting, so 'for the Hellespont I imagine our Thames here; and then Leander, I make a Diers sonne, about Puddle-wharfe: and Hero a wench o' the Bankeside, who going over one morning to old fish-street; Leander spies her land at Trigsstayers, and falls in love with her: Now do I introduce Cupid, having Metamorphos'd himselfe into a Drawer, and hee strikes Hero in love with a pint of Sherry' (V. iii. 120). Thus the ludicrous performance continues, bringing in also the story of the trial of friendship between Damon and Pythias, 'two faithfull friends o' the Bankside'. It is true that Heywood was capable of this kind of thing, and that Shakespeare touched upon it in *A Midsummer Night's Dream*, but neither of them, surely, in such a spirit of bitterness. Beaumont mocks the tastes of the popular stage and the citizen audiences in *The Knight of the Burning Pestle*, but not with the scorn and contempt which Jonson shows in *Bartholomew Fair*. It may fairly be said that if Dekker set out to be the servant of his audiences, Jonson was determined to be the master of his, and their treatment and presentation of similar material reflects this difference clearly.

Heywood, although much closer to Dekker, reveals from time to time a curious admixture of Jonson's spirit. His claim to have had a hand in some two hundred and twenty plays puts him squarely in the class of journeyman-dramatist. His surviving plays show that he was willing to turn his hand to practically every popular type: chronicle plays, plays on classical themes, domestic drama, current events, romantic adventure plays, and pageants for the Lord Mayors' Shows. Yet his latest biographer could title his book *Thomas Heywood et Le Drame Domestique Élizabéthain*, for more than any of his contemporaries he emphasized domestic themes. On the one hand, Jonson rarely deals with domestic subjects as such: the relationship between Corvino and

Celia in *Volpone*, that between the Littlewits in *Bartholomew Fair*, and the strange liaisons of *Epicoene*, to mention three obvious examples, are far from being serious treatments of domesticity and form only a small section of the general human scene that Jonson is surveying. In Heywood, on the other hand, domestic virtues are always in the picture, even when his ostensible subject seems far removed from the domestic scene.

Heywood's views on the stage are well set out in his *Apology for Actors* (1612), a conscious justification of his art which aligns him with Jonson rather than with Dekker. In the third section he deals with the purpose and benefits of the stage:

> First, playing is an ornament to the City . . . Secondly, our English tongue, which hath ben the most harsh, uneven, and broken language of the world . . . is now by this secondary meanes of playing, continually refined, every writer striving in himselfe to adde a new florish unto it . . . Thirdly, playes have made the ignorant more apprehensive, taught the unlearned the knowledge of many famous histories, instructed such as cannot reade in the discovery of all our English Chronicles: & what man have you now of that weake capacity, that cannot discourse of any notable thing recorded even from William the Conqueror, nay from the landing of Brute, untill this day, beeing possest of their true use. For, or because Playes are writ with this ayme, and carryed with this methode, to teach the subjects obedience to their King, to shew the people the untimely ends of such as have moved tumults, commotions, and insurrections, to present them with the flourishing estate of such as live in obedience . . . (F3–3ᵛ).

He shows how tragedies and histories in particular teach these lessons, and goes on to say of moral plays that their purpose is 'to perswade men to humanity and good life, to instruct them in civility and good manners, shewing them the fruits of honesty, and the end of villany'. Of comedy, 'it is pleasantly contrived with merry accidents, and intermix with apt and witty jests, to present before the Prince at certain times o solemnity, or else merily fitted to the stage. And what is then the subject of this harmlesse mirth? either in the shape of a Clowne to shew others their slovenly and unhansome behaviour, that they may reforme that simplicity in themselves, which others make their spor . . .', to reprove foolish lovers, to refresh the weary or the melancholy to warn young men against usurers and whores. 'Briefly, there neither Tragedy, History, Comedy, Morrall or Pastorall, from which an infinite use cannot be gathered' (F3ᵛ-4).

Here are almost all the principles upon which he worked in his own plays: the inculcation of civic pride, of nationalism and patriotism, the duty of the learned towards the unlearned, the domestic virtues of loyalty, civility, and good manners, the right use of entertainment, and the importance of balance in character and temperament. Jonson would have approved of most of these, sometimes perhaps with reservations; but he did not approve of the methods that Heywood used. Dekker, had he thought about the matter at all, would have sided with Heywood in both respects.

Heywood's civic and national pride are well illustrated in the series of pageants which he wrote for the Lord Mayors' Shows, with such significant titles as *Londons Ius Honorarium*, *Porta Pietatis*, and *Londini Status Pacatus*. It is also noticeable in a play such as *The Four Prentices of London, with the Conquest of Jerusalem*, in which Eustace, Godfrey, Charles, and Guy carry the fame of their beloved city and the reputation of their fellow-apprentices to the eastern world in a series of fantastic adventures, resolved only by still more fantastic coincidences. In his address 'To the honest and hie-spirited Prentises The Readers' when the play was published in 1615, Heywood touches on a few points which are important:

> To you (as whom this Play most especially concernes) I thought good to dedicate this Labour, which though written many yeares since, in my Infancy of Judgement in this kinde of Poetry, and my first practise: yet understanding (by what meanes I know not) it was in these more exquisit and refined Times to come to the Presse, in such a forwardnesse ere it came to my knowledge, that it was past prevention, and knowing withall, that it comes short of that accuratenesse both in Plot and Stile, that these more Censorious dayes with greater curiosity acquire, I must thus excuse. That as Playes were then some fifteene or sixteene yeares agoe it was in the fashion. Nor could it have found a more seasonable and fit publication then at this Time, when, to the glory of our Nation, the security of the Kingdome, and the honour of the City, they have begunne againe the commendable practise of long forgotten Armes . . .

There is pride in London and in England, praise for the apprentices, and, with them, regret for the passing out of fashion of plays of this kind[1] and lack of concern for the *publication* of his own works. These last two points are exemplified frequently elsewhere in his writings; two important instances may be given. In the address to the reader prefacing Part 2 of *The Iron Age* (1632) he remarks: 'These Ages have beene long since Writ, and suited with the Time then: I know not how they may bee received in this Age, where nothing but *Satirica Dictaeria*, and *Comica Scommata* are now in request: For mine owne part, I never affected either, when they stretched to the abuse of any person publicke, or private'. In a similar address prefacing *The Rape of Lucrece* (1608) we read:

> It hath beene no custome in mee of all other men (Curteous Readers) to commit my plaies to the presse, the reason, though some may attribute to my own insufficiencie, I had rather subscribe in that to their seveare censure then by seeking to avoide the imputation of weakenes, to incurre a greater suspition of honestie: for though some have used a double sale of their labours, first to the Stage, and after to the presse, For my owne part I heere proclaime myselfe ever faithfull in the first, and never guiltie of the last.

It was through the presentation of his plays on the stage, and for the most part at the public theatres, that Heywood intended his lessons to be taught. Even the notorious pirates, Purser and Clinton, on their way to execution in *Fortune by Land and Sea* (1607?), are permitted an atrocious pun and a patriotic sentiment for the amusement and edification of the audience: 'And set sail from the fatal Marshal seas, and Wapping is our harbour, a quick sand that shall swallow many a brave Marine souldier, of whose valour, experience, skil, and Naval discipline, being lost, I wish this land may never have need' (F2^v–3).

Heywood's stress on domestic virtues is too well known to need emphasis here. Two plays in particular, *A Woman Killed with Kindness* (1603) and *The English Traveller* (1624?–27?), are almost entirely devoted to them. Eliot thought that in the latter Heywood had found his best plot, 'a plot especially modern among Elizabethan plots; for the refinement of agony of the virtuous lover who has controlled his passion and then discovers that his lady has deceived both her husband, who is his friend, and himself, is really more poignant than the torment of the betrayed husband Frankford' (in *A Woman Killed*). Eliot goes on

---

[1] The 1615 title-page claims, however, that it was 'diverse times' acted at the Red Bull, a theatre built in 1604–6.

to refer to Heywood's 'refinement of sentiment' and 'sympathetic delicacy' in these two plays, and although he finds, as one would expect, that the interest is 'always sentimental, and never ethical', he comes to a conclusion which is important from our point of view: 'Heywood's sense of pity is genuine enough, but it is only the kind of pity that the ordinary playgoer, of any time, can appreciate. Heywood's is a drama of common life, not, in the highest sense, tragedy at all; there is no supernatural music from behind the wings. He would in any age have been a successful playwright; he is eminent in the pathetic, rather than the tragic' (pp. 111–16). Heywood would probably have agreed, and would have been satisfied that it was so.

There are other points about his 'drama of common life' which tend to be overlooked. His contempt for the unlettered is not so fierce as that of Jonson's, but it is still there. More than Jonson, however, he seems prepared to make allowances for it, and even to feel that he should do something about it. This didactic purpose sometimes leads him into trouble, for he will cheerfully hold up the action of his play to give a long explanation of what is going on; *The Brazen Age* (1612?), for example, has two such pauses, one to discuss the history and interpretation of the Golden Fleece, and the second to discuss similarly the labours of Hercules, while the audience of *2 The Iron Age* (1613?) was regaled with an account of the Amazons. When he was not concerned to teach the unlettered, Heywood was prepared to recognize their right to be entertained and his duty to give them the kind of entertainment they wanted. One of the best examples of this occurs in *Londini Speculum* (1627): 'The third Pageant or Show meerly consisteth of Anticke gesticulations, dances, and other Mimicke postures, devised onely for the vulgar, who are better delighted with that which pleaseth the eye, than contenteth the eare'. And why should this not be done, he asks, since in the great concourse of people who are looking on there are a great many different tastes to be satisfied? And 'grave and wise men have beene of opinion, that it is convenient, nay necessitious, upon the like occasions, to mixe *seria iocis*; for what better can set off matter, than when it is interlaced with mirth?' (C2).

Lastly there is his ability to poke fun at things which elsewhere he will take seriously, a facet of his character which seems to have something in common with Jonson's anti-romanticism. This is often done by the introduction into a serious scene of one of Heywood's typical clowns, with his earthy realism, shrewd comment on the action, bawdy jests and word-play. A clown in *The Golden Age* confuses 'Jupiter' with 'gibbet-maker', and keeps the attention of the old women while Jupiter makes love to the imprisoned Danae. Clem in *The Fair Maid of the West* (1600?–10?) entertains us with the reactions of a country yokel suddenly set down in the court of an eastern potentate. Gallus of *The Brazen Age* is set to keep watch while Mars and Venus are sleeping together. Most striking of all is the clown of *Love's Mistress* (1634), who educates the swains with the truth, as he sees it, about Pan and Cupid and the story of the Trojan War, and shows them how they have been deceived by the versions put about by poets:

> Menelaus was a farmer, who had a light wench to his wife call'd Hellen, that kept his sheep whom Paris, one of Priam's mad lads, seeing and liking, ticeth over the brooke, and lies with her in despight of her husbands teeth: for which wrong, he sends for one Agamemnon, his brother, that was then high Constable of the hundred, and complaines to him: he sends to one Ulisses, a faire spoken fellow, and Towneclarke, and to divers others, amongst whom was one stout fellow called Ajax, a Butcher . . .

and so on, until the Trojan War is reduced to the status of an afternoon's bout with a pair of cudgels 'for a broken pate' (D3).

All the time Heywood had his eye firmly on the stage, and lost no opportunity for dramatic effect and swift-moving incident. At least three of his plays open with a murder; and coincidence, accident, disguise, non-recognition between close relatives, dumb-show—all the tricks and paraphernalia of the Elizabethan and Jacobean stage are used with astonishing gusto. If the first part of a play proved popular, a second part was added, either with new adventures or with similar ones in slightly different surroundings. Jonson and his followers may have looked down their noses at this kind of drama, and did indeed succeed very largely in putting it out of business. There can be no doubt, however, that in its heyday, with authors like Dekker and Heywood to serve it, London audiences were supplied with a citizen comedy (and tragedy) and a domestic drama which appealed to every one of their senses, and to their hearts—and from time to time even to their heads. By the nature of things it could rarely be great drama; an isolated scene here and there might have the seeds of greatness in it, but the plays as a whole were ramshackle in construction and were not concerned to hammer home any one central point. Jonson and his followers realized this, and approached the matter in a different way. Once satire became the purpose of comedy a ruthless pruning was necessary. It was no longer enough to have characters throwing off unimpeachable sentiments, whether in the domestic or in wider fields, when the rush of incident was the audience's main concern. Comedy, therefore, both in form and content, must become an intellectual concern; wit and satire must replace broad, farcical humour, incident must be strictly controlled, and the moral purpose, which Heywood and Dekker thought of in general terms, must become specific.

Note

Biography: John Marston, 1576–1634
Son of a Shropshire lawyer and his Italian wife, he was probably born in Coventry. He studied at Brasenose College, Oxford (being admitted to a degree in 1594), and was afterwards resident at the Middle Temple. In 1608 he was imprisoned in Newgate. In September 1609 he was ordained deacon, and in the following December, priest. In 1619 he married Mary Wilkes, daughter of one of James I's chaplains.

Works. His first publications, in 1598 under a pseudonym, were *The Metamorphosis of Pigmalion's Image, and Certain Satires,* and *The Scourge of Villainy.* From 1599 to 1601, he wrote and revised plays for the Paul's Boys, and became involved in a theatrical flyting with Jonson. *The Dutch Courtesan* (1603-4) and following plays were written for the Queen's Revels boys' company. In 1605, he joined Chapman and Jonson to write *Eastward Ho* for them. It seems that William Barksted completed the tragedy, *The Insatiate Countess,* which Marston left unfinished in 1608.

Modern Editions. A. Davenport edited the *Poems* (1960) and A. H. Bullen the *Works* (3 vols., 1887); the *Plays* were also edited by H. H. Wood (3 vols., 1934-9). Quotations in the following chapter are from the Quartos, with line-references to Bullen. Webster is quoted from the edition of F. L. Lucas (1927), Sharpham's *Fleer* from that of H. Nibbe, in *Materialien* (1912). All these are modernized.

Scholarship and Criticism. One general book on Marston is J. A. Axelrad, *Un malcontent Élizabéthain, John Marston* (Paris, 1955). T. S. Eliot has an essay on his plays in *Elizabethan Essays* (1934), Una Ellis-Fermor a chapter in *Jacobean Drama* (1936), and Theodore Spencer an essay in *Criterion* (1933). F. T. Bowers, *Elizabethan Revenge Tragedy* (1940) discusses *Antonio and Mellida,* and B. Spivack, *Shakespeare and the Allegory of Evil* (1958), relates the Machiavellian villain of Elizabethan drama to the medieval 'Vice'.

J. Enck discusses the novelty of the realism and judgement in *Every Man Out of His Humour,* in *Jonson and the Comic Truth* (1957); T. Bogard, *The Tragic Satire of Webster,* investigates Marston's influence on Webster. M. Praz has discussed Elizabethan attitudes to Italy in *Shakespeare Survey* (1954). O. J. Campbell's *Comicall Satyre and Shakespeare's 'Troilus and Cressida'* (1938) examines the vogue for satirical plays.

IV

English Folly and Italian Vice
The moral landscape of John Marston

G. K. HUNTER

★

THE year 1599 is generally supposed to have seen the first productions of two very different plays, by authors whose attitudes and controversies were to keep the next decade entertained, and to provide between them much of the impetus for its dramatic development—the two plays were Jonson's *Every Man Out of His Humour* and Marston's *Antonio and Mellida* (parts one and two). The power and the newness of Jonson's play do not require any laborious exposition: here is a comic logic coupled to an unsparing social realism, and an insistence on judgement, which is completely new in Elizabethan comedy. Marston's play, on the other hand, is seldom seen as more than a sophisticated variant of the old 'Tragedy of Blood'; and it is certainly not an obvious example of what, in normal language, we would call 'realism'. Yet if we listen to what Marston says about his own play in the Prologue to Part Two of *Antonio's Revenge*, we find that it is in such terms that he speaks about its horrors:

> Therefore we proclaim
> If any spirit breathes within this round
> Incapable of weighty passion
> (As from his birth being hugged in the arms
> And nuzzled twixt the breasts of happiness)
> Who winks and shuts his apprehension up
> From common sense of what men were, and are,
> Who would not know what men must be—let such
> Hurry amain from our black-visaged shows;
> We shall affright their eyes.

How are we to treat this curious appeal from the abattoir to the Stoa? Does it in any way explain the Italianate horrors of the play, and does it justify any association of Marston with Jonson as a pioneer of Jacobean 'realism'?

We should begin by noting that the central idea found in the Prologue to *Antonio's Revenge*, the idea of 'what men were, and are . . . what men must be' is not mere window-dressing; it is found in the play itself. At the end of the revenge, when the tyrant Piero Sforza has been disposed of, a grateful senate offers the revengers 'what satisfaction outward pomp can yield':

> 1. SENATOR. You are well seasoned props,
> And will not warp or lean to either part.
> *Calamity gives man a steady heart.*
> ANTONIO. We are amazed at your benignity;
> But other vows constrain another course.
> PANDULPHO. We know the world, and did we know no more
> We would not live to know; but since constraint
> Of holy bands forceth us keep this lodge
> Of dirt's corruption till dread power calls
> Our souls' appearance, we will live enclosed
> In holy verge of some religious order
> Most constant votaries.   (V. ii. 141)

The first lines of Pandulpho's speech here are very close to Fulke Greville's 'I know the world and believe in God';[1] and in that light we may see our quotation from the Prologue as another statement of the Christian-Stoic position so characteristic of the Jacobean outlook. Given the reality of the world—'this lodge of dirt's corruption'—suicide would be (says Pandulpho) the natural conclusion to the action, but under Christianity this is not possible, and monastic retreat until death is the only alternative way of dissociating the soul from the world.

The image here of the real nature of the world—'what men were, and are . . . what men must be'—is not a sunny one, but it provides a natural tragic counterpart to the equally unrelenting language of the Induction to *Every Man Out of His Humour*:

> Who can behold such prodigies as these
> And have his lips sealed up? . . .
> I fear no mood stamped in a private brow

[1] Quoted by G. Bullough, *Poems and Dramas of Fulke Greville* (1939), I. i,

> When I am pleased t'unmask a public vice
> I fear no strumpet's drugs, nor ruffian's stab,
> Should I detect their hateful luxuries;
> No broker's, usurer's, or lawyer's gripe,
> Were I disposed to say, they are all corrupt.
> I fear no courtier's frown, should I applaud
> The easy flexure of his supple hams.

and indeed it should be related to a whole group of Jacobean statements preferring the downward (realist) estimate of man's potentialities to the upward (romantic) vision of many Humanists. As Bacon remarks,

> we are much beholden to Machiavel and others, that write what men do not what they ought to do.[2]

Plainly, Marston and Jonson were as 'beholden' as Bacon himself. In *Every Man Out*, however, Jonson is not 'disposed to say' the worst that can be said about such a world: the play is to be a *comicall* satyre and the gripe of the satirist will content itself with squeezing out 'the humour of such spongy souls As lick up every idle vanity'. It is the function of such a play 'to sport with human follies not with crimes'; but tragedy is, by definition, concerned with crimes, and with the magnified world in which crime may be expected and observed. The most obvious of such worlds is the world of power.

If we transfer the judgements of *Every Man Out* to the world of courtly power we arrive at attitudes very close to those of *Antonio and Mellida*. The private and privileged vantage-points of Jonson's commentators—Asper or Macilente—cannot be preserved in the more violent world of tragedy, and the evils of court life have to be focused from the viewpoints of those who endure them (Antonio, Andrugio, Pandulpho); but what they see is the same 'monster bred in a man by self love and affectation',[3] which is 'humour' in a person without power, and political crime in a sovereign. Both dramatists assume that this is the reality of human nature, which romantic or sentimental outlook may keep concealed, but whose truth must become apparent to any unprejudiced and experienced spectator. In one case the care for reality produces an anatomy of

> deeds and language such as men do use

---

[2] *Advancement of Learning*, ed. J. M. Robertson (1905), p. 140.
[3] *Every Man in His Humour* (quarto version), III. i. 157 f.

since the reality of folly is most easily seen in the petty everyday pretensions of our contemporaries. In the other case, however, the reality of man's criminal corruption demands both 'the rarity of Art' in language and a dramatic scene remote enough from the pettiness of everyday life to allow those simplifications and exaggerations that tragedy requires.

It is then as an image of the 'realities' of power (i.e. *Realpolitik*) that Marston defends his *Antonio and Mellida*, and it is in this respect that we ought to see the newness of his play. This is not the same thing, of course, as propounding its aesthetic success. Compared with the maturer version of the same outlook which we find in Jonson's *Sejanus*, Marston's play only weakly realizes the potentialities of political tragedy. It lacks both the unity of tone which Jonson preserves and the historical 'truth of argument' which Jonson attests by his continuous reference to Tacitus, Suetonius, Dio, etc. Yet the decisive advance or distinction that is achieved in *Antonio and Mellida* cannot be ignored if we set it against its predecessors (in many cases its sources).

The play has often been viewed in relation to earlier 'tragedies of blood', but always (I think) in terms of the mechanics of the revenge plot—how the delay is motivated and drawn out—and in the shadow of its potent relative, *Hamlet*. This I take not to represent the central interest of Marston himself (the Marston who wrote *Certain Satires*), nor the resting-place of his excellences, and certainly not the gift he bequeathed to his successors. I shall, in consequence, ignore it.

Antonio and Mellida is based almost everywhere on the tried favourites of the earlier Elizabethan period—Sidney's *Arcadia*, Kyd's *Spanish Tragedy*, Lyly's pageboy comedies, and (in its two-part structure) Marlowe's *Tamburlaine*. It was natural for a young dramatist to play safe by imitating proved successes; but it was also natural for a self-conscious graduate into the new age to see what he imitated with new eyes, and this is just what we find in this transitional and unsatisfactory play—a tension between the interests of the writer and the natural tendency of the plot-material he has selected. Andrugio, the deprived father of the play, is obviously modelled on Kyd's Hieronimo, but the effect of his tirades is quite different. The role of Hieronimo, like that of Titus Andronicus, is a martyr role: we see human suffering pushed up to (and beyond) the extreme edge of endurance. The structure of the play lines up trial after trial and the force of the speeches depends on the passionate eloquence with which they reveal the depths of human love and suffering:

> Where shall I run to breathe abroad my woes,
> My woes, whose weight have wearied the earth?
> Or mine exclaims, that have surchargad the air
> With ceaseless plaints for my deceased son?
> The blust'ring winds, conspiring with my words,
> At my lament have mov'd the leafless trees,
> Disrobed the meadows of their flowered green
> Made mountains marsh with spring-tides of my tears
> And broken through the brazen gates of hell
> (III. vii. 1)

The rhetoric of *pathos* here, the repetitions, exaggerations, and pathetic fallacy, serves to concentrate our interest on the woes of Hieronimo himself, freed from any background of people or ideas. Hieronimo is placed in a court which is fixed geographically, and one which will not hear his appeals:

> Go back, my son, complain to Aeacus,
> For here's no justice; gentle boy, be gone,
> For justice is exiled from the earth.
> (III. xiii. 137)

But no political image of the court is presented to us, no image of how courtly intrigue really works. In Marston's play, on the other hand, most of the energy of the dramatist goes into a vivid and detailed picture of life in a court from which justice has been exiled. The underlying thematic structure of the play is a series of contrasting philosophic and political poses: flattery at court is set against the honesty of exile; the unhappiness of the Stoic at court against the fulfilment of the Stoic in penury, the kingdom of the self-sufficient man against the kingdom of the successful politician. Inside such a framework the tirades of the deprived father, Andrugio, take their place less as exposures of human nature in extremity and more as demonstrations of an attitude to courtly corruption:

> Come soul, resume the valour of thy birth;
> Myself, myself, will dare all opposites;
> I'll muster forces, an unvanquished power;
> Cornets of horse shall press th'ungratefull earth;
> This hollow-wombed mass shall inly groan
> And murmur to sustain the weight of arms;

> Ghastly amazement with upstarted hair
> Shall hurry on before, and usher us
> While trumpets clamour with a sound of death.
> LUCIO. Peace, good my lord! Your speech is all too light.
> Alas! survey your fortunes, look what's left
> Of all your forces and your utmost hopes!
> A weak old man, a page, and your poor self.
> ANDRUGIO. Andrugio lives, and a fair cause of arms.
> Why, that's an army all invisible!
> He who hath that hath a battalion royal,
> Armour of proof, huge troops of barbed steeds,
> Main squares of pikes, millions of harquebus.
> O, a fair cause stands firm and will abide.
> Legions of Angels fight upon her side.
> (III. i. 72)

This is at once more personal and more political than the corresponding passages in *The Spanish Tragedy*. Andrugio is meaningful to us less as a representative of human misery and more as a philosophic stance, in a world which can be commented on and exposed from this point of view—though the point of view will hardly serve as a basis for action or 'improvement'.

Here is another essential difference between the world of *The Spanish Tragedy* and that of *Antonio and Mellida*: Hieronimo's bewilderment is not one that we share—not, at least, outside the individual speeches in which it is so powerfully expressed—for we know (through the Induction figures of Andrea and Revenge) that a whole supernatural machinery is directing and guaranteeing the revenge. When Hieronimo calls

> O sacred heavens, may it come to pass
> That such a monstrous and detested deed
> So closely smothered and so long concealed
> Shall thus by this be venged or revealed?
> (III. vii. 45)

there is no real surprise that the sword so long suspended over the head of the evil-doers should begin to fall. In *Antonio and Mellida*, however there is no external reason why (in the world of the play) one political attitude should conquer another, and this is perhaps the central weakness of the development. The story is a violent one, and to motivate it violence we feel the need for passionate involvement; but the interest of the author is in the cold realities of power, revealed in detached satiric portraiture, and in philosophic stances which comment on one another, but never really engage or necessarily issue into action. Given this lack of momentum, all the events in the play are equally surprising; the central actions seem as accidental as the others (Mellida's death is a case in point), and the conclusion completes nothing but the thematic picture of a world of Hobbesian individualism. Clearly, this is what Marston cared about, and it is certainly what his successors borrowed from him. As an author he is notoriously careless and probably contemptuous of his means of expression. His satires rejoice in a barbarity of diction and discontinuity of structure. The theory of the genre no doubt encouraged this, but Marston took to the genre like a duck to its dirty water, and shows no great willingness to abandon its methods even when he writes for the stage. Given all this, the plot and counter-plot intrigue of the revenge play can be seen to be ludicrously unapt to his genius, though one can see why he was attracted to the Hamlet-like problems of philosophic minds required to engage in the corrupted world of political action.

What are apt to his genius are the scenes of satiric social observation which spread the action of *Antonio and Mellida* across ten acts. From the point of view of revenge plotting these are tedious irrelevancies, but in terms of the leading ideas they supply a complementary social image to the political one of sovereign corruption and tyranny. The frivolous courtiers, denied responsibility, punished for truth and advanced for flattery, present a coherent image, no less moral for being comic, of what indeed 'men were, and are . . . what men must be'. If we regard simply as sensationalism the horrific elements in the intrigue of *Antonio and Mellida*, we can only support F. T. Bowers' temperate remark, 'Marston was no artist in comic relief' (p. 120); but if we try to understand what Marston was doing in terms of the ideas he himself presents in his Prologues, we may see the social satire as an integral part of a new vision, though a vision only imperfectly realized in this play.

Perhaps the most obvious aspect of Marston's innovation in tragedy is his discovery of a suitable background for his vision of reality. Critics who handle the 'Italianate' element in English drama usually speak as if attitudes to Italy were simple, and equally diffused throughout the whole period; but early tragedies like *The Spanish Tragedy* and *Titus*

Andronicus have 'Italianate' subject-matter (as the most distinguished exponent of literary relations between the two countries has recently remarked[4]) only in a very special sense. Villainy of an individualistic, self-justifying kind was often called Machi-villainy by the Elizabethans themselves, but the relation of this attitude to any image of Italy as a whole was very tenuous, especially in the drama before *Antonio and Mellida*. Marlowe brings Machiavelli himself on to the stage, but he is a spirit, and he is not confined to Italy: he ranges through France and appears in England itself. In fact, the atheism, political opportunism, and libertine views about love and family, supposed to be characteristic of the Machiavellian villain on the Elizabethan stage, are all natural enough as extensions of the Medieval 'Vice', given the substitution of political and social manners for the direct moral presentation of the later Middle Ages—and this substitution is already a cliché of literary history. Marlowe's Lightborne (in *Edward II*)

> Learned in Naples how to poison flowers,
> To strangle with a lawn thrust through the throat,
> To pierce the windpipe with a needle's point
> ... Or open his mouth and pour quicksilver down
> (2362–9)

but his name is that of a devil in the Chester Cycle, presumably equivalent to Lucifer.

The earliest Italians on the English stage[5] appear as comic foreigners, comic because foreign; and there is nothing particularly sinister about them. Concurrently, we find the traditional romantic image of Italy, as 'the country which to Shakespeare's fellows was the hallowed land of romance',[6] a land of rich and elegant young students whiling away the golden time of youth in

> fruitful Lombardy,
> The pleasant garden of great Italy.[7]

---

[4] Praz, p. 96. More tenable is his statement in 'L'Italia di Ben Jonson' (*Machiavelli in Inghilterra ed altri saggi* (1943), p. 173) that *The Spanish Tragedy* is set in 'un generico Mezzogiorno'; but even this is to avoid the stated fact that the scene is Spain.

[5] For example, in *The Rare Triumphs of Love and Fortune* (1582), *Three Ladies of London* (1582), Haughton's *Englishmen for my Money* (1598).

[6] H. B. Charlton, *Shakespearian Comedy* (1938), p. 33.

[7] *Taming of the Shrew*, I. i. 3.

This is the Italy of the *Cortegiano*, of courtship in both senses of the term, and of Euphues' proverb, 'If I be in Crete I can lie, in Greece I can shift, if in Italy I can court it'.[8]

There is little enough in all this to make Italy appear a natural home for sin. Indeed, when heinous deeds appear on the stage before 1599, or characters of monstrous wickedness, the background of the Vice is made obvious by the choice of specifically anti-Christian nationalities —Turkish in *Selimus* and *Alaham*, Moorish in *Titus Andronicus*, *Lust's Dominion*, and *The Battle of Alcazar*, Jewish in *The Jew of Malta*. It was only when the dramatists became politically minded[9] and saw tragedy as concerned (in Greville's phrase) 'to trace out the high ways of ambitious governors, and to show in the practice that the more audacity, advantage and good success such sovreignties have, the more they hasten to their own desolation and ruin',[10] to analyse the human motives in power politics, that the Italian court became the natural *venue* for lurid criminal behaviour. The applicability of Greville's idea of tragedy to the Italian background is obvious in the dedication of Robert Gomersall's Italianate *Tragedy of Lodovic Sforza* (1628), which is designed (he claims), to 'make the ambitious see that he climbs but to a fall, the usurper to acknowledge that blood is but a slippery foundation of power, all men in general to confess that the most glorious is not the most safe place'.

Of course, Marston's use of Italian courts as a setting for the personal abuse of power drew on expectations which were fixed before his day. Protestant polemic had kept up a running fire at Papistry and Epicurism (not always clearly distinguishable) which must have had an

[8] J. Lyly, *Euphues* (ed., 1916), p. 13.
[9] By 'politically minded' here I mean, 'concerned with politics as the art of exploiting human weakness, and with history as a chart of political success or failure'. Political problems had been presented on the stage before this time (as in Shakespeare's histories) and had bulked large in books like the *Mirror for Magistrates*. But political action is seen in the chronicles and the *Mirror* largely in the light of what men ought to do, and essentially as the fruit of God's will; so that 'all men seeing the course of God's doings may learn to dread his judgement and love his providence' (Preface to Grafton's *Chronicle*, 1569). Shakespeare's politics are not as blatantly moralized as this, but he does not seek to make a scientific separation of political from moral activity. This was the avowed aim of the new historiographers—like Sir John Hayward and Sir Francis Bacon—and it is to this I am referring when I speak of 'politically minded'.
[10] *Life of Sidney*, ed. N. Smith (1907), p. 221.

influence, but the effect in terms of art is neither obvious nor simple. A certain continuity in the English idea of Italy may be seen if we consider the spectrum of words associated with 'wit'—cleverness, cunning, artfulness, artistic power, originality, individualism, etc.—but there is no evidence that any Elizabethan saw these different aspects, some admirable, some the opposite, in this organized way. We can see that Spenser is naïve (or virile) where Tasso is sophisticated to an almost pathological degree, or that Byrd is fresh where Marenzio (not to mention Gesualdo) is on the edge of decadence; but we should beware of importing this perception into the period: Spenser and Byrd themselves seem to have felt only admiration and kinship with these contemporary Italian masters.[11]

The dangers affecting 'le jeune Anglais brusquement jeté dans ce milieu corrompu'[12] seem to have been much simplified and therefore much exaggerated. Euphues, like other Elizabethans, sees Italy as a land of opportunity open to conquest by wit, where the rooted pieties of a traditional way of life are broken up. But this does not argue 'Italofobia';[13] the 'Naples' of Euphues is London to the same extent as its 'Athens' is Oxford; 'Italian' vices are metropolitan vices and in fact duplicate those in the home life of their own dear Queen. We seriously distort relations between the two countries in this period if we ignore the fact that Italian culture was at least fifty years ahead of English in urban sophistication, in political and capitalistic theory, in philosophy, in casuistry, and in family relations, and that much of the English reaction is rustic distrust of urban manners.

In Jacobean comedy the breakdown of traditional values in the face of the new sophistications becomes a central issue, with the dramatists asserting the old pieties against the new opportunism of knights and merchants.[14] Likewise it was only in the Jacobean period that the background of ultra-modern opportunist Italy (familiar from the *novelle*) acquired sinister connections with tragedy; Italy was an awful warning about the state of Hobbesian individualism into which England

[11] On Marenzio see T. Watson's Latin sonnet, set before his *Italian Madrigals Englished* (1590)—a volume with which Byrd seems to have been closely connected.
[12] A. Feuillerat, *John Lyly* (1910), p. 51.
[13] I take the word from L. Torretta, 'L'Italofobia di John Lyly', *Giornale Storico della Letteratura Italiana* (1934), but the idea is fully developed in Feuillerat, *op. cit.*
[14] See L. C. Knights, *Drama and Society in the Age of Jonson* (1937).

seemed to be moving. Comedy satirized knights and city ladies for their failure to keep their appointed places; tragedy and tragicomedy revealed the new Hell around the corner, when the alternatives of eat or be eaten were all that remained to man. Italy became important to the English dramatists only when 'Italy' was revealed as an aspect of England.

F. T. Bowers has remarked that 'it is curious that Marston who with Webster and Tourneur was one of the most Italianate of Elizabethan dramatists in the sense that he more correctly portrayed the Italian scene and character as the Italians themselves would have recognised it, was at the same time one of the most Senecan' (p. 124). The dilemma that is proposed here, between real-life Italy and an ethical code remote from it, is one which we may now see as not strictly applicable. The real Italy of the turn of the seventeenth century is not one that appears in the plays. The Italy of the Counter-Reformation, of Spanish hegemony and of Baroque art is not one that we hear mentioned. The Italy of Marston and his successors is, in fact, chosen out of Italian history with as much deliberation and artifice as Jonson used when he came to choose the reign of Tiberius out of Tacitus. The world of competing petty princelings, bearing names like Sforza, Gonzaga, d'Este, and Medici, belongs to the period portrayed in Guicciardini's *Storia d'Italia* (1492–1534). It was a world long vanished when Marston wrote: the Sforza line was extinct by 1535 and the others seem to have become submerged in the responsibilities rather than the excitements of their roles. In his choice of the period of Guicciardini Marston is in fact very close to Jonson in the latter's choice of Tacitus as a principal source, for the two historians were favourites at the same time, of the same men, and for the same reasons. Overbury's 'Mere Fellow of an House' (a kind of Oxford Politic-Would-Be) feeds his self-regard on 'state-policy' out of 'Tacitus, Guicciardine or Gallo-Belgicus'. Justus Lipsius, the great editor and interpreter of Tacitus for this age, himself one of its prime formative influences,[15] calls Guicciardini 'inter nos summus historicus', and again, 'prudens peritusque scriptor et qui tales lectores suos facit'.[16] Both writers may be called Jacobeans before the letter; both see clearly the incapacity of individual virtue to outmanœuvre tyranny, or succeed in politics, lost as it is bound to be in the bewildering

[15] See L. Zanta, *La Renaissance du Stoïcisme au XVIᵉ Siècle* (1914).
[16] *Politicorum libri sex* (1589), annotations on Bk. I, cap. ix. Dallington's *Aphorisms* (see below) quotes the former on its title-page.

variety of causes and contingencies that rule the world. Both seem to belong by nature to that 'Counter-Renaissance' movement which denied the interpenetration of Divine and Natural Law, and both saw the world of power as a jungle of *homo homini lupus*. In the tract of history he covered Guicciardini showed to the world 'la grande tragedia di una nazione che rovina per l'egoismo dei propri governanti',[17] and pointed to the key figure of Lodovico Sforza (Il Moro) whose egotism destroyed the whole Italian nation when he called in the French to assist his own private usurpation. The figure of Lodovico clearly fascinated the English dramatists: Marston's 'swart' Piero Sforza must be meant to recall Lodovico, and two other plays (Gomersall's *Sforza* and Massinger's *Great Duke of Milan*) use him as the central character.

Both Tacitus and Guicciardini were closely associated with the spread across Europe of ideas about *ragione di stato*: while the name of Machiavelli himself was being vilified, his political philosophy was purveyed under their names; and this is the philosophy we find in Marston and Jonson, derived, it would seem, not from the sensational Machiavelli of the earlier English stage, but from the real Machiavelli, mediated by historians and scholars. The spread of *Tacitismo* (this political use of Tacitus) at the end of the sixteenth century, and the relationship with Machiavelli has been amply described by G. Toffanin,[18] but since Toffanin does not mention England we ought to point to Jonson's apparent knowledge of the tradition—where he speaks of

> a chrysolite, a gem, a very agate
> Of State and Policy, cut from the quar
> Of Machiavel; a true Cornelian
> As Tacitus himself.
>   (*Magnetic Lady*, I. vii. 29)

It is presumably no accident that Tiberius, who stands at the centre of Jonson's tragedy, is called by Toffanin 'questo capolavoro di "ragione di stato" lavorato da Tacito' (p. 51) and was selected by the Tacitisti as one who used the techniques of Machiavelli's prince in their full per-

---

[17] N. Orsini, *Studii sul Rinascimento Italiano in Inghilterra* (1937), see p. 77. Also H. Haydn, *The Counter-Renaissance* (1950).

[18] *Machiavelli e il Tacitismo* (1921). That Jonson got his Machiavellism from the classics was long ago recognized by E. Meyer in *Machiavelli and the Elizabethan Drama* (1897), p. 101; but the method by which it reached him has not, I think, been noticed.

fection. The political conclusion that one must draw from *Sejanus* is very close to that which Toffanin describes as derived from Tacitus' Tiberius by the Tacitisti: 'in spite of Tacitus' antipathy to Tiberius the logic of his history is that Tiberius' iniquity *worked*, and this logic is undoubtedly one of the motives inspiring the *Principe*' (p. 52 f.).

The case of Guicciardini is more problematical. It may be approached, however, by considering the evidence of the English 'discourses'—historical essays in the empirical and disenchanted manner of Machiavelli. Machiavelli's *Discorsi* were not printed in English till 1636, but by then the *Discorso* approach to history was well attested in England. In 1600 Sir Clement Edmondes published his *Observations on the first five books of Caesar's Commentaries*, with a clear reference to Machiavelli as one of the 'pregnant wits who have presented decades of History to these later ages' (p. 3). Edmondes' book claims to be a discourse on war, 'for the better direction of our modern wars', but an approach to war implies an attitude to politics, and this we find Edmondes to handle in a strictly empirical and coldly scientific manner extraordinarily like that later recommended by Bacon:

> for, unless the understanding be in this sort qualified and able by logistical discourse to ascend, by way of composition, from singularity to catholic conceptions [i.e. from particular to general]; and return again the same way to the lowest order of his partitions, the mind cannot be said to have the perfection of that art, nor instructed in the true use of the knowledge. (p. 2)

Edmondes' words did not fall on stony soil: the book came bearing commendations from Camden, Daniel, Sylvester, and Ben Jonson: it was enlarged by command of Prince Henry, and went through four editions in the next ten years.

There are no less than two of these English discourses to show the convenience of Guicciardini's material for this kind of treatment. In 1601 Remigio Nannini's book of discourses (Bacon possessed a copy of the original) was Englished as *Civil considerations upon many and sundry histories as well ancient as modern, and principally upon those of Guicciardine*. In 1613 Sir Richard Dallington published his *Aphorisms civil and military . . . out of the first quaterne of Fr. Guicciardine*. Both of these approach the *Storia d'Italia* as a natural landscape for political observation. Commonplace books of the time tell the same story. N. Orsini has pointed to the dozen or so manuscript commonplace books in the British Museum and Bodleian Libraries which contain extracts from the *Storia d'Italia*; indeed Guicciardini himself had pointed to this use of his material in his own *Ricordi* or *Precetti*, which appear in both Nannini and Dallington, and had appeared earlier still in Hitchcock's translation, *The Quintessence of Wit* (1590). Indeed, the large number of derivatives from Guicciardini, all over Europe, show the extent to which he had made Italian history what one of these compilations uses as its title—a *speculum aulicorum*, a mirror for courtiers, wherein they might see (as in Jacobean tragedy) the methods of political action, and its fruits. It need not surprise us that the political interests of Jacobean tragedy turn it naturally towards material that had been, as it were, predigested.

The evidence would suggest then that the Guicciardini period of Italian history was well known to the Jacobeans as a *corpus vile* for political dissection by the new scientific methods. I suggest further that it was this rather than any general reputation of Italy for immoral behaviour or any heritage of the popular Machiavel that drove Marston to choose it as a background for a tragedy of the individual under tyranny.

The image of warring states selfishly absorbed in the effort to betray one another, together with a variety of philosophic and satirical poses is not, however, enough to convey any idea of the political seriousness needed to relate Stoicism to a tyrant's court. When Marston shows us

> Young Galeatzo? Ay, a proper man,
> Florence, a goodly city: it shall be so.
> I'll marry her to him instantly.
> Then Genoa mine by my Maria's match,
> Which I'll solemnize ere next setting sun.
> Thus Venice, Florence, Genoa, strongly leagued.
> Excellent, excellent! I'll conquer Rome,
> Pop out the light of bright religion;
> And then, helter skelter, all cocksure!
> (*Antonio's Revenge*, IV. i. 260)

he gives us *material* which might have come out of the *Storia d'Italia*, but the jauntiness of the manner blurs any sense of the cold and unpredictable web of politics which we find in Guicciardini himself. If Marston is to express throughout this material 'what men were, and are

'... what men must be', and achieve a standpoint as expressive as that of the Jacobean essayists, or writers of Characters, clearly he must acquire a voice which can sound both knowing about the situation and yet detached from it, an individual and personal point of view which can focus both the attraction and corruption of the world of power. The fairy-tale figure of the disguised prince has obvious potentialities in this direction, and Marston utilizes some of these in *Antonio and Mellida*, though in a typically incoherent way. Antonio, the disinherited heir, stays at court disguised as a fool in order to observe the reports of his own death:

> ANTONIO. Antonio's dead, the fool will follow too; he, he, he.
> Now works the scene; quick observation scud
> To quote the plot, or else the path is lost.
> (IV. i. 225)

But this stance can provide no more than one element in the complicated plotting of the revenge, though it is an effective element in itself:

> I never saw a fool lean: the chub-faced fop
> Shines sleek with full-crammed fat of happiness;
> Whilst studious contemplation sucks the juice
> From wizards' cheeks; who making curious search
> For Nature's secrets, the first innating cause
> Laughs them to scorn, as man doth busy apes
> When they will zany men. Had Heaven been kind,
> Creating me an honest senseless dolt,
> A good poor fool, I should want sense to feel
> The stings of anguish shoot through every vein.
> I should not know what 'twere to lose a father,
> I should be dead of sense to view defame
> Blur my bright love, I could not thus run mad
> As one confounded in a maze of mischief,
> Staggered, stark felled with bruising stroke of chance.
> (IV. i. 42)

The status of the fool is an obvious vantage-point for moral comment, but commentary on government is hardly within its scope.

When Antonio puts on his fool's coat, however, his confidant, Alberto, suggests another disguise:

> Rather put on some trans-shaped cavalier,
> Some habit of a spitting critic, whose mouth

> Voids nothing but gentile and unvulgar
> Rheum of censure. (IV. i. 3)

This reads like a first idea for the plot of Marston's best play, *The Malcontent* (1604), where the disguised prince (Altofront) does in fact assume the guise of a 'spitting critic' or Malcontent in order to observe and describe (with loathing and relish) the decadent court of the usurper. In this play Marston has avoided the difficulties of his revenge plot in *Antonio and Mellida*, yielding to his natural bent for satiric observation. The plot is one which keeps passion, by constantly satirizing it, at the reduced level of a somewhat ridiculous distance. The aims of the wretched eminent beings, whose lives we observe, are all frustrated, but frustrated without bloodshed and almost without violence. The function of the Malcontent, Malevole, is to expose (and if possible convert) rather than punish, and the play concludes naturally with a judgement rather than a bloodbath. The satiric (or, rather, *satyric*) violence of language, which made farce out of many of the strained revenge poses in *Antonio and Mellida* is here harnessed to a coherent though violently disillusioned outlook:

> Now good Elysium, what a delicious heaven it is for a man to be in a prince's favour! O sweet God! O pleasure! O Fortune! O all thou best of life! what should I think? what say? what do? to be a favourite! a minion! to have a general timorous respect observe a man, a stateful silence in his presence, solitariness in his absence, a confused hum and busy murmur of obsequious suitors training him; the cloth held up and way proclaimed before him; petitionary vassals licking the pavement with their slavish knees, whilst some odd palace lampreys that engender with snakes and are full of eyes on both sides, with a kind of insinuated humbleness fix all their delights upon his brow. O blessed state! what a ravishing prospect doth the Olympus of favour yield! (I. i. 325)

In *Antonio and Mellida*, exuberant satire of the courtlings had made it difficult to refocus on the solitary Stoics who provide the only possible alternative to the world of flattery, corruption, and power. The Stoicism of Pandulpho and Feliche was so pure that it was difficult to see what they were doing at the court of the tyrant Piero. But in *The Malcontent* the materials are more genuinely mixed into a tragicomic compound—and much borrowing from Guarini's *Pastor Fido* may indicate that Marston had been reading up this prototype of tragicomedy while preparing his own *aspera Thalia*. Malevole, as his name suggests, is eaten into by the evil he beholds. He is the cynical *observer* (the word is a favourite of the period), disillusioned almost beyond sanity and scornful of remedies or ameliorations. It is his voice we hear behind the exchange.

BILIOSO. Marry, I remember one Seneca, Lucius Annaeus Seneca.
PIETRO. Out upon him! He writ of Temperance and Fortitude, yet lived like a voluptuous epicure and died like an effeminate coward.
(III. i. 26)

Sic transit philosophia! The Malcontent is sufficiently close to the emperical scientist to know (and demonstrate) that there is no substitute for experience, and that experience is only available to those who are, in some sense, part of the world they observe. Hence, of course, the tension between the different desires of the disguised prince figure who is so common in the first decade of the seventeenth century[19]—between the desire to participate in the life of power, and the desire to condemn and withdraw. It is this that makes Malevole their prototype, rather than Jonson's Macilente who had preceded him by several years. Macilente is the envious man of *Every Man Out of His Humour*: he is both contemptuous of the fools and envious of their success, and so anticipates the complex of attitudes in Malevole. But Macilente is presented as superior to and unmenaced by the follies he observes. He is detached from the main current of the action; the well-weighed quality of his vocabulary and the rounded organization of his speeches give his attitudes a coolness very different from the half-crazed involvement of Malevole inside affairs he is helpless to control. Macilente is quite clear about what he believes; the Malcontent is only really clear about what he disbelieves. The anticlericalism of *The Malcontent* presents this position with a directness rarely attempted in Elizabethan drama; here Protestant individualism has reinforced Stoicism in its rejection of corporate values. The hero is left alone with

> that Eternal Eye
> That sees through flesh and all[20]

—and this means the hero's flesh no less than that of the others.

In creating the type and the tone of the Malcontent (or deriving

---
[19] See Shakespeare's *Measure for Measure*, Marston's *Malcontent* and *Fawn*, Sharpham's *Fleer*, Day's *Law Tricks*, Middleton's *Phoenix*.
[20] *The Revenger's Tragedy*, I. iii. 74.

these from *Hamlet*[21]) Marston has created an instrument which can expose and anatomize the pettiness of individual effort in a world of chance, emptied of effective moral norms and governed by competing power-politicians. 'Let's mutiny and die', says Celso (Malevole's confidant). Malevole replies

> O no! climb not a falling tower, Celso;
> 'Tis well held desperation, no zeal,
> Hopeless to strive with fate. Peace! Temporize.
> (I. i. 238)

The patience of Malevole here is very different from the patience of Hieronimo or Titus: it is the patience of the poker-playing individualist who knows that his turn will come when the others (inevitably) make their mistakes:

> MALEVOLE. Discord to malcontents is very manna; when the ranks are burst, then scuffle Altofront.
> CELSO. Ay, but durst?
> MALEVOLE. . . . Phewt! I'll not shrink
> He's resolute who can no lower sink (I. i. 250)

The Malcontent is a philosopher who knows the ineffectiveness of philosophy, and the brutality of action; yet still seeks for power. Hence his vocabulary is deprived of ideals, and even of self-regard:

> I'll . . . be a right man then, a man o' the time;
> For to be honest is not to be i' the world.[22]

The most he can be is an 'honest villain' (I. i. 130).

In fixing this figure, and handing him on as an effective presenter of the individual's fate in a world of power politics, Marston gave a clear indication of how the problem of 'what men were, and are . . . what men must be' could be treated on the public stage. It is hardly to be doubted that the Italianate tragedies of Tourneur, Webster, and Middleton owe much of their tone and their technique to the example set by Marston. It was he who discovered in the world of Guicciardini's Italy a natural background for the self-torturing individualism of the Malcontent observer, who saw that the atmosphere of corrupted power could be crystallized by setting a solitary, cynical 'observer' against a

---

[21] H. R. Walley and E. E. Stoll discuss the relative dates of *Hamlet* and *The Malcontent* in *The Review of English Studies* (1933 and 1935).
[22] *The Revenger's Tragedy*, I. i. 101–3.

procession of sophisticated and self-confident vice. The opening pageant of *The Revenger's Tragedy* (1606?) shows what poetic power the method can achieve. As a mere location for sin other places were as effective as Italy, and went on being used; but for the background for political plotting and counterplotting Italy remained, from the time of Marston, the favourite location.

This does not mean, of course, that Marston or his successors had any desire to complicate the 'realism' of political outlook with the *reality* of Italian life. How much Marston and Tourneur are concerned with ideas, and how little with places, is indicated by a brief glance at their *dramatis personae*. Florio's Italian dictionary gives us the key to what is, in the main, a Morality company. Thus in *The Revenger's Tragedy* we have *Supervacuo*, 'too much, superfluous, overmuch, vain, not necessary, unprofitable, to no use'; *Spurio*, 'a bastard, a base born. Also adulterate or counterfeit', etc., etc. In Marston's *Fawn* we find *Nymphadoro*, 'an effeminate fellow, a spruce ladies' courting fellow'; and *Frappatore*, 'a bragger, a boaster, a vaunter, a craker. Also a crafty prattler, a coney catcher, a cheater'. These occur in a play where the Duke of Ferrara is called Hercules (no doubt intended to recall the real Ercole d'Este) and the Duke of Urbino is named Gonzago (*sic*). To see any contradiction here is to forget the tradition which set historical plays on the Elizabethan stage, where *Stephen Langton* and *Sedition* can be alternative names for one character, with *Usurped Power* and *The Pope* as another interchangeable pair. For Bale (from whose *King John* these names are taken), as for Spenser, there is here no contradiction; the importance of history was just this, that it made actual the preordained patterns of vice and virtue: if the Pope is the living embodiment or incarnation of Usurped Power, one must expect to find in his court characters like Treason, Private Wealth, or Dissimulation, wearing the flesh and individuality of named men. The pattern of historical thinking in Marston and Tourneur is different from this, but if we substitute social observation for the intense moral scrutiny of Bale or Spenser we find that the corrupt court of a Renaissance prince is in fact no less a Morality masque of skulls beneath the skin, no less a parade of Lussurioso and Spurio and Sordido and Bilioso and Maquerelle.

This treatment of Italy, as a mode of human experience rather than as a country, may seem to apply less to Webster than to Marston and Tourneur; since Webster's two Italian tragedies are probably the greatest plays in the tradition, the exception would have some importance.

F. L. Lucas has remarked: 'Again and again critics have cried out at characters like Flamineo or Francisco or Ferdinand with the refrain of Judge Brack—"But people do not do such things". And to that the only answer is, "They did"; and the only remedy is to read the history of the time' (i. 92). This may be true, but it has little relevance to the art-form that Webster was working in, which can only seem incredibly ramshackle if judged by the standards of any school of historical realism. It is true that Morality structure is not obvious in Webster: his characters do not generally have significant names (though Zanche, Cariola, and Doctor Julio seem to be exceptions[23]). It is only possible to regard the plays in a realistic way, moreover, if we disregard the explicit gnomic statements which stud every scene. This is, of course, regularly done; I. Jack tells us that the moral statement 'has nothing to do with the action of the plays',[24] and Una Ellis-Fermor has elaborated this attitude quite fully. If we approach Webster's plays via Marston's it is possible, however, to see within his dramatic actions a structure and an attitude which may be able to reconcile their sententiousness and their liveliness. In Webster, as in Marston, we have the political conditions of Guicciardini's Italy, the mazes of Princes and Cardinals with their plots and counterplots, their dynastic ambitions and their ruthlessness, to provide a natural milieu for the discontented scholar or 'spitting critic' who stands at the centre and mediates all the action. Flamineo and Bosola, like Malevole (and Vindice), are also the centre of the plays' gnomic activity; they keep before us an idea of virtue which may be helpless in the world and therefore rejected, but which continues to exercise its appeal

> to scorn that world which life of means deprives.

They, like Malevole, are the individualists who know all the rules for individualists, know the meaninglessness of success, yet carry on, as if hypnotized by their own expertise. They indeed of all characters in the plays are least able to achieve any of their desired ends. As tool-villains they have to obey the rules of those who have hired them, and lack even the satisfaction of a Lodovico in 'limning' the night-piece of *The White Devil* (1612)—a satisfaction which seems to survive even when the artist himself is about to be 'dis-limbed'. They end their lives where

---

[23] See *Notes and Queries* (1957), p. 55.
[24] *Scrutiny* (1949), pp. 38–43.

the plays started them—intelligent, self-aware, disenchanted, poor, envious, and damned.

Webster's Malcontents, like Marston's, hold together in their minds a world which involves obvious logical contradictions and which (in another presentation) might fall apart—a world of greed, cunning, madness, ambition, melancholy and contempt for the world, priggishness, and cynicism—but since the play *is* what they see (and since the dramatist has found a compelling language for their vision of it) the play does not fall apart. Indeed we can see the dramatist altering his Italian narrative so that the pressure of real life will not obscure his obsessive rephrasing of it into Morality terms, so that it will fulfil what the Malcontents tell us:

> This busy trade of life appears most vain
> Since rest breeds rest, where all seek pain by pain.
> (*White Devil*, V. vi. 273)

The choice allowed here is so narrow as to be inadmissible in any but Morality terms, but it supplies the framework for Webster's Italy, where the only rest is the rest of innocuousness, unimportance, and death (the rest that Spenser's Despair offers Red Cross Knight), and where the only activity that is effective is what leads through 'policy' to wickedness and punishment.

The intense gnomic activity of the plays is not irrelevant to their action; for the action is organized on principles that depend on such gnomic understanding. Webster is obsessively concerned with certain patterns of action which show man to be lost, isolated, or in a state of servile subjection; but these patterns are only important if the author can convey some sense of the values they exclude, the sense of loss in the world of power, the tension between Virtue and Fortune, or (as the Humanists would have put it) between *vita comtemplativa* and *vita activa*.[25] Webster carries to its logical extreme the concern with 'what men were, and are', assuming that it is only in action that men are truly themselves, and that contemplation or pure knowledge is beautiful but ineffective. This was the basic assumption that the Humanists handed on to these dramatists and to the modern world. The line of tragic drama from Marston to Webster explores the assumption in terrifying detail, facing the Italianate or modern world of success-at-all-costs

[25] See especially the *Dialogue between Pole and Lupset* by T. Starkey.

with scorn and horror. The scorn and horror remain relevant to us in the modern world of today.

* * *

The vision of Italian vice that descends through *Antonio and Mellida* and *The Malcontent* to Tourneur and Webster may seem at a great remove from London citizen comedy as written (for example) by Middleton. The fact that Middleton also wrote *Women Beware Women* ought, perhaps, to make us pause; but a clearer demonstration of the relationship may be given if we consider the comic descent from Marston parallel to that which we have already traced for tragedy.

In *Antonio and Mellida* the corrupt Italian court is set against a variety of Stoic poseurs and disguised persons who comment on the scene, but do not dominate or distance its horrifying and extraordinary activities. In *The Malcontent* the commentator stands fairly and squarely between us and the life of the court; the detachment with which we view this world is consequently greater and its comic potentialities increased. In Marston's later comedy, *Parasitaster, or The Fawn* (1604-6), we meet once again a disguised Duke commenting cynically, and even encouraging malevolently, the excesses of court folly and vice. But here the detachment of the audience from the scene is still greater: the court observed is not the commentator's own court; there is an absence of the intense involvement which marks Malevole; and the end in view is not power, but love:

> So may we learn that nicer love's a shade—
> It follows, fled; pursued, flies as afraid—
> And in the end close all the various errors
> Of passages most truly comical
> In moral learning; with like confidence
> Of him who vowed good fortune of the scene
> Should neither make him fat, or bad make lean.
> (V. i. 19)

The intrigue, in short, has become more important in its own right, as a maze traced through courtly follies, without losing itself in the violent reactions these give rise to. 'Moral learning' remains important, but largely as a means of controlling and winding up the 'passages most truly comical'.

The course of comic development from *The Fawn* may be conveniently indicated by jumping a few stages and looking now at a little-known and hideously disorganized, but (for that reason) historically revealing play—Edward Sharpham's *The Fleer* (1606). *The Fleer* is disorganized just because it tries to move from Italian melodrama to citizen comedy inside the action of one play, and without any subtlety of modulation. The central character is a dispossessed Italian duke (called Antifront, in obvious imitation of Marston's Malcontent duke, Altofront), whose disguise as an old serving man, Fleer, allows him to spy on his two daughters, who have (of all things!) moved from Florence to London and set up a bawdy-house. Once the disguised duke reaches London, the play turns into pure citizen intrigue of weak knights and cheeky servants, improbably dragged back by a restitution of the forgotten dukedom in the last few lines. The play contains evil —an attempt to poison (frustrated by the usual benevolent apothecary); the one thing it does not contain is Marston's 'moral learning', a coherent response to vice or folly, which does not allow intrigue simply to carry away what is repugnant. Sharpham seems to have taken Hamlet's 'poison in jest; no offence i' the world' as a motto for his action, and to suppose that deeds done among citizens need no such integrity of judgement as is required when the actors are great men.

The same weakness of response might be thought to be present in other plays that Sharpham brings into relation with his own:

FLEER. And will you to the Southward i' faith? will you to the confines of Italy, my gallants? take heed how ye go Northwards; 'tis a dangerous coast; jest not with 't in winter; therefore go Southwards my gallants; Southwards ho! (II. 397)

Dekker and Webster's *Northward-Ho* (1605), to which this seems to refer, has only a tenuous relation to the tradition we are describing, but the first play of the series, *Westward-Ho* (1604), is clearly related to it as a further variant on the Marston situation of the disguised Italian. The Italian is now only an Italian merchant, resident in London, who disguises himself as a writing-master to watch the supposed infidelities of his wife; and who, in this disguise, malevolently enjoys and encourages the adulterous plottings of other citizens' wives:

if... all wives love clipping, there's no fault in mine. (II. i. 232 f.)

The disguised husband is here principally an intriguer and hardly at all a commentator; and our sense of vice and corruption is further softened or sentimentalized into a view that it is all a harmless if spicy frolic.

The *dénouement* is achieved without moral judgement, but simply by showing that the husbands are just as bad as the wives they accuse, and by arranging the reconciliation on this *quid pro quo* basis. There is, of course, in *Westward-Ho*, the highly rhetorical episode of the Italian's wife and her would-be seducer, the Earl, with its blank-verse orations, pseudo-corpse, husband disguised as his own wife, etc. It is true that this presents an image of virtue; but it is of virtue so melodramatic that it does not modify our judgement of the realistic main intrigue. The impression we get is that virtue is a matter of theatrical extremes, while casual vice is the real substance of living.

That such attitudes did not satisfy Marston seems to be clear enough from the reply concocted with Jonson and Chapman under the title of *Eastward-Ho* (1605). There is good ground for supposing that Marston was the leading spirit behind this venture, and that he constructed the general outlines of the play. In *Eastward-Ho* it is made clear that a background of citizen life need not infringe the strictest moral judgement; the methods of the Morality play are used, without reducing the social documentation or the precise local allusions. The story of the good apprentice and the wicked apprentice is as authentic and as diagrammatically moral as the images it so strangely resembles in Hogarth's Idle Apprentice and Industrious Apprentice series of engravings:

> As I have two prentices, the one of a boundless prodigality, the other of a most hopeful industry; so have I only two daughters, the eldest of a proud ambition and nice wantonness, the other of a modest humility and comely soberness. (I. i. 83)

In this play Security, the usurer, encourages his own wife (supposing her to be the wife of his colleague and neighbour) to liberal infidelity. The contrast with the Italian merchant of *Westward-Ho* is that we are never in any doubt about the moral status of Security; and his end (shipwrecked at Cuckoldshaven, and then put in prison) is entirely appropriate to the strictest canons of justice:

> Alas I am a cuckold,
> And why should it be so?
> Because I was a usurer
> And bawd, as you all know.
> (V. v. 147)

It is in the context of this conflict of dramatic ideals that we should look at Marston's one independent London comedy, *The Dutch Courtesan* (1603–4). This play has sometimes been supposed to bear some relation to Dekker's *The Honest Whore* (part one) (1604). Whether or not one play was written in answer to the other is not certain, but the two plays have enough points of similarity to make the contrast between them a profitable mode of exposition. The two titles sound as if they had been designed in competition with one another, and this sense is strengthened by the note that Marston appends to his Prologue: 'The difference betwixt the love of a courtesan and a wife is the full scope of the play'. It is just this difference that *The Honest Whore* is concerned to smooth away. Bellafront, Dekker's honest whore, is a sinner who is brought to repentance, and so (the play assumes) to virtue, by a fine poetic speech and a handsome face in the speaker. She is made an attractive figure, even in the days of her sin; but the play concentrates, in any case, on her subsequent, Magdalen-like state. There is much talk about sin, but the play (it might be said) is not prepared to show the nastiness that dwells in real-life sin: certainly the dramatic emphasis falls on the graces of repentance.

Marston could never be accused of wishing to avoid the nastiness of real-life sin. But his play is not simply a slice of nasty life. Like *Eastward-Ho* and unlike Dekker's play it is braced by a rigid Morality framework, which shows itself most clearly in the names and the strict *decorum* of his persons—however their lives may be illustrated by real-life vignettes. It is one of the oldest dramatic rules that courtesans should always behave like courtesans, and this Dekker's Bellafront does not do. Francischina, Marston's Dutch courtesan, bears a famous Venetian prostitute's name, which was also the type-name of the *Commedia dell' Arte* servant-girl; in its English equivalents, often used in the play—Frances or Frank—the name implies one who is frank or free with her favours. Nothing complicates the simple moral discriminations on which the play is founded. But though the structure of the play is as simple as that of a Morality, the Everyman (or Prodigal Son) who stands at its centre is no simple moralist's conception. Here the average self-centred man of Machiavelli and Bacon can be seen in the process of becoming the *gallant* of Caroline or Restoration Comedy, the man whose virtue (if that is the correct word) comes to him by his experience of vice and not at all by precept. In *The Honest Whore* virtue triumphs because it is shown as more eloquent than vice in appealing to the softer emotions; in *The Dutch Courtesan* it triumphs because one character (Freevil) steps aside to direct the plot and interpret it; the method does not presuppose any natural bias towards virtue in the life depicted. The centre of *The Dutch Courtesan* lies in the soliloquies with which Freevil explains his move into disguise and into control of a medicinal or purgative plot—that is, one which will end with punishment for the vicious Francischina, and self-knowledge for the rigid Malheureux, who has succumbed to her influence. Freevil himself is actuated by no romantically simplified emotions, but is obliged to rest on what is useful:

> But is this virtue in me? No, not pure;
> Nothing extremely best with us endures,
> No use in simple purities; the elements
> Are mixed for use; silver without alloy
> Is all too eager to be wrought for use;
> Nor precise virtues ever, purely good,
> Holds useful size with temper of weak blood.
> (IV. ii. 40)

By this rough ethic the gallant is able to justify his manipulation of other people's weaknesses, but this is not the whole ethic of the play. Freevil can justify his earlier resort to Francischina by the argument that he (unlike Malheureux) was never besotted, could handle pitch without being defiled; but the 'full scope' of the play is that there is no compromise between love and lust, and we judge Freevil accordingly. *The Dutch Courtesan*, no less than Marston's tragedies, is concerned with 'what men must be'. Though here it is sex and not power that is the motive force in the play, the position of Freevil, as one who has to be part of the depraved world before he can accurately describe it, or effectively manipulate it, makes him obviously parallel to Malevole. Though never encouraging a tragic response, *The Dutch Courtesan* moves throughout in a world of fallen creatures, where depravity may be checked but cannot be forgotten. It is this that explains Freevil's desire to test and retest virtue, his unwillingness to trust its existence, till he has proved it against his pulses; the speech in which he expresses this aim may serve indeed as a comment on the whole Jacobean movement to overload human virtue till it breaks under the rigour of mad inquisition (as, in a sense, the inquisitors must wish it to):

FREEVIL. I will go and reveal myself; stay! no, no;
Grief endears love. Heaven! to have such a wife

Is happiness to breed pale envy in the saints.
Thou worthy dove-like virgin without gall,
Cannot that woman's evil, jealousy,
Despite disgrace, nay (which is worst) contempt,
Once stir thy faith? O Truth, how few sisters hast thou!
Dear memory! With what a suff'ring sweetness, quiet modesty,
Yet deep affection, she received my death!
And then with what a patient yet oppressed kindness
She took my lewdly imitated wrongs.
O' the dearest of Heaven! Were there but three
Such women in the world, two might be saved.
Well, I am great with expectation to what devilish end
This woman of foul soul will drive her plots.
But Providence all wicked art o'er-tops.
'And Impudence must know (though stiff as ice)
'That Fortune doth not alway dote on vice.'
                              (IV. iv. 85)

The victory of Providence is scored throughout in this minor key; the comedy avoids the obvious trap of a falsely romantic ending only by conveying this sense of restriction in the victory. Indeed this local victory even gives us a renewed sense of the prevalence of tragic disorder in ordinary human life; its integrity may serve to remind us that English folly and Italian vice are in this period only complementary images to express a single vision of the human state.

Note

Biography: Ben Jonson, 1573–1637
The posthumous son of a 'grave minister of the gospel', he was born in or near London and educated at Westminster School under the antiquary, William Camden. At 17 he was put to the trade of bricklayer, but left this to serve as a soldier in the Low Countries and, later, to join a company of actors. By 1595 he was married and writing plays for the impresario, Philip Henslowe. In 1598 he killed an actor in a duel (for which he was imprisoned and branded as a felon), became a Roman Catholic while in prison (and remained one for 12 years), and saw his *Every Man in His Humour* performed by the Chamberlain's Men, the best company of the time. He boasted of his high aims as a dramatist and engaged in a 'war of the theatres', writing *Poetaster* (1601) which contains a satirical portrait of Marston. On the accession of James I, he was commissioned to write court masques and, despite a brush with the censor of plays (see pp. 126 n.8 and 226), wrote 30 masques during this reign. In 1616 James granted him a pension of 100 marks a year for life; he was now at the height of his fortunes, having friends, patrons, and followers among the nobility, men of affairs, scholars, and poets. He helped with the publication of the folio edition of Shakespeare's plays in 1623, writing verses for it and, probably, Heminge and Condell's letter to the readers. In 1628 he had a stroke which rendered him an invalid until he died, but in the same year he was appointed Chronologer to the City of London.

Works. His greatest comedies are *Volpone* (1606), *Epicoene* (1609), *The Alchemist* (1610), and *Bartholomew Fair* (1614). Seven comedies, masques, non-dramatic poems, and his two tragedies, *Sejanus* (1603) and *Catiline* (1611), were published under Jonson's close supervision, as his *Works*, in a folio of 1616. This was reprinted in 1640, and a second volume published containing five further comedies, as *Bartholomew Fair, The Devil is an Ass* (1616), and *The Magnetic Lady* (1632), and masques, two dramatic fragments, poems, a translation of Horace's *Art of Poetry*, a grammar, and 'Observations on Poetry and Eloquence', called *Timber.*

Modern Editions. The Works are edited by C. H. Herford and P. & E. M. Simpson (11 vols., 1925–52); quotations in the following chapter are from this edition. There is an edition in the Everyman Library (2 vols., 1910). Editions of selected plays are numerous.

Scholarship and Criticism. L. C. Knights has a concise treatment in *The Age of Shakespeare*, ed. B. Ford (1955), and E. B. Partridge a fine study of the major comedies in his *Broken Compass* (1959). J. Barish's *Ben Jonson and the Language of Prose Comedy* (1960) provides an illuminating 'rhetorical' approach to the plays. The political background may be studied in L. C. Knights, *Drama and Society in the Age of Jonson* (1937) and C. Hill, *Puritanism and Revolution* (1958).

V

The World's Proportion

Jonson's dramatic poetry in 'Sejanus' and 'Catiline'

GEOFFREY HILL

★

> The worlds proportion disfigured is
> That those two legges whereon it doth rely,
> Reward and punishment are bent awry.
> (John Donne, *The First Anniversary*)

JONSON, in his two Roman tragedies, is either a monumental victim of the New Learning, or a brilliant satirist of the contemporary political situation. By an act of secular faith one takes the latter assumption to be true. It is the less respectable choice since, to many, politics is forever loitering about the vestal precincts of Art. There is a lack of enthusiasm in the voices of the Oxford Editors when they discuss the social relevance of *Catiline*:

> And Jonson's *Catiline* hardly affects to have any more specious aim than to assert the claim of the have-nots against those who have—a claim, moreover, here presented in its least persuasive form, as the revolt of a needy and debased aristocracy against the state at large. (ii. 124)

Both Coleridge and Swinburne, however, have intelligent notes on the relationship of these plays to the Jacobean political dilemma. They are at least prepared to accept that Jonson's choice, and treatment, of his themes may have been governed by something other than scholarly perverseness.

In both *Sejanus* and *Catiline*, Jonson manages to blend a forthright dogmatism with an astute trimming. This makes him, in a way, an epitome of the disturbed decades preceding the outbreak of the Civil

War. This was the time of Selden, the troubled democrat; and of Falkland, the troubled Royalist; and Jonson knew them both. And, at a period when the tensions between Court and City were becoming increasingly felt, Jonson abandoned the public theatres for ten years to become a writer and producer of masques for royalty and aristocracy. A despiser of the crowd, he yet said 'Words are the Peoples' ' and captured in his comedies the idioms and inflexions of common speech. And modern critics have, of course, sufficiently appraised Jonson's 'accurate eye for oddities', his 'quick ear for the ordinary turns of speech' (Chute, pp. 74, 85). Nevertheless, this very admiration produces its own kind of danger. To suggest that art, to be significant, must grow from vernacular roots is so much a contemporary necessity that it becomes, almost, a required cliché. And to say that, in Jonson,

> the tricks of shysters and crooks, mountebanks, lawyers, newsvendors, and monopoly-hunters are transferred to the stage with all the relish of one who sees for himself what is under his nose (*Age of Shakespeare*, p. 304)

is to make his satire seem more indulgent than it is. 'Relish' and 'under his nose' suggest a slightly myopic gourmet.

Moreover, the recent and thorough evaluation that the comedies have received from various hands appears to leave a residual implication: that, compared to the tough contact with life in plays like *The Alchemist* or *Bartholomew Fair*, the world of the Roman tragedies is an abstraction, a retreat into formulas and commonplaces. The cadences and imagery of these plays are certainly at a remove from those of Busy or Dol Common; but it could be argued that the 'grand commonplaces'—even those that refer back to Latin originals—are as much part of the seventeenth-century 'climate' as are the idioms of the great comic characters. It seems to be a modern scholastic fallacy that 'living speech' can be heard only in the smoke-room or in bed; in fact the clichés and equivocations of propaganda or of 'public relations' are also part of the living speech of a society. Character writers of the seventeenth century used Roman allusions, as modern political cartoonists employ a kind of visual short-hand, to 'tune in' to a required stock response.[1] It could be argued that the high-pitched invective that

[1] See D. Nicol Smith, *Characters of the Seventeenth Century* (1918), pp. 2, 63, 223 (both James I and Charles II are there likened to Tiberius and 'Silla's Epitaph' is applied to Strafford) and Fulke Greville, *Life of Sidney* (ed., 1907),

runs through *Sejanus* and *Catiline* is superb 'cartoon' language, with all the serious over-statement and polemic relevance of that art:

> CICERO. What domesticke note
> Of private filthinesse, but is burnt in
> Into thy life? What close, and secret shame,
> But is growne one, with thy knowne infamy?
> (*Catiline*, IV. 316)

The vituperative 'filthinesse', 'shame', 'infamy' could, perhaps, be taken too easily as a mere stage-anger, as an abstraction from the tensions, the 'humanity' of real experience. The stresses of Jacobean and Caroline society, culminating in the Civil War, were real enough; yet men declared their living angers, their immediate and pressing problems, in a language comparable to that of *Catiline*. The *Declaration of the County of Dorset, June 1648* was framed in the following terms:

We demand . . .
(iv) That our liberties (purchases of our ancestors' blood) may be redeemed from all former infringements and preserved henceforth inviolable; and that our ancient liberties may not lie at the mercy of those that have none, nor be enlarged and repealed by the votes and revotes of those that have taken too much liberty to destroy the subjects'. . . .
(vii) That we may no longer subjugate our necks to the *boundless lusts* and unlimited power of *beggarly and broken* committees, consisting generally of the tail of the gentry, men of *ruinous fortunes* and despicable estates, whose *insatiable desires* prompt them to continual projects of pilling and stripping us. . . .[2]

The 'boundless lusts' and 'ruinous fortunes' anathematized in the *Declaration* may be set against Cicero's denunciation of Catiline and his fellows, their 'filthinesse', their 'shipwrack'd mindes and fortunes' (IV. 413).

Moreover, Jonson shares with the authors of the *Declaration* a dual attitude towards the name and nature of liberty. The 1648 testament puts liberty in two poses: the first respectable; the second disreputable. 'Liberty' in the first case is plainly involved with property and heredity

---

p. 39 ('nor yet like that gallant Libertine Sylla . . .'), and Pope, *Epistle to Cobham*, l. 212. These polemic analogues share a common field of classical reference with Jonson's two plays. See also p. 96 above.

[2] Bayley, *The Great Civil War in Dorset*, quoted by C. Hill and E. Dell, *The Good Old Cause* (1949), p. 368 (my italics).

('purchases of our ancestors' blood'). Opposed to this is a second, destructive 'liberty', synonymous with licence ('boundless lusts', 'insatiable desires'). In Jonson's moral world, also, a stress and counterstress is evoked from the conflicting connotations of words such as 'liberty' or 'freedom'. In the Roman tragedies 'liberty' seems frequently equated with irresponsible power:

> CATILINE. Wake, wake brave friends,
> And meet the libertie you oft have wish'd for.
> Behold, renowne, riches, and glory court you . . .
> And, being *Consul*, I doubt not t'effect,
> All that you wish, if trust not flatter me,
> And you'd not rather still be slaves, th[a]n free.
> CETHEGUS. Free, free. LONGINUS. 'Tis freedom. CURIUS. Freedom we all stand for. (I. 409)

As parallel to this grotesque shout there is, in *Sejanus*, the 'Senates flatterie' of the new favourite Macro; their weak cries of 'Liberty, liberty, liberty' as he takes Sejanus' place. The irony here is that the Senators cry out to celebrate the return of that liberty which is a concomitant of property and stability; but we know that 'liberty', under Macro, will still be only 'licence'—a renewal of 'pilling and stripping'.

The civic alternatives to such dissolute, destroying forces are 'industry', 'vigilance' (*Cat.*, III. 33) and a proper reverence for the gods. The Second Chorus in *Catiline* speaks of the need 'to make a free, and worthy choice' (II. 373); and the good soldier, Petreius, instructs his army in the fundamentals for which it is fighting:

> PETREIUS. The quarrell is not, now, of fame, of tribute,
> . . . but for your owne republique.
> For the rais'd temples of th' immortall gods,
> For all your fortunes, altars, and your fires,
> For the deare soules of your lov'd wives, and children,
> Your parents tombes, your rites, lawes, libertie,
> And, briefly, for the safety of the world.   (V. 11)

It is clear from this that the word 'liberty' regains, in the oratory of Petreius, its respectable associations, being securely anchored next to 'lawes' and preceded by the pietist sequence: 'gods', 'altars', 'wives', 'children'. There is danger in the handling of such deliberately emotive catalogues. At worst, such rhetoric can become a confusion of apparent humility and actual hectoring. William Wordsworth, a late democrat beginning the drift back to conservative orthodoxy, employs a similar imagery in his sonnets of 1802:

> altar, sword and pen,
> Fireside, the heroic wealth of hall and bower . . .

Wordsworth's invocation is more raucous than Jonson's, being somewhat burdened by the self-imposed romantic role of poet-as-prophet. Jonson, exploiting the dramatic medium, is able to 'distance' his orthodox eloquence by projecting it through the mouth of a persona.

Elsewhere, too, the essentially conservative rhetoric is handled with persuasive charm, as in the *Catiline* dedication to the Earl of Pembroke:

> MY LORD. In so thick, and darke an ignorance, as now almost covers the age, I crave leave to stand neare your light: and, by that, to bee read. Posteritie may pay your benefit the honor, & thanks: when it shall know, that you dare, in these Jig-given times, to countenance a legitimate Poeme. I must call it so, against all noise of opinion: from whose crude, and ayrie reports, I appeale, to that great and singular faculty of judgement in your Lordship, able to vindicate truth from error. It is the first (of this race) that ever I dedicated to any person, and had I not thought it the best, it should have beene taught a lesse ambition. Now, it approcheth your censure cheerefully, and with the same assurance, that innocency would appeare before a magistrate.

This is a well-contrived amalgam of religious, political, and literary connotations. The keywords embody dual-associations of order, authority, and harmony in more than one field. 'To vindicate truth from error' sounds like Hooker; and 'judgement' and 'innocency' have theological overtones, even though Jonson's prime application is in secular self-vindication. 'Innocency' thus serves to fuse the ideas of divine order and human law. 'Censure' is the province of priest and magistrate and satirist; it is also the privilege of master-patron to servant-poet as Jonson suggests. The dedication is not only an extremely bland and suasive piece of self-defence; it is also a testament to conservative legitimist order; within the bounds of such prose, the tenure of kings and magistrates is unquestionably secure. The very 'assurance', the intuitive rightness of Jonson's usage, stems from a familiar rhetoric, a vision of order typified by Sir Thomas Wilson:

> I thinke meete to speake of framing, and placing an Oration in order, that the matter beeing aptly setled and couched together: might better please the hearers, & with more ease be learned of al men. And the rather I am earnest in this behalf, because I knowe that al things stande by order, and without order nothing can be.[3]

Again, in Jonson's own *Epistle to Selden*, the statesman is praised for his 'manly elocution', a phrase in which a way of speaking and a way of living become one and the same.

Such evocative vindications of 'wholeness' exist, of course, in a social and dramatic context where the unity of ethic and action is a rarity. For the world of Jonson's Roman tragedies is a world 'bent awry', distorted chiefly by the perverted lust for private gain at the expense of public good. Against all the evidences of tawdry chaos Jonson poses the orthodoxy of Cicero and Cato: rather as Pope, in the *Epistles to Several Persons*, celebrates the 'decency' of agrarian Order in the face of the Whig financiers; and as Yeats sets the 'great melody' of Burke against all manifestations of imperial Whiggery.

In both the Roman plays Jonson's vision of moral and civic disorder —though embodied in several forms—is most immediately presented as a reversal of roles in man and woman; as an abdication of power and choice by the former, a usurpation of private and public control by the latter. In *Catiline* the aborted natures of the protagonists is stressed. Sempronia has a very 'masculine' wit; she is 'a great stateswoman', 'a shee-Critick' who can also 'play . . . the orator'. And, in her conversation with Fulvia she acts and sounds like Brutus in his tent:

> SEMPRONIA. I ha' beene writing all this night (and am
> So very weary) unto all the *tribes*,
> And *centuries*, for their voyces, to helpe Catiline
> In his election. We shall make him *Consul*,
> I hope, amongst us. . . . FULVIA. Who stands beside?
> (Give me some wine, and poulder for my teeth.
> SEMPRONIA. Here's a good pearle in troth! FULVIA. A pretty one.
> SEMPRONIA. A very orient one!) There are competitors, . . .
>
> (II. 96)

The derangement is here stressed by the abrupt parenthesis of womanish trivia, chatter about pearls and dentifrice. Sempronia's strength is an errant thing, a matter of coarse presumption and gesturing.

As moral and dramatic corollary to this 'roaring girl' is the sharp

[3] *Arte of Rhetorique* (1560); ed. G. H. Mair (1909), p. 156.

depiction, throughout the play, of lasciviousness and hysteria in the men of Catiline's party. There is the incident of the homosexual attempt on one of Catiline's pages (I. 506–11), an episode which so disturbed Coleridge that he suggested emending it out of existence; he called it 'an outrage to probability'. This is precisely its point! The nineteenth century preferred a half-remorseful majesty in its great apostates, a power which Jonson is not prepared to depict in the Catiline conspiracy. Catiline is not Captain Ahab. His rebellion *is* an outrage to probability where 'probability' is more-or-less synonymous with 'Nature' and the 'moral law'. What Jonson does give, is a dramatic relevance to outrage and abnormality; and where the actions of the protagonists seem most to elude the patterns of reason, that is the point of Jonson's attack. These opponents of Cicero are 'men turn'd furies', whose 'wishings tast of woman'; into whose mouths Jonson puts a deliberately grotesque hyperbole:

> CETHEGUS. Enquire not. He shall die.
> Shall, was too slowly said. He' is dying. That
> Is, yet, too slow. He' is dead.   (III. 663)

In this projection of a world of spiritual and physical disorder the Roman tragedies are close to certain of the comedies. In *Epicoene* (1609), varied strata of imagery and action are explored, to discover intricate evidence of ethical and sexual abnormality; of dangerous (even if trivial) perversion in the private and public functioning of human natures.[4] Sejanus, too, was once

> the noted *pathick* of the time . . .
> And, now, the second face of the whole world.
>   (I. 216–17)

And here the theme of sexual inversion is absorbed into that of broken status, debauched hierarchy. It was by trading his body that Sejanus rose from serving-boy to be potential master of Rome.

In *Catiline*, the play of action and imagery, though less intricate than the machinations of *Epicoene*, has its own manner of involvement. Apart from the 'logical' balancing of illogical sexual conditions in men and women, there is a recurring pattern of significant epithets. The conspirators are described (even self-described!) as 'needy' and 'desperate', 'wild', 'lost'. But they are also shown to be possessed by 'sleep'

[4] E. B. Partridge has a brilliant discussion of imagery and action in *Epicoene*.

and 'sloth' (V. 235, 380). At moments of crisis they shout like excited women, or make passes at boys. To be both 'wild' and 'sleepy', 'desperate' yet 'slothful' is gross indecorum, even in rebellion's own terms. It is a double inconsistency, a double irony.

In fact Jonson's method, in both the Roman plays, might be termed an anatomy of self-abuse. It is clear that the *Catiline* conspirators are destroyed as much by their own grotesque self-contradictions as by the bourgeois virtue of Cicero. And in both plays a dangerous apathy or rashness on the part of the body politic is a contributor to the tragedy. Rome, 'bothe her owne spoiler, and owne prey' (*Cat.*, I. 586), is always as much sinning as sinned-against. Jonson has Sejanus say:

> All *Rome* hath beene my slave;
> The *Senate* sate an idle looker on,
> And witnesse of my power; when I have blush'd,
> More, to command, th[a]n it to suffer.   (V. 256)

At first sight this might appear an inappropriate hyperbole, since Sejanus is presented throughout as a blushless villain. It is certainly no sign of regeneration on the part of the evil-doer; but rather a late outcropping of the morality-technique. Sejanus, though villain, is allowed an 'objective' condemnation of the ills of the State, is even, for a moment, permitted a 'Ciceronian' touch. Compare:

> CICERO. O *Rome*, in what a sicknesse art thou fall'n!
> How dangerous, and deadly! when thy head
> Is drown'd in sleepe, and all thy body fev'ry!
> No noise, no pulling, no vexation wakes thee,
> Thy *lethargie* is such.   (*Cat.*, III. 438)

In some respects Jonson has Sejanus fill a dual role. He blends some of the characteristics of 'Scourge'—bringing torment to a corrupt world —with all the attributes of the *arriviste*, the supposedly amoral disrupter of society's settled decency. As *Sejanus* progresses, Jonson's moral scathing is directed more and more against the blushless dereliction of Senate and people; their abandonment of moral choice. Rome displays the vice of apathy rather than the virtue of patience. This deliberate duality is again stressed at the end. Although it would be quite inappropriate to speak of Jonson's 'sympathy' for Sejanus, nevertheless, the drive of the satire is here against society-at-large rather than against the solitary villain. There is dramatic 'pity' for Sejanus and his children at this point; not because, as human-being, Sejanus deserves it, but because his immediate role as mob-victim makes such treatment necessary.

* * *

Jonson's dramatic rhetoric, in these two Roman tragedies, is so constructed as to work on two levels, yet to a single end, a comprehensive moral effect. The hyperbole of the protagonists is often so excessive as to be a parable of the spiritual and physical debauchery. At the same time, varied sequences of keywords signal the ethical truth of the action, like spots of bright marker-dye in a greasy flood. In Catiline's wooing of Aurelia, the satiric method is one of profound parody:

CATILINE.   Wherefore frownes my sweet?
Have I too long beene absent from these lips,
This cheeke, these eyes? What is my trespasse? Speake.
AURELIA. It seemes, you know, that can accuse your selfe.
CATILINE. I will redeeme it. . . .
AURELIA. You court me, now. CATILINE. As I would alwayes, Love,
By this *ambrosiack* kisse, and this of *nectar*. . . .   (I. 102)

Here is an epicene savouring, a ludicrous distinction between flavours in the kisses, each one mincingly appropriated by the demonstrative. It is the absurdity of over-meticulousness. It is the Spenserian-Petrarchan sexual reverence employed in a context which makes its very euphuism obscene. Marvell adapts the method in *To his Coy Mistress*:

Two hundred to adore each Breast

where the point is to satirize the idea of virginity as good bargaining-material. In Marvell, as in Jonson, the perspective requires the utterance of deliberate cliché, but cliché rinsed and restored to function as responsible speech. As the lover in *Amoretti* asks for 'pardon' and 'grace' from the beloved and fears lest he 'offend', so Catiline and his paramour toy with a sacramental idiom ('trespasse', 'accuse', 'redeeme'). The suggestive rhetoric is finely used. Catiline is made to utter an effective *mélange* of portentousness and off-hand cynicism. We know that he takes himself too seriously and humanity too lightly (his Petrarchan 'fidelity' is pasted nicely upon a cynical confession of wife-removal). The total irony of this scene, of course, depends on the fact that this tiny Petrarchan mock-trial is the nearest Catiline ever gets to an understanding of trespass, or of redemption. He and Aurelia utter, unknowingly, a punch-and-judy burlesque of the play's great meanings. It is significant that this evocative scene should be an act of courtship. It is through such sexual attitudinizing and mutual titillation, through such an exposé of the mechanics of allurement, that Jonson presents his broader commentary on the corrupt-world practices of self-seeking and preferment. The forwardness of the female, the decorative word-spinning of the male, are far from being dramatically inconsistent. And though the gaudy Petrarchan is elsewhere seen as a cold destroyer it is, in fact, the pervading odour of blood that gives a poignant ruthlessness to Catiline's dalliance, his calling Aurelia 'sweet'.

As in Marvell's *To his Coy Mistress*, or Pope's *Epistle to Dr. Arbuthnot*, Jonson's language is frequently 'literary' in the best sense of the term. That is, its method requires that certain words and phrases, by constant repetition in popular literary modes, shall have been reduced to easy, unquestioned connotations. These connotations are then disturbingly scrutinized. Pope's:

> Oblig'd by hunger and Request of friends

requires for its effect the common formula of gentlemanly apologia, on the part of coy amateurs bringing out verse. It is 'hunger' that blasts the cliché into a new perspective. Marvell's wit feeds off Suckling's *Against Fruition* as much as it does off Marlowe's *Passionate Shepherd*. Jonson needs the Petrarchan mask even while, in the Catiline-Aurelia scene, he tears it into paper streamers. And, in the following soliloquy from *Sejanus*, Jonson is able to blend the authoritarian tones of Hall-like satire with suggestions of tongue-in-cheek duplicity on the part of the speaker. Sejanus has just concluded his scene of apparently forthright discussion with Tiberius and is alone:

> SEJANUS.   Sleepe
> Voluptuous Caesar, and securitie
> Seize on thy stupide powers, and leave them dead
> To publique cares, awake but to thy lusts.
>   (III. 598)

This holds good on two levels. Tiberius *is* voluptuous and does neglect public affairs (though not nearly so much as Sejanus imagines). So far, Sejanus' words may be taken as choric, as in a morality or a satire, setting the scene for the imminent fall of princes. The difference is that Sejanus is gleeful rather than sorrowing or indignant, and that the 'prince' whose fall is imminent is not Tiberius. Tiberius is, in fact, far from stupefied, and succeeds in shepherding Sejanus to the slaughter.

Hence, Sejanus' choric comment (still true in its essential commentary on an evil prince) becomes also a statement, by implication, of the fatal blindness of hubris, of Sejanus' own recklessness and greed. In the light of what the audience knows but Sejanus does not, the imperatives of the confident puppet-master ('Sleepe, voluptuous Caesar') slide into the subjunctives of a wishful-thinker ('and [may] securitie seize on thy stupide powers . . .').

From a study of such examples one would conclude that Jonson is able to employ ambiguity—of word, phrase or situation—to give what is ultimately a quite unambivalent expression to moral preference or decision. There is, however, a secondary form of ambiguity at work in both plays—more subjective, more cunning even; and with roots in the Janus-like situation of the professional moralist in Jacobean England.

In *Sejanus*, for instance, crucial political implications are guided into a kind of dramatic cul-de-sac; as in the scene where Sabinus is tempted into self-betrayal by Sejanus' hirelings:

> SABINUS. No ill should force the subject undertake
> Against the soveraigne, more than hell should make
> The gods doe wrong. A good man should, and must
> Sit rather downe with losse, than rise unjust.
> Though, when the *Romanes* first did yield themselves
> To one mans power, they did not meane their lives,
> Their fortunes, and their liberties, should be
> His absolute spoile, as purchas'd by the sword.
> LATIARIS. Why we are worse, if to be slaves, and bond
> To Caesars slave, be such, the proud Sejanus!
> He that is all, do's all, gives Caesar leave
> To hide his ulcerous, and anointed face,
> With his bald crowne at *Rhodes*. . . .   (IV. 163)

The opening of Sabinus' argument is orthodox, reflecting Tudor statecraft as expressed in the Tenth Homily (1547), and anticipating the Canons of 1606 and the Laudian Canons of 1640. James I's considered opinion that 'it was unfit for a subject to speak disrespectfully of any "anointed king", "though at hostility with us",[5] gives the orthodox viewpoint succinctly enough. Sabinus' acceptance of the official dogmas comes out even in the pithiness of the trotting couplets with which his

[5] Quoted by G. P. Gooch and H. J. Laski, *English Democratic Ideas in the 17th Century* (1927), p. 53.

speech opens. The thought clicks neatly into place together with the rhyme. Then, as a kind of conditional afterthought, Sabinus suggests that very scrutiny of the tenure of kings which he appears to reject at the beginning. The Tudor apologist suddenly begins to speak like a moderate post-Restoration Whig, one to whom: 'government exists, not for the governors, but for the benefit of the governed, and its legitimacy is to be judged accordingly.'[6] Compare, too, the tone of the opening three lines ('hell', 'the gods') with the ironic use of 'absolute' to qualify, not 'kingship', but 'spoile'. Dramatically speaking, this argument (absolutist dogma and Whig qualification) is delivered with the appeal of a Lost Cause. Sabinus is innocently speaking his own doom; his 'fault' is predetermined; his stage-audience is wholly composed of agents provocateurs and concealed spies, so that his appeals to civic rectitude are sealed off from directly influencing the outcome of the tragedy. It is the theatre-audience or the reader ('invisible' witnesses) who are exposed to the full vision of the noble conservative humiliated and betrayed by exponents of corrupt Power, of cynical *Realpolitik*. And it is arguable that the celebrated line:

> To hide his ulcerous, and anointed face

gains much of its power through a 'suspension' (rather than a 'union') of opposites. It is at once a well-turned translation of Tacitus' Latin, and an ambiguous metaphor juxtaposing two hostile connotations. These are: 'anointed' in the sense of 'smeared with (ointment or cosmetic)' and 'anointed', meaning 'marked with sacramental authority' (compare 'The Lord's anointed'). Hence, the phrase pivots Jonson's two most powerful social attitudes—disgust at corruption; and reverence for consecrated power—thus: 'Tiberius is corrupt and, what is worse, tries to paint over that corruption'; or: 'Tiberius is corrupt, nevertheless he is the anointed of the gods.' 'Face' continues the deliberate ambivalence; it is both physiognomy and 'cheek' (one is reminded of the character called 'Face' in *The Alchemist*); 'bald crown' signifies both 'hairless head' (a private impotence) and 'stripped authority' (a public impotence). As these words are spoken by Latiaris, the hireling, only in order to trap Sabinus they cannot, therefore, be taken as 'active' radicalism. The image is securely bedded down in a web of tangential implication.

This scene in particular makes nonsense of the view of Jonson's

[6] L. I. Bredvold, *The Intellectual Milieu of John Dryden* (ed. 1956), p. 143.

'originally non-dramatic nature'.[7] He so deploys his conservative philosophy as to give it the attraction of Resistance idealism. He commits himself less deeply than, say, Marvell who, in the *Horatian Ode on Cromwell's Return from Ireland*, speaks—in his own voice, and without dramatic 'distancing'—of Charles' 'helpless Right' and of the 'bloody hands' of the spectators round the scaffold. And Jonson's dramatic cunning is also in significant contrast to the procedure of Donne, in his *Elegie XVII*:

> The golden laws of nature are repeal'd
> Which our first Fathers in such reverence held;
> Our liberty's revers'd, our Charter's gone,
> And we're made servants to Opinion,
> A monster in no certain shape attir'd,
> And whose originall is much desir'd,
> Formlesse at first, but goeing on it fashions
> And doth prescribe manners and laws to nations.
> Here love receiv'd immedicable harmes,
> And was dispoiled of his daring armes. . . .
> Only some few strong in themselves and free
> Retain the seeds of antient liberty,
> Following that part of love although deprest
> And make a throne for him within their breast,
> In spight of modern censures him avowing
> Their Soveraigne, all service him allowing.

The keywords here are like those in Jonson's Roman plays: 'Liberty'; 'free'. But it is clear that their significance is far from the 'Ciceronian' ideal. Donne's 'liberty' is not the state of civic wisdom based on 'industry and vigilance', nor is it a concomitant of inherited property. 'Strong *in themselves* and free' smells more of the dangerous anarchism that, in *Catiline*, yearns to use the 'free sword' (I. 230). And the implications of 'Our liberty's revers'd' and 'retain the seeds of antient liberty' sing out much more sharply and defiantly in Donne's lyric than do the equivalent but 'well-buffered' iconoclasms in Jonson. And, at the crux of his argument, Donne, in offering fealty to a Soveraigne clearly not 'anointed of the Lord' commits a kind of witty high treason. In his own voice he pays homage to 'libertine' nature in terms that Shakespeare preferred to put into the mouth of a branded villain, the bastard Edmund in *Lear*. And, in Jonson, this kind of 'freedom' belongs to

[7] Una Ellis-Fermor, *The Jacobean Drama* (1936), pp. 99–100.

degenerate conspirators, rather than to Cecil-like 'new men' such as Cicero. Both Jonson and Shakespeare, though prepared to give an airing to subversive statements in their work, tend to 'contract-out' of direct commitment; whereas Donne pursues, with a cynical faithfulness, the conclusions made inevitable by his accepted premisses. It could be argued that such distinctions are the product of the time; distinctions between 'revolutionary' ideas circulating in manuscript verses among a small, cultured *élite* and ideas handled in the drama, a medium struggling against official censorship, and always in the blast of public scrutiny and comment.[8] The ambivalence is certainly there. It was noted by Coleridge, when he said of *Sejanus*:

> The anachronic mixture in this Arruntius, of the Roman republican, to whom Tiberius must have appeared as much a tyrant as Sejanus, with his James-and-Charles the First zeal for legitimacy . . . is amusing.[9]

* * *

In *Catiline*, Jonson's treatment of the 'Ciceronian' virtues, and his attitude to the Cicero-Catiline struggle provide a working example of the dramatist's capacity for 'suspended' judgement. Sempronia describes Cicero as:

> A meere upstart,
> That has no pedigree, no house, no coate,
> No ensignes of a family? FULVIA. He' has vertue.
> SEMPRONIA. Hang vertue, where there is no bloud: 'tis vice,
> And, in him, sawcinesse. Why should he presume
> To be more learned, or more eloquent,
> Than the nobilitie? or boast any qualitie
> Worthy a noble man, himselfe not noble?
> FULVIA. 'Twas vertue onely, at first, made all men noble.
> SEMPRONIA. I yeeld you, it might, at first, in *Romes* poore age;
> When both her Kings, and *Consuls* held the plough,
> Or garden'd well; But, now, we ha' no need,
> To digge, or loose our sweat for't.   (II. 11)[10]

---

[8] Dramatists frequently fell foul of the censors: *Sejanus* itself, despite Jonson's caution, barely scraped past official disapproval; Fulke Greville destroyed a tragedy in manuscript because he thought it 'apt enough to be construed or strained as a personating of vices in the present Governors and government' (Greville, *op. cit.*, p. 156).

[9] S. T. Coleridge, *Lectures and Notes on Shakespeare* (ed. 1904), p. 413.

[10] The whole question of the 'new man' is obviously one of the great thorny

Jonson so places the virtue of old Rome in the mouth of a 'modern' degenerate that he gets away with a good deal. To dig or to lose one's sweat honestly at the plough becomes the sweet untainted antithesis to the 'sloth', 'fatness', 'lethargy' of the present. Any scepticism we might have had regarding the tireless virtue of simple poverty is ruled out of court together with Sempronia's gibes. All that she sees as laughable or contemptible we are to receive as serious and worthy. 'Rome's *poore* age' is unquestionably Rome's *great* age. Similarly, in *Cynthia's Revels* (1600):

> the ladie Arete, or *vertue*, a poore *Nymph* of Cynthias traine, that's scarce able to buy her selfe a gowne (I. 89)

is, in fact, a powerful chastiser of prodigality and corruption. By a connotative slide, therefore, 'poor' is made synonymous with 'pure'.

Jonson is noted for the hard precision of his images; and justly. He builds magnificently so that he may destroy:

> we will eate our mullets,
> Sous'd in high-countrey wines, sup phesants egges,
> And have our cockles, boild in silver shells,
> Our shrimps to swim againe, as when they liv'd,
> In a rare butter, made of dolphins milke,
> Whose creame do's looke like opalls . . .
> (*The Alchemist*, IV. i. 156)

The 'moral pleasure' here stems from Mammon's lavishing of such imaginative effort on shrimps; and 'rare *butter*' is a good, serious joke. Jonson's recreation of the bulk and weight of corruption, of criminal-farcical expenditure, is superb. On the other hand, the persuasive weight of such imagery is sufficient to commit the listener to the acceptance of a good deal of simple and evocative language, as part of Jonson's vision of the Good Life. In the First Chorus of *Catiline*, the pejorative vision of the effeminate men of new Rome (a terse set of epithets: 'kemb'd', 'bath'd', 'rub'd', 'trim'd', 'sleek'd') works into a

---

problems of the era. It cannot be fully discussed here; the fact remains that Cicero, the *arriviste*, is 'good'; Sejanus, the *arriviste*, is 'wicked'; and the necessity to cajole us into the acceptance of the fact influences both action and imagery in the two Roman plays. Cicero is an approved 'new man' but feels some need for self-justification. 'Cecil noted in 1559 that "the wanton bringing up and ignorance of the nobility forces the Prince to advance new men that can serve" ' (*Age of Shakespeare*, p. 16). The 'new man' versus the 'wanton' nobility is, essentially, the situation of *Catiline*.

passage of much more tenuous verbal 'gesturing' when old Rome is evoked:

> Hence comes that wild, and vast expence
> That hath enforc'd *Romes* vertue, thence,
> Which simple poverty first made.   (I. 573)

And Fulvia's reply to Sempronia is also a case in point. Her:

> 'Twas vertue onely, at first, made all men noble

is plainly on the right side of the moral fence. 'All men' sounds very liberal and fine; so does the easy juxtaposition of 'vertue' and 'noble'. In practice, though, Jonson's social vision is as far from a Leveller's dream as it is from any real faith in a natural aristocracy. Phrases like 'all men' make gestures; they do not define or ever truly perform.

Such evasions are to be distinguished from the valid workings of dramatic and rhetorical persuasion. Take, for contrast, this sequence from *Catiline*:

> CHORUS. The voice of Cato is the voice of *Rome*.
> CATO. The voice of *Rome* is the consent of heaven!
> And that hath plac'd thee, Cicero, at the helme, . . .
>   (III. 60)

Here, the anadiplosis, linking Cato's word to the authority of heaven, appears as a legitimate rhetorical parable of the great chain of Being. And, in this context, the commonplace of ship-of-state (as, elsewhere, the commonplace for body-politic) appears as an authentic, even though limited, statement of civic faith. Jonson *is* pedantic, but his pedantry has little or nothing in common with the supposedly neurotic crabbedness of the 'unworldly' scholar. He is pedantic as Fulke Greville in his *Life of Sidney* is pedantic: each is prepared to risk appearing over-scrupulous in the attempt to define true goodness:

> he piercing into mens counsels, and ends, not by their words, oathes or complements, all barren in that age, but by fathoming their hearts, and powers, by their deeds, and found no wisdome where he found no courage, nor courage without wisdome, nor either without honesty and truth.[11]

In Jonson, too, the insistent comparison, qualification and paradox sometimes appearing 'in-grown'—is made in the teeth of a barren age.

[11] *Op. cit.*, p. 36.

The world of the Roman plays, like that of many of the comedies, is a world full of false witness:

> We have wealth,
> Fortune and ease, and then their stock, to spend on,
> Of name, for vertue.   (*Cat.*, II. 131)

If 'name' is a mere commodity, an advertisement without relation to substance or property or ethic, how can 'name' alone be trusted? 'Name' must be demonstrated as belonging or not-belonging to 'thing'; its properties plainly discussed. Hence, in Jonson's dramatic rhetoric, antithetical pairings are frequent: 'inward' opposes 'outward'; 'justice', 'law'; 'private gain' is won by 'public spoil'. In the world of the Roman plays, this degree of moral scrutiny is painful, but necessary. This is the celebration of a good man, the dead Germanicus, in *Sejanus*:

> He was a man most like to vertue'; In all,
> And every action, neerer to the gods,
> Than men, in nature; of a body' as faire
> As was his mind; and no lesse reverend
> In face, th[a]n fame: He could so use his state,
> Temp'ring his greatnesse, with his gravitie,
> As it avoyded all selfe-love in him,
> And spight in others.   (I. 124)

Here, the heavy antitheses are wrenched across the line, with considerable moral and muscular effort. They do not fall harmoniously within the line-period—and within the limits of their own predetermined world—as do Dryden's fluent couplets to the good man, Barzillai:

> In this short file Barzillai first appears;
> Barzillai, crowned with honour and with years . . .
> In exile with his godlike prince he mourned
> For him he suffer'd and with him return'd.
> The court he practic'd, not the courtier's art:
> Large was his wealth, but larger was his heart,
> Which well the noblest objects knew to choose,
> The fighting warrior and recording Muse.
>   (*Absalom & Achitophel*, 817–28)

In terms of Dryden's bland wit, Charles is unquestionably 'godlike'.

I

This is the very point that Jonson labours to verify in the portrait of Germanicus: 'In all | And every action neerer to the gods, | Than men ...' Jonson's qualifications worry the verse into dogs-teeth of virtuous self-mistrust. If his passage is painfully spiky, Dryden's approaches fatty degeneration. 'For him ... with him', 'Large was ... larger was' are syntactically flabby, embodying the elevated complacency of the thought. The repeated 'Barzillai ... Barzillai' gestures in the general direction of virtue and goodwill. The over-all tone of the Barzillai panegyric, it can be argued, has much to do with Dryden's thorough-going acceptance of his lot as laureate of the Tory oligarchy. The famously smooth irony of the opening of *Absalom & Achitophel* is, ultimately, an indulgent cherishing irony, making such a smiling, gentlemanly thing of equivocation that only a puritan cit could object.

Jonson's sense of the complexity of Order is very different, both poetically and politically, from Dryden's *practical* political attack and defence. Jonson's awareness can produce both the richly suggestive ambiguities of the Catiline-Aurelia courtship, or Latiaris' speech about Tiberius, and the fine assurance of the Pembroke Dedication. But there are occasions when, it seems, Jonson succumbs to the contradictions of the age; when he is unable, even reluctant, to tie down and tame the airy, 'floating' connotations in words such as 'noble', or 'vertue', or 'poverty'. The *Catiline* Chorus, for example, speaks of 'simple poverty' as though this, and this alone, accounted for the 'vertue' of Old Rome. A moral slogan such as this is as blandly shallow as anything produced by Dryden's political partisanship. And in *The New Inn* (1631) there is this, equally emotive, exchange:

> NURSE (*who is Lady Frampul disguised*). Is poverty a vice? BEAUFORT.
>   Th' age counts it so.
> NURSE. God helpe your Lordship, and your peeres that think so,
> If any be: if not, God blesse them all.
> And helpe the number o' the vertuous,
> If poverty be a crime ...   (V. 56)

Yet, in *Catiline* it is made explicit that 'need' is the reason that so many flock to the conspirators' support. And Volturtius, a turn-coat and minor villain, is contemptuously dismissed by Cato without punishment; is even promised:

> money, thou need'st it.
> 'Twill keep thee honest: want made thee a knave.
>   (V. 299)

Poverty, then, is a virtue only when it is associated with a remote, lyrically evoked agrarian order, a world so distant that it appears static; or when it provides a temporary refuge for missing persons of good family. The poverty that really preoccupies Jonson is the reverse of simple and is far from static; is, in fact, a prime mover in that constant flux of demand and supply; the seventeenth-century urban predicament.

This world of savage indecorum, which, like Tiberius, 'acts its tragedies with a comic face', which to Donne appears 'bent awry', is a world that Jonson struggles to subdue. It may be true that:

> In *Catiline* as in *Sejanus*, Jonson appears wholly inaccessible to the attraction of the profound 'humanity' and psychology of Shakespearian tragedy (Herford and Simpson, ii. 122)

but it is equally true that he is inaccessible to that periodic debauching which the Shakespearian 'humanity' suffered at the hands of, say, John Webster. There is nothing in Jonson's Roman tragedies to equal the celebrated 'syrup' speech in the Duchess of Malfi's death-scene; and we should at least be grateful for this. One ought to be sceptical of 'timeless moments' in any art. Jonson redeems what he can:

> It is not manly to take joy, or pride
> In humane errours (we doe all ill things,
> They doe 'hem worst that love 'hem, and dwell there,
> Till the plague comes) The few that have the seeds
> Of goodnesse left, will sooner make their way
> To a true life, by shame, than punishment.
> (*The Devil is an Ass* V. viii. 169)

Note

The Tempest was probably written in 1611; the first recorded performance was at Court by the King's Men on Hallowmas night, 1611. The New Arden Edition, by F. Kermode (1954), provides the fullest introduction, and reprints accounts of voyages to the West Indies (which Shakespeare knew) and the surviving contemporary music for the play.

E. Law has an interesting *Shakespeare Association Pamphlet* on the play 'as originally staged at Court' (1921). G. W. Knight considers the recurrent images and ideas in *The Shakespearian Tempest* (1932), and B. Dobrée usefully distinguishes its achievement from that of Shakespeare's other 'romances' in *Essays and Studies* (1952). There is a provocative chapter on the play with suggestions for its production in J. Kott, *Shakespeare our Contemporary* (tr. 1964).

W. H. Auden's *The Sea and the Mirror* (1945) is a sequence of speeches for the *dramatis personae* and is probably the most imaginative and useful commentary written in this century.

Studies of Shakespeare's Plays in Performance. H. Granville-Barker's *Prefaces* (5 vols., 1927-47) are the best attempt to discuss the plays as in performance. G. W. Knight's *Principles of Shakespearian Production* (2nd ed., 1949) is a 'symbolistic' treatment.

Current productions of the plays are reviewed annually in *Shakespeare Survey* and *Shakespeare Quarterly*: both journals provide a more documented account than those printed in daily or weekly papers. Muriel St. C. Byrne has discussed past productions in *A History of Shakespearian Production in England: 1700-1800* (1948) and 'Fifty Years of Shakespearian Production, 1898-1948', *Shakespeare Survey* (1949). T. C. Kemp and J. C. Trewin have written on *The Stratford Festival* (1953). A. C. Sprague has recorded many details in *Shakespeare and the Actors: the Stage Business in his Plays: 1660-1905* (1944) and *Shakespearian Players and Performances* (1953).

Past productions are considered historically by H. Child and C. B. Young in each volume of the New Cambridge Shakespeare; some New Arden volumes also contain Stage Histories.

W. M. Merchant's *Shakespeare and the Artist* (1959) is a most valuable account of stage-settings and illustrations.

VI

'The Tempest' on the Stage

DAVID WILLIAM

★

THE stage-history of *The Tempest* is one of regular revivals and frequent popularity. Yet most productions differ little from each other, either in their interpretations of the play, or methods of staging it. For all its formal simplicity, it is a difficult play, and most producers have taken (and continue to take) the easiest (though not always the least expensive) way with it. We are fairly safe in expecting 'a liberal provision of the scenic and musical embellishments which have long been deemed essential in an efficient representation of the play'—a tradition which a critic of a production in 1871 evidently regarded as already well established.

Whilst modern productions may not quite emulate Charles Kean's in 1857, in which 'the scenic appliances are of a more extensive nature than have been attempted in any theatre in Europe', (though a production at Stratford in 1951 ran it fairly close), the play's visual opportunities are still apt to be the chief priority. Nor, of course, should it be doubted that a play so rich and suggestive in atmosphere warrants the highest possible imaginative treatment by both producers and designers; yet how rarely this is achieved. In no play is the visual trap more tempting or more dangerous. Regardless of what belongs to a frippery, and lacking in confidence in the demands which the play makes on the ear (especially in the big exposition at the beginning), producers offer a visual accompaniment that more often than not distracts from the action instead of illuminating it. This, and a tendency to sentimentality (particularly in the sub-plot) are the most recurrent blemishes in modern productions. Time and again, the strength and violence that lie so near the surface of the play are submerged in layers of charm and hocus-pocus; the urgent directness of action, which moves from beginning to end with such narrative skill, is interrupted and weakened by exaggerated detail and peripheral fuss.[1]

The climax of *The Tempest* is a moral decision. The moment occurs early in Act V. Ariel ends his description of the 'distracted' lords with the strangely personal reflection:

> Your charm so strongly works 'em
> That if you now beheld them, your affections
> Would become tender.
> PROSPERO.   Dost thou think so, spirit?
> ARIEL. Mine would, sir, were I human.
> PROSPERO.   And mine shall.
> Hast thou, which art but air, a touch, a feeling
> Of their afflictions, and shall not myself,
> One of their kind, that relish all as sharply,
> Passion as they, be kindlier moved than thou art?
> Though with their high wrongs I am struck to the quick,
> Yet with my nobler reason 'gainst my fury
> Do I take part: the rarer action is
> In virtue than in vengeance: they being penitent,
> The sole drift of my purpose doth extend
> Not a frown further.
>
>   (V. i. 17)

The reluctance to see in this the stuff of drama, different in kind, but equal in dramatic effect to, say, the death of Desdemona or the meeting of Viola and Sebastian, narrows the range of available theatrical experience (on both sides of the footlights).

Prospero's renunciation of vengeance is the resolution of the play; everything else leads up to it, and upon it the destinies of all the characters (himself included) depends. The creative objective, therefore—to invoke Stanislavsky's useful terminology—is 'To pardon the deceiver.' Hence, the guiding aim of any responsible production must be to organize the action of the play (main-plot and sub-plot) so that

---

[1] An encouraging step in the other direction was taken by Peter Brook's production at Stratford in 1957. This had the advantages of a most convincing and adventurously conceived Prospero from Sir John Gielgud, and a simple, formal setting, consisting of a parallel series of cut-outs reminiscent of Inigo Jones' designs for the *Salmacida Spolia*. Unfortunately the rest of the production did not measure up to these assets. But there was a splendid shipwreck produced by comparatively simple means.

it is related, however indirectly, to this moment. Only thus can such a climax achieve its explicit dramatic effect.

Like the great tragic heroes, Prospero is a man of strong passions, but, unlike them, does not yield to their promptings. With his enemies entirely in his power, he discards that power entirely. It is not an easy victory; he knows what must ensue from it—not only the pardoning of the guilty, but his own return to the world of governments and younger brothers. The ending of *The Tempest* is very moving, not least because it is so reticent. Beyond the stated issue lies a sense of deprivation as poignant as it is necessary. The liberation of Ariel seems to involve a contraction of Prospero's personality which he both recognizes and accepts. It is as if the powers of the spirit, vested in him on the island, cannot operate in Milan, for Milan bodies forth the real world, in which the life of the spirit is at all points compromised. For one who has seen through the deceptions of that world, a return to it is indeed a sacrifice, but the rising generation find it beautiful, and while their vision lasts, they must put it to the test of practical experience. Beyond this, there is, perhaps, the more ironic hint that even the life of the spirit is susceptible of corruption, and the 'Thing of darkness', which Prospero acknowledges his, may serve as a reminder that, for those seeking the consummation of the spirit in this life, there can be no final satisfaction. So the staff must be broken, the book drowned, and the journey home begun while there is yet promise of calm seas and auspicious gales.

The possibility of some such dramatic experience, then, lies at the very heart of this play. Though it eschews the ranges of tragedy, it charts a no less powerful landscape. It is the noblest of the revenge-plays.

THE UNFOLDING OF THE PLAY

An analysis of *The Tempest*'s structural craftsmanship may indicate why Shakespeare gave it such a form and how that form determines its theatrical qualities.

With the exception of *The Comedy of Errors*, it is the shortest of the plays. It has fewer scenes than any. The action is continuous and confined; in fact, the unities of time and place are observed more stringently than any formulation demands. These facts alone bespeak a deliberate restriction of subject unusual for Shakespeare. Moreover, nearly a quarter of the play is devoted to exposition. That is a very high proportion—too high for theatrical comfort, if it is *mere* exposition. Fortunately, it is not, for it is animated and sustained by continually inventive characterization, and integrated with the establishment of the physical and moral background of the play.

The play opens with violent action: 'A tempestuous noise of thunder and lightning heard: Enter a Ship-master, and a Boatswain.' The first four lines tell us where we are. The problems of staging this scene are easily outweighed by its advantages as an opening-scene. Not only is it exciting in itself (what shipwreck would not be?), but its very violence of incident arrests the audience's attention at the outset, so that it is readier for the long exposition than it would have been if the play began at I. ii. Shakespeare's method with his audience is akin, in fact, to the schoolmaster's, who sends his class twice round the playing-field before a lesson. A further merit of the scene, of course, is the introduction of nearly half the *dramatis personae*. Although Shakespeare allows himself little time for assigning appropriate dialogue to the respective characters, what chances arise are aptly taken. Antonio's arrogant indifference and Gonzalo's humorous fortitude are immediately planted. Even if we are unable to identify the members of the royal party (and if the stage-action is as coherently frantic as it should be, that is very likely), we shall recognize them as soon as they reappear in their next scene.

The temperature of the play, then, at its opening, registers well above normal. The second scene begins at a scarcely lower pitch, with Miranda's impassioned anguish. Prospero's affectionate reassurances begin to relax the tension:

> Be collected:
> No more amazement: tell your piteous heart
> There's no harm done.

But the generous distress needs repeated assurances. These are tenderly forthcoming before Prospero begins to divert her attention to more pressing matter:

> No harm.
> I have done nothing but in care of thee,
> Of thee, my dear one, thee, my daughter, who
> Art ignorant of what thou art, nought knowing
> Of whence I am, nor that I am more better
> Than Prospero, master of a full poor cell,
> And thy no greater father.

Within the first twenty-five lines of the scene, Shakespeare establishes Miranda's instinctive unselfishness and innocence, and Prospero's love for her, blended with a protective authority (note his eight imperatives in less than twice as many lines), and his magic power.

The temper of the scene is now one of eager moderation. Soon it is to change again. Prospero begins his remarkable story. His sense of the momentousness of the occasion is touchingly attested by the solicitude with which he leads Miranda to the dark backward, gently probing in the recesses of her own memory to assist her response to what must follow. He spares nothing in his care of her, but forgets himself, for, as he draws nearer to the picture of the past, its contents begin to unsettle him:

> The direful spectacle of the wreck, which touch'd
> The very virtue of compassion in thee,
> I have with such provision in mine art
> So safely ordered that there is no soul—
> No, not so much perdition as an hair
> Betid to any creature in the vessel
> Which thou heard'st cry, which thou saw'st sink.

At this point, the editors, quivering with indignant vigilance over so sound a text, scent trouble. A solitary anacoluthon is arraigned, brought to trial, and sentenced as an impostor. Dr. Johnson leads the way, emending 'soule' to 'soil'; the editor of the New Temple Shakespeare, defending, in turn, the acceptance of the emendation by the editors of the New Cambridge Shakespeare, justifies his position as follows: 'there are of course plenty of anacolutha in Shakespeare; *but Prospero is in no sort of excitement or disorder of mind*; on the contrary he is explaining with calm satisfaction how well his schemes have worked; and a violent anacoluthon would be undramatic.' The italics are mine, and I suggest the Prospero therein described is not Shakespeare's.

A little later in the same scene he tells Miranda:

> I find my zenith doth depend upon
> A most auspicious star, whose influence
> If now I court not but omit, my fortunes
> Will ever after droop.

That is to say, the moment is critical, and therefore hardly conducive to a mood of 'calm satisfaction'. Nor is this all. For twelve years Prospero has lived alone with the secret of his dukedom. At last he has resolved to break the long silence, to emerge from the isolation which such a secrecy must impose. His further intentions for Miranda are, for the time being, withheld from her, but they are in his mind: if she is to become the queen of Naples, she must be shown the darkest corners of the house into which she marries. She must also know her own father. Little wonder, then, if the hand that lifts the family skeleton from its long resting-place begins to tremble. He has made the attempt before, but given up, 'Concluding, "Stay: not yet" '. But 'The hour's now come.' Regaining outward composure, and searching the warranty of her remembrance to its little limit, he begins the brave and painful recapitulation:

> Twelve year since, Miranda, twelve year since,
> Thy father was the Duke of Milan and
> A prince of power.

As the story develops, so its narrator's feeling heightens. The pace of the speeches quickens, the syntax twists and turns in abrupt, sharp phrases; inversions and subordinate clauses pile up, as, for the first time, he publishes his remembrance of the old high wrongs. The agitation and urgency beget an extraordinary compression of diction:

> To have no screen between this part he play'd
> And him he play'd it for, he needs will be
> Absolute Milan. Me, poor man, my library
> Was dukedom large enough: of temporal royalties
> He thinks me now incapable; confederates—
> So dry he was for sway—wi' the King of Naples
> To give him annual tribute, do him homage,
> Subject his coronet to his crown, and bend
> The dukedom yet unbow'd—alas, poor Milan!
> To most ignoble stooping.

The actor's task here is to suggest the growing opposition between the rational wish to tell the story with objective truth and the passion which the recollected experience gradually engenders. As the story hastens to its climax, we may trace the emerging paradox which is to exercise Prospero's imagination throughout the play—the dual experience of the blackness of the corrupted nature and the innate goodness of the innocent soul.

Despatching Miranda to sleep, Prospero summons his servant to continue the work already begun. Even for those who know the play, Ariel's first entrance ought never to fail of its magic in the theatre. Personally, I find myself waiting for it (in all but the dreariest productions) with no less excitement than for the first appearance of the Ghost in *Hamlet*. It is finely situated. The material background of the play has been established: it is now time to extend its spiritual dimensions. Prospero's invocation prepares us for no ordinary creature:

> Come away, servant, come. I am ready now.
> Approach, my Ariel, come.

And back, as if down the wind, comes the unearthly answer, with sustained monosyllables and echoing long vowels (what a contrast to Caliban's response to *his* summons):

> All hail, great master! grave sir, hail!

If an adequate acoustic perspective can be achieved, these seven words surely warrant an off-stage delivery, for their verbal magic, in the context, will be strongest if the appeal is solely to the ear.

Nothing daunted by having managed nearly two hundred lines of exposition, Shakespeare embarks on more. Ariel's dramatic function is established, and, by means of the violent extremes of love and anger which the relationship of master and servant encompasses, Shakespeare reaches further into the depths of Prospero's nature. It is only the inattentive who will find his treatment of Ariel unduly harsh. Under the circumstances, his reaction to Ariel's display of reluctance is understandable. Exclusively, and for the best of reasons, committed to his zenith, he cannot at this juncture think of anticipating Ariel's liberation. That, and of course the power of his love, stretch his already tensed nerves beyond the limits of moderation. Also, the scene is a fine example of Shakespeare's craftsmanship (never more resourceful than when surmounting technical difficulties). For the reproach of master to servant provides a dramatically legitimate opportunity to tell the audience the story of Ariel's duress. The device, if properly managed by the actors, should be entirely successful. Finally, the tenderness with which Prospero despatches Ariel leaves no doubt as to the true state of his feelings.

The recapitulatory device is repeated with audacious success in the scene with Caliban. The appearance of a new character (and such a character) revitalizes the audience's attention, so that it may receive the last (and shortest) of the three expositions. Once again, of course, there is much more to the scene than mere narrative. First, there is a finely inventive touch to heighten the very moment of Caliban's approach. We have already heard his voice, terse, savage, and resentful: 'There's wood enough within.' Prospero repeats the summons:

> Come forth, I say! there's other business for thee:
> Come, thou tortoise! when?

And suddenly, instead of the lumbering monster we expect, the incarnation of debased nature, there flashes across the stage its very opposite: 'Enter Ariel like a water-nymph.' He pauses for his master's bidding and is gone. Nothing could more potently charge our first experience of Caliban than this exquisite juxtaposition.

To the social and spiritual picture of the island so far projected Caliban now adds the darker tones of guilt and brutality. It is surely part of Shakespeare's intention that the conflict with Prospero is not one-sided, that there is more to it than one of them being 'right' and the other 'wrong'. As the wrath of Prospero fills the stage once more, an ironic undertone accompanies it. For Caliban is his failure, and he knows it. The account which Prospero now gives of his attempts at regenerating the monster is not unfair, though its blame may seem a trifle over-urged:

> I endow'd thy purposes
> With words that made them known. But thy vile race,
> Though thou didst learn, had that in't which good natures
> Could not abide to be with; therefore wast thou
> Deservedly confined into this rock,
> Who hadst deserved more than a prison.[2]

But it is not the full account, and comes the terrible answer to repudiate it:

> You taught me language; and my profit on't
> Is, I know how to curse.

To the impotent fury of that accusation the raiser of tempests has no fit answer:

[2] The Folio is surely mistaken in assigning this speech to Miranda; she nowhere else speaks so aggressively, and the narrative content is more appropriate to what we already know of Prospero.

> Hag-seed, hence!
> Fetch us in fuel; and be quick, thou'rt best,
> To answer other business . . .

Regulated severity masks the remorse and frustration which is to inform his consciousness of Caliban until the final dispensation.

Caliban's exit completes the exposition, leaving Shakespeare free to develop the external action. The mood is immediately lightened. The transition is consummate: as Caliban crawls, muttering, from view, the song of Ariel ushers in the play's ideal of romantic love. The music's effect on Ferdinand—a lyrical dissolvement of his sense of the actual—leads to the haunting poignancy of 'Full fathom five'. As the sea-nymphs add their burthen, Shakespeare matches the rapture of the senses with the magic of his language. Prospero bends over the unsuspecting Miranda, and, with exquisite under-statement, delivers her to her destiny:

> The fringed curtain of thine eye advance
> And say what thou seest yond.

Not since the ball of the Capulets has Shakespeare staged so wonderful a lovers' meeting.

Nothing remains of the occasion but for Prospero to impose that test of love, 'least too light winning make the prize light', which calls up the long tradition of patient lovers hallowed in literature since Jacob served seven years for Rachel.

The scene ends with a glimpse of another ideal:

> Thou shalt be as free
> As mountain winds: but then exactly do
> All points of my command.

And after, perhaps, a moment's gaze at the vanishing figure, Prospero turns, and with a brave assumption of severity, marshals the lovers on their way.

The next scene re-introduces the royal party. By dramatizing their response to the situation, it establishes both their relationships with each other, and their respective places in the moral pattern of the play. Gonzalo's zealous, if unsuccessful, consolation of the king, coupled with the courteous tolerance with which he endures the insults of his other superiors, endorses the sympathetic disposition of Prospero's account of him in the previous scene. Alonso, accessory before the fact of Prospero's banishment, now comes before us as a bereaved father, and his numbed distress speaks instantly of better scruples, which later scenes are to confirm. Sebastian's spiteful recriminations and the cheapness of his badinage arouse immediate aversion. Adrian and Francisco barely engage attention. The strongest figure in the group is the darkest —Antonio. In him, we are to find the continuing principle of corruption, its appetite having grown by what it has fed on. To usurpation and extrusion he now proposes to add murder. The duologue in which he tempts Sebastian is brilliantly managed—from the deliberate hesitancy of its inception, through the confident ease with which he dismantles the weaker man's objections, to the arrogant indifference of its climax:

> but I feel not
> This deity in my bosom: twenty consciences,
> That stand 'twixt me and Milan, candied be they
> And melt ere they molest!   (II. i. 277)

One last twitch of pusillanimity from Sebastian gives Ariel his cue to wake Gonzalo, and the plot is foiled. The power of the island has declared itself to the purest consciousness among those present, and prompts immediate action. Alonso's assurance of his son's death weakens, and he leads his companions on a further search, whilst Ariel departs to bear fresh evidence for his master's judgement.

The image of corruption in its most sophisticated form now gives place to one in its most primitive. The next scene opens with Caliban's curse on Prospero. Through its blend of hatred and terror we perceive the glimmerings of that frustrated sensibility which adds depth to the perspective of Shakespeare's portrayal.

With Trinculo's entrance the language drops into graphic prose. The gaberdine antics and the re-union with Stephano provide an energetic comic diversion from the sustained seriousness of the main plot, whilst the irony of Caliban's transfer of allegiance and vision of freedom should satisfy the impatient moralist. The business which Shakespeare has in hand for these three does not allow him much time to spare for comic relief; but he does not waste his opportunities, and the physical humour of the scene should be as uninhibited as the text implies.

Between this scene and III. ii, Shakespeare interposes the brief idyll of the love-scene. Here, both Prospero and the audience are given honourable guarantee of the worth of Miranda's purchaser. Then we return to the sub-plot, its protagonists now well-advanced in liquor, and easy prey to the temptations of lust and ambition that now confront them. Producers should guard against a tendency to sentimentalize this scene. *Pace* the *mores* of English stage-culture, not all drunkards are endearing: the brutality and cowardice of these are an integral part of their characters, which alcohol merely releases. Not since *Measure for Measure* has Shakespeare given us such morally loaded comedy. While the murderous plot is being formed, the magic of the island intervenes, and Shakespeare draws a powerful irony between the selfish insensitivity of the humans' reaction to the music and the poignant fantasy of the monster's. Fortified by Caliban's example, butler and jester follow the strange taborer, and, like their masters, draw closer to the waiting judgement.

With the next scene, the urgency of the main plot is restored. From now on the play moves in a sublimity of atmosphere which is sustained with very little interruption until the end. As the royal people advance upon the tempting viands, the island puts forth a mightier magic, and the guilty men are served with their tremendous indictment. (That it is only they who hear it, is proved by Gonzalo's astonished interrogation of Alonso after the banquet vanishes.) Alonso's reply, attesting the witness which the elements themselves have borne against his guilt, is a magnificent prelude to the high miracle that awaits them. In suicidal despair he rushes from the place. Characteristically, the 'distraction' of Antonio and Sebastian takes a different form. Excluding the slightest hint of remorse, it expresses itself in aggressive defiance, as, with drawn and futile swords, they follow the king. Gonzalo remains to point the moral (more accurately than he suspects) to the attendant lords, and then fearful of ensuing violence, they hurry in pursuit. The magic circle is not far off.

Here, I suggest, the interval, if there must be one, should come. But with so short a play, it is a questionable amenity. Played with proper pace, the performance should last little over two hours, and the advantages which accrue from such uninterrupted concentration are well worth considering. But if the demands on the audience's powers of attention (not to mention the bar receipts) seem to warrant an interval, this seems the best place. Certainly it can come no later, for two-thirds of the play is already done. Some producers put it at the end of III. i, but this breaks the continuity of the sub-plot which—

though it can afford the brief intermission of the love-scene—is not strong enough to sustain an additional delay. It also involves opening the second act on a weak note. Another alternative interval—after III. ii—is no less unsatisfactory, as it involves too long a time-lapse between the appearances of the royal party. With so concentrated a play it is important to preserve at least an impression of continuous action, and the least damaging pause seems to be after III. iii. Producers, of course, are not above contriving their own artificial intervals. A production at the Old Vic several years ago, for example, transposed III. iii. 94–109 to follow l. 81, and cut the lines:

> And in these fits I leave them, while I visit
> Young Ferdinand, whom they suppose is drown'd,
> And his and mine loved darling.

Then, on the phrase 'my meaner ministers', a few lines earlier in the same speech, Prospero was joined by his 'shapes', who, at the cue 'they now are in my power', shrieked and writhed with felicitatory relish as the curtain fell. The object of this nonsense was to gerrymander an 'effective' act-ending, but its achievement was to diminish the grandeur of the scene, and, in particular, to stress Prospero's prestidigitation at the expense of his humanity.

If, therefore, the first act ends after III. iii, the second can begin firmly with the betrothal of Ferdinand and Miranda. From this moment Prospero never leaves the stage. The dramatic demands on him are many and various, and test his power and authority to the utmost. But all through—the betrothal, the invocation of the goddesses, the imminent arrival of his old enemies—everything is encompassed with royal composure. There is a moment's wavering, as he suddenly recalls yet another claim on his attention:

> I had forgot that foul conspiracy
> Of the beast Caliban and his confederates
> Against my life.   (IV. i. 139)

But his recovery is prompt and disciplined, and brings with it a touching solicitude for the younger hearts:

> Bear with my weakness; my old brain is troubled:
> Be not disturb'd with my infirmity:
> If you be pleased, retire into my cell
> And there repose . . .

And so, with the frustration of Caliban's plot ensured, he is now ready to receive his guests. Perhaps not quite as ready as he seems, for, at Ariel's delicate prompting, he must first make his great renunciation. Up to this moment, there must surely be some doubt in his mind (and hence, the audience's) about the kind of dispensation to be made. In the event, it could not be nobler. Indeed its disinterested magnanimity transcends the barrenness of some of the responses. For although Alonso's penitence is full and imaginative, and Caliban himself at last covets grace and wisdom, no word of remorse falls from the lips of the principal offenders. And this is surely Shakespeare's dramatic intention. The ultimate impenitence of Antonio and Sebastian is all of a piece with their behaviour throughout the play. Even when addressed directly by Prospero, they say nothing in reply, and this final silence, broken elsewhere by no more than an occasional flippancy, has its own dramatic effect. But that effect is largely ironic, and I have seldom seen it expressed on the stage. In the very moment of his spiritual triumph, Prospero is brought face to face with the harsher and irreconcilable values of the world.

But his resolution does not alter. With ineffable tenderness, he gives Ariel a last assignment, and ushers the royal party into his cell. He turns before following them (what better moment for the breaking of the staff?), and then, faced only with the dissolution of the strongest spell of all, comes down to speak the Epilogue.

The end of *The Tempest* is so rich in feeling that it may accommodate many kinds of meaning. Only a perverse response, for instance, can refuse to see, within the orbit of Prospero's abdication, some image of Shakespeare's farewell to the creative life. Yet there is far more to the end of the play than this, and we must be careful how explicitly we state the ideas it seems to contain. Too deliberate an unravelling of the threads of poetic suggestion may result in a dramatized lecture instead of a high imaginative experience. Provided he is sure of his territory, a producer may be wiser to make the appeal to the audience indirectly, and thus, by avoiding too explicit a committal of their sympathies, capture them far more securely. Conversely, the merits of letting the play speak for itself are nullified if the company is unaware of its fundamental utterance. The vague approach has little chance of arrival. The ideal production is perhaps a rarity we may never encounter, but, at least, an attentive and talented enthusiasm is the indispensable point of departure.

For only thus can an audience discern, through this composition of tempest and calm, anger and gentleness, the remorse of the sovereign intelligence and the tormented aspiration of the spirit imprisoned by the senses, the sacrificial love of the old for the young, and the self-increasing love of the young for one another, the assertion of happiness ever after and the negation of the noblest by the basest—only thus can it apprehend the vision of a great dramatic masterpiece, and the victorious sanity of its creator.

THE VERSE AND ITS SPEAKING

Much confusion seems to exist about the speaking of Shakespearian verse. Complaints at the inability of most modern actors to speak it even adequately are frequent, and sometimes justified. But any critical postulates on the matter which imply a distinction between good verse-speaking and good acting are quite adrift. Shakespeare's dramatic poetry is drama at the same time as it is poetry, and any delivery which tends to separate the two is at fault. The self-indulgent arabesques of the 'voice beautiful' are no less deplorable than the rhythmic fractures sustained in the cause of so-called naturalism. The only valid test of good verse-speaking is that, in its dramatic context, it should sound necessary and inevitable.

Hence, there is no one particular 'style' for speaking Shakespeare, any more than there is a fixed style of singing. No soprano in her right musical senses would attempt to sing Mozart as she would sing Wagner; furthermore, the style appropriate to Fiordiligi differs no less significantly from Donna Anna's than Senta's from Brünnhilde's. So it is with Shakespeare. The Oberon style will not suit Othello, nor should a delivery that encompasses the lyrical symmetries of *Richard the Second* be transferred without appropriate adjustment to the muscular directness of *Julius Caesar*. But whilst, at the moment, no responsible opera-companies allow singers to appear as Carmen or Don Giovanni until they are at least familiar with the technical requirements of their art, neophyte Romeos and Titanias are far from rare in the English theatre. This might not be so bad if producers paid some attention to the matter once they were confronted with inadequate delivery. But their irresponsibility is extraordinary. Nor is it as if the problems of speaking Shakespeare were unduly formidable. With adequate training, the technical principles can be learnt by all but the rhythmically insensitive (who should not attempt it anyhow). And it should not be too much to ask that such training should not be carried out quite so haphazardly, or so blatantly *coram populo*, as at present. We have surely earned a respite from those productions of Shakespeare which imply that the use of verse is some kind of defective compromise on the part of the author.

The verse of *The Tempest* bears all the qualities to be expected from Shakespeare at the full flow of his creative maturity. It is very varied, and, as with all good styles, always appropriate to the expressive requirements put on it. In the main, it is energetic, compressed, sparing of imagery (especially sensuous imagery), and rhythmically very flexible. There is the intense, nervous rush of:

> like one
> Who having into truth, by telling of it,
> Made such a sinner of his memory
> To credit his own lie, he did believe
> He was indeed the duke; out o' the substitution,
> And executing the outward face of royalty,
> With all prerogative. . . .   (I. ii. 99)

or the graver power of the following, with its adroit combination of ellipsis and accumulated subordinate clauses:

> and do pronounce by me
> Lingering perdition, worse than any death
> Can be at once, shall step by step attend
> You and your ways; whose wraths to guard you from—
> Which here, in this most desolate isle, else falls
> Upon your heads—is nothing but heart-sorrow
> And a clear life ensuing.   (III. iii. 76)

In more majestic mood, there is:

> I have bedimm'd
> The noontide sun, call'd forth the mutinous winds,
> And 'twixt the green sea and the azur'd vault
> Set roaring war: (V. i. 41)

in which Shakespeare could not more plainly be demanding the sonorous exploitation of the expansive internal rhymes. By contrast, there is the limpid directness of certain lines which entrance the ear with their rhythmic ease and simplicity of syntax:

> Sit still, and hear the last of our sea-sorrow
> (I. ii. 170)
>
> Be not afeard; the isle is full of noises
> (III. ii. 144)
>
> Bravely, my diligence. Thou shalt be free.
> (V. i. 241)

For further variation, the rhyming couplets of the Masque relieve the bold austerity of the language of the rest of the play; their verbal flavour is of profusion and sensuous bounty:

> Who, with thy saffron wings, upon my flowers
> Diffusest honey-drops, refreshing showers,
> And with each end of thy blue bow dost crown
> My bosky acres and my unshrubb'd down,
> Rich scarf to my proud earth.   (IV. i. 78)

If Shakespeare avoids delaying the swift flow of the main stream of the dialogue with the decorative metaphors of earlier styles, there is no decrease in the vitality of the language. The play abounds in compounds and coinages. In addition to words already quoted, we may find 'fraughting', 'over-topping', 'sight out-running', 'still-vext', 'wave-worn', 'urchin-shows', 'cloud-capp'd', 'pinch-spotted', 'spell-stopp'd', all of which colour the vocabulary with an authentic strangeness of tone that is conducive to the character of the play.

The verse-speaking in *The Tempest* requires considerable variety. It is not the easiest of styles to master. The flexibility of its rhythms alone is remarkable, even for Shakespeare. But the text never imposes demands beyond the range of a sensitive and athletic delivery. Thorough familiarity is, of course, the safest method of approach, and this involves a good deal more than merely learning the lines. By becoming properly conscious of all the items in Shakespeare's technical equipment—vocabulary, punctuation, syntax, tempo, rhythm—the actor may discover from the text indications of Shakespeare's dramatic intention no less reliable than the stage-directions in a modern script or a composer's markings in a musical score. A fine style is its own interpreter.

STAGING, COSTUME, AND MUSIC

On 5th November 1897, William Poel produced *The Tempest* for the Elizabethan Stage Society in the Mansion House. Shaw's review of the production may serve as an apt introduction to the problems of staging the play:

> Mr. Poel says frankly, 'See that singers' gallery up there. Well, let's pretend that it's the ship'. We agree, and the thing is done. But how could we agree to such a pretence with a stage ship? Before it we should say, 'Take that thing away: if our imagination is to create a ship, it must not be contradicted by something that apes a ship so vilely as to fill us with denial and repudiation of the imposture. . . .' The reason is not that a man can *always* imagine things more vividly than art can present them to him, but that it takes an altogether extraordinary degree of art to compete with the pictures which the imagination makes when it is stimulated by such potent forces as the maternal instinct, superstitious awe, or the poetry of Shakespeare. . . . It requires the nicest judgment to know exactly how much help the imagination wants. There is no general rule, not even for any particular author. You can do best without scenery in *The Tempest* and *A Midsummer Night's Dream*, because the best scenery you can get will only destroy the illusion created by the poetry; but it does not at all follow that scenery will not improve a representation of *Othello*.

Poel's strict Elizabethanism is still unacceptable to most modern producers of Shakespeare. But recently there are signs that Shakespeare behind the proscenium arch is declining in favour. The splendid open-stage at the Mermaid Theatre has not yet accommodated a satisfactory Shakespearean production, but that, and the modifications to the Stratford-upon-Avon stage are hopeful signs that the ascendancy of pictorial Shakespeare is at least being questioned. Certainly the basic facilities of the Elizabethan stage (provided, for example, in the stage at Stratford, Ontario)[3] are appropriate to all the mechanical requirements of *The Tempest*. The inner-stage for Prospero's cell, the various galleries for Ariel as harpy, the appearance of Juno, the hell-trap for the ship's cabins (and Caliban's rock?) and the platform for the main action. No modern proscenium-stage can match its opportunities for swift, continuous action, and that flexibly intimate style of speech which so much of the text requires. The problem of speaking Prospero's text in I. ii is enormously increased by the distances between actor and audience in our proscenium theatres—and the apron-stages at Stratford and the Old Vic are only slight modifications. The Elizabethan stage (or, to be more practical, a stage which preserves its advantages, adding to them needful modern facilities of sound and lighting) rightly throws all

[3] Not to mention other open stages built since the first appearance of this book.

stress on the play itself. Anyone who has seen Shakespeare performed in these circumstances, or 'in the round', is struck by the instant gain in intimacy and access to the play.

Given a proscenium-stage, however, producers should aim for a setting which accords as closely as possible with the play's structure. Presumably a basically permanent set will be an initial prerequisite, and no alterations to this during the play should be obtrusive or hold up the action. Designers should be restrained from trying to transgress the play's scenic data ('this bare island') and smothering the play with subaqueous gew-gaws and the rest of the botanical farrago. But gorgeousness and mystery should accompany the Masque, and it is up to the collective ingenuities of producer, designer, and choreographer to ensure that the audience shall be no less transported than Ferdinand.

Distinctive costumes can do much to strengthen the play's impact. One should not dogmatize here beyond certain essentials which the text makes plain. The lords are the easiest problem. The prime requisite is clothes that will establish their social identities. Seventeenth-century contemporary style (English or European) would place the real world firmly (and becomingly) in the play's visual scheme. The islanders are less straightforward. We know that among his luggage Prospero was enabled to include:

> Rich garments, linens, stuffs and necessaries,
> Which since have steaded much . . .
> (I. ii. 164)

So, if these are to be seen, they must obviously harmonize in style with what the courtiers wear—though an inventive designer may find it helpful to point the passage of twelve years by changes in fashion for the latest visitors to the island.

For the *dénouement*, Prospero must have a royal robe of Milan. If the transformation from the master of a full poor cell to Duke restored is to have the strongest impact possible, then there is a good argument in favour of Prospero's earlier costume being markedly different in style from the courtiers'. His condition of scholar and recluse may provide the designer with helpful points of departure. And, of course, the magic garment must carry the right associations of power and mystery. Miranda, too, will benefit from whatever appearance of detachment from the style of the 'real' world can be designed that is both apt and becoming.

A good many Ariels resort to varying degrees of undress, offset by bizarre tones of body make-up and sundry articles of vegetation. It is, however, salutary to remember that, nearly always, the more clothes are removed the less spiritual the appearance becomes. Perhaps an apter approach to the very difficult problem of designing for Ariel may be to begin with the salient features of his dramatic condition—'an airy spirit', once imprisoned in a pine, aspiring towards total liberty, rapid transformation. The elemental associations are air and fire:

> I flamed amazement: sometime I'ld divide
> And burn in many places . . .
> (I. ii. 198)

> Hast thou, which art but air . . .
> (V. i. 21)

The disguises of water-nymph and harpy are explicit and therefore easier to encompass.

Caliban's elements, on the other hand, are earth and water, and the 'salvage and deformed slave' of the Folio list of characters should present a credibly grotesque debasement of physical humanity. Caliban is capable of not a few human conditions (e.g. lust, drunkenness, and pleasure in music) so that his appearance, however brutal, must indicate an aspiration towards human nature, whereas Ariel's is away from it.

With the goddesses the play should reach its peak of sumptuousness. All three of them are well contrasted in character and function: Juno, grand, and consummate, the highest queen of state; rich and bounteous Ceres, symbol of nature's bounty; and Iris, about whom Shakespeare has virtually written a note to the designer:

> . . . many colour'd messenger. . . .
> Who with thy saffron wings. . . .
> (IV. i. 76–8)

The ship's crew, and Stephano and Trinculo, present no great problem. They should wear whatever harmonizes with the other costumes and at the same time suggests their professional occupations.

Music plays a very important part in establishing the successive atmospheres of the play. In no other play of Shakespeare is it so organically integrated. If special composition can be afforded, it should be borne in mind, first and foremost, that whoever hears the music of the island is immediately enchanted by it. Purveyors of *musique concrète* are apt to tax an audience's credulity when Caliban speaks of the sounds and *sweet* airs. Certainly the structure of the songs warrants a melodic setting. If, on the other hand, existing music (recorded or live) has to be used, the more recondite ensembles (including harp and/or harpsichord) are likely to provide the most suitable accompaniments. There is so much wonderful early seventeenth-century music that is almost completely unknown that, if the play is being given a contemporary setting, producers need look no further.

CHARACTERS AND CASTING

Prospero

Prospero so dominates the play both in length and dramatic function that the choice of actor for the part must largely determine the character of the whole production.

In performance the part presents certain hazards. One is a tendency to stress the magician at the expense of the man. This generally results in a delivery of booming tedium and an appearance of minor prophet, with costume and make-up vaguely after William Blake. The intention is to match the great hieratic moments, but these are only effective if the inner tension of the personal conflict has been first suggested. Sir John Gielgud's performance at Stratford-upon-Avon in 1957 offered an exemplary re-assessment of the character. Ascetic, wiry, and middle-aged in appearance, he admirably combined the three identities of father, duke, and magician.

Those who prefer their Prosperos old adduce evidence from the text: 'Bear with my weakness; my old brain is troubled' (IV. i. 159) and, 'Every third thought shall be my grave' (V. i. 311). But the first of these remarks is addressed to Ferdinand and Miranda under particularly exacting circumstances. It is a common habit of the older generation to exaggerate its age to the younger. Moreover, Shakespeare's contemporaries regarded fifty and over as older than we do. The second quotation seems even less convincing. Even to a modern quinquagenarian one thought out of three on any topic as absorbing as the grave may not seem unduly excessive.

Another aspect of Prospero which is apt to worry actors, producers, and, in consequence, the audience, is his puritanism. The puritanism of *The Tempest* is similar to that of *Comus*. That is to say, it is both positive and idealistic. Its frankest and fullest expression occurs in Prospero's adjurations to Ferdinand before the Masque:

> If thou dost break her virgin-knot before
> All sanctimonious ceremonies may
> With full and holy rite be minister'd
> No sweet aspersion shall the heavens let fall
> To make this contract grow . . .   (IV. i. 15)

and again:

> Look thou be true; do not give dalliance
> Too much the rein: the strongest oaths are straw
> To the fire i' the blood: be more abstemious,
> Or else, good night your vow.   (IV. i. 51)

To both these injunctions, Ferdinand replies with prompt and ardent acquiescence. The modern error is to present this kind of feeling in the spirit of Thou Shalt Not. There is no space here to go into the spiritual background of the Renaissance ideal of chastity. It must suffice to say that Shakespeare in *The Tempest* is writing in full accord with that ideal. Nowadays our attitude to the matter is supposedly more pragmatic. But in the seventeenth century glandular determinism did not enjoy the cultural ascendancy it does today.

If Prospero's sacramental attitude to sex can be presented as a thing of joy and love rather than as the restrictive suspiciousness of a prurient *voyeur* then it should be dramatically acceptable to all who can respond to the imaginative presentation of ideas different from their own.

'*The Lords*'

Thus theatrical parlance has named them, and, on the whole, disparagingly. Most actors regard them as unrewarding parts. Yet they are all (even Adrian and Francisco) firmly characterized. Their superficial penalty as parts is that they seem to begin much better than they finish. Antonio and Sebastian, for instance, say very little in the last two acts, and Alonso's and Gonzalo's best scenes occur before the last act. Yet the play requires that these characters become increasingly passive with the approach of the *dénouement*. Viewed as deliberate rather than casual, this tapering of individuation may seem a dramatic advantage if the actors concerned will play their later silences and responses for what they are worth.

More often than not the parts are undercast. What, above all, they must have is an aristocratic quality. If the implicit assumption that what they say and do and think carries public consequences is lacking, then indeed, they are insufficient strands in the play's texture. Given this quality, however, they are all good parts, and will repay vigilant interpretation.

Alonso develops most. Beginning as an accessory before the fact of Antonio's usurpation, he subsequently shows that the roots of evil do not lie deep in his nature. A sense of bereavement numbs him into frigid isolation. The kindly solicitude of Gonzalo merely jars upon his nerves:

> You cram these words into mine ears, against
> The stomach of my sense ...   (II. i. 106)

Then, increasing awareness of the quality of the island revives his hopes until the indictment of the banquet-scene brings him his purgation. It is a sign of the importance Shakespeare attaches to this moment that he gives Alonso one of the greatest speeches in the play:

> O, it is monstrous, monstrous!
> Methought the billows spoke and told me of it;
> The winds did sing it to me, and the thunder,
> That deep and dreadful organ-pipe, pronounced
> The name of Prosper: it did bass my trespass.
>   (III. iii. 95)

From this moment he is ready for arraignment and acquittal. Shakespeare adds sympathetic touches to the portrait right up to the end. There is the poignant honesty of:

> But, O, how oddly will it sound that I
> Must ask my child forgiveness! (V. i. 197)

An even more delicate moment comes a little later. It falls to Gonzalo to invoke divine blessing on the betrothal of the lovers, and then his sovereign quietly adds: 'I say, Amen, Gonzalo' (V. i. 204). The humility of that echo is conclusive guarantee of Alonso's regeneration.

Both Sebastian and Antonio are established with brilliant clarity.[3] What a wealth of characterization, for instance, there is in Sebastian's:

>   to ebb
> Hereditary sloth instructs me
>   (II. i. 222)

with its overtones of decadent complacency and passive arrogance. He is the perfect victim for Antonio's strength and eloquence. Nor is Antonio's power over him broken at the end. 'What things are these, my Lord Antonio?' (V. i. 264), with its blustering flippancy, expressive

[3] W. H. Auden's *The Sea and the Mirror* is perhaps nowhere more perceptive and illuminating than in its portraits of Antonio and Sebastian.

of the man's discomfiture but also of his impenitence, tells us that Antonio is not the only younger brother whom Shakespeare leaves unredeemed. The strength of Antonio's will and the weakness of Sebastian's are what raise their respective resistances to the possibility of spiritual growth.

Gonzalo is a more conventionally drawn character. If, in addition to suggesting the warmth and humour of the man, the actor can match Shakespeare's audacity in allowing him every now and again to slip over the edge of tedium (to his companions, of course, not to the audience), then the part becomes a valuable and restful element in the total composition.

Ferdinand and Miranda

The contemporary theatrical climate is not conducive to the breeding of Shakespeare's golden lads and girls. There is a marked deficiency in young actors and actresses who can encompass the poetic, physical, and social qualities without which such parts become otiose. Yet, when they are well played, both parts emerge with charm and vitality. Miranda is alive and individual from the breathless anxiety of her opening speech. She is never afraid—for all her delicacy of mind—of expressing her feelings, and this candour of soul reaches an exquisite climax with her famous exclamation on first seeing the royal visitors

> O, wonder!
> How many goodly creatures are there here!
> How beauteous mankind is! O brave new world,
> That has such people in 't!   (V. i. 181)

And, although her father, with his gentle aside, is not slow to point out the irony of her observation, for a moment the audience will do right to see the world through Miranda's eyes. (It seldom happens like this, however, as the speech invariably raises a laugh in the theatre, a depressing reflection on the chances of a reasonable hearing for idealism.)

Ferdinand is a prince charming worthy of such a paragon. Courage, rapture, and nobility are written into the part with enough dramatic *raison d'être* for the right sort of actor to make him a real person as well.

Ariel and Caliban

Ariel is probably the most difficult part in the play to cast satisfactorily. The sheer spirituality of the character puts it beyond the range of most actors (and further still beyond actresses). Add to this the need for extreme physical mobility and grace, a highly developed vocal technique both in speaking and singing, and it is clear that the demands of the part are indeed difficult to meet. Yet the problem of casting Ariel and Caliban is not made easier by the tendency to conceive both characters in terms that are vague and sentimental. For Ariel this involves overtones of Peter Pan, and for Caliban that of Our Dumb Friends' League.

Perhaps it is a mistake to approach either character in terms solely of itself. In fact, I find it difficult to think of either of them apart from Prospero, and believe that they only make full imaginative sense if apprehended as externalized aspects of Prospero—the one of his spiritual, the other of his sensual appetencies. The conditions of earthly existence do not permit either of these appetencies to over-reach themselves, or gratify themselves at the expense of one another, without some injury to the total organism of the self; in this way, the violence of some of Prospero's encounters with both his servants may find its aptest dramatic manifestation in terms of some such symbol of tension. Moreover, both Ariel and Caliban acquire, at certain moments, phenomenal accesses of energy, and these always occur in sight of their own particular horizon of liberation. 'What shall I do? say what? what shall I do?' cries Ariel after Prospero has promised to discharge him within two days; and we should feel there is no limit for the answer. Correspondingly, Caliban's, 'Freedom, high-day, high-day freedom, freedom, high-day, freedom' is nothing if not the natural and exultant expression of the brute instinct glorying in its sudden discovery of independent vitality, when the social inhibitions laid upon it by authority have been released by alcohol.

It is, of course, very difficult, perhaps impossible, to suggest such concepts at all *specifically* on the stage. But one can suggest their *possibility*. That is to say, the appeal must be made to the imagination rather than to the intellect. One cannot be too careful about introducing such notions into the overall concept of a production, but if such a triune relationship as I have indicated can be encompassed—and it can certainly be *assisted* by discreet costuming as well as casting—then I am sure it can only enhance the extraordinarily powerful impression which the supernatural element in the play is capable of making.

Stephano and Trinculo

Here, again, the watch must be set up against mawkishness, without sacrificing any of the comic opportunities. Both characters are firmly integrated in the sub-plot, and this involves them in a programme, the items of which include rape and murder. Though their plan is abjectly mismanaged, it is still a serious project, and brings out the worst in both of them. Stephano's domination over Trinculo echoes, in cruder terms, Antonio's over Sebastian. His immediate reactions to all predicaments are selfish, greedy, and unimaginative. Of all Shakespeare's drunkards, he is the least acquainted with delight. His apology to Trinculo is the only generous action he performs, and that is hardly disinterested.

With the possible exception of Malvolio, Trinculo is the most neurotic of Shakespeare's comic characters. His stage-life is a progress from fear to fear, beginning with the weather. His mind is more sensitive than Stephano's, but its only introductions are to terror and misery. The decadence of the Neapolitan court could receive no more conclusive attestation than when its jester and its butler are rejected by the sea.

Note

Biographies: John Fletcher, 1579–1625; Francis Beaumont, 1584?–1616; Philip Massinger, 1583–1640
Fletcher was the son of a clergyman who became Bishop of London; Beaumont came from the landed gentry, the son of a Justice of Common Pleas; Massinger's father was a confidential secretary to the second Earl of Pembroke. Beaumont and Massinger went to Oxford, Fletcher to Cambridge.

Works. Beaumont and Fletcher began collaborating in plays written for boys' companies about 1607 or 1608, but soon came to write for the King's Men. A folio was published in 1647, called, *Comedies and Tragedies Written by Francis Beaumont and John Fletcher*; it contained 34 plays and a masque. A second folio of 1679 contained 52 plays. Although no credit is given him in the folios, there is strong internal and external evidence that Massinger took Beaumont's place as chief collaborator. Daborne, Field, Rowley, and Shirley were among others working with Fletcher; *Two Noble Kinsmen* and the lost *Cardenio* he probably wrote with Shakespeare, while some scholars have seen his hand in *Henry VIII*.

Modern Editions. A. Glover and A. R. Waller edited *The Works of Beaumont and Fletcher* (10 vols., 1905–12); this is a reprint of the second folio, with collation of the first folio and earlier quartos. A. H. Bullen edited a Variorum Edition of 20 plays (4 vols., 1904–12); quotations in the following chapter are from this edition where possible.

Selected plays are available in the Mermaid Series (2 vols., 1904) and the Everyman Library (1911); both collections include *A King and No King* and *The Maid's Tragedy*. Other plays discussed in this chapter are seldom reprinted, but *The Island Princess* is in Brooke and Paradise's *English Drama, 1580–1642* (1933), and nineteenth-century editions of the complete *Works* (ed., H. Weber, G. Darley, or A. Dyce) are often to be found in secondhand bookshops. *A King and No King* has recently been edited in the Regents Renaissance Drama Series by R. K. Turner (1964).

Scholarship and Criticism. No published attempt to partition the work of the collaborators in the Beaumont and Fletcher plays can be regarded as authoritative. E. H. C. Oliphant's *The Plays of Beaumont and Fletcher* (1927) attempts the task, and recent work by C. Hoy is published in *Studies in Bibliography* (1956–62).

There is much useful information about criticism of the plays in L. B. Wallis, *Fletcher, Beaumont and Company* (1947). A suggestive study with information on sources and backgrounds is E. M. Waith's *The Pattern of Tragicomedy* (1952). Two stimulating essays are by Una Ellis-Fermor in *Jacobean Drama* (1936) and A. Mizener on *A King and No King* in *Modern Philology* (1941). A. C. Sprague has a study of *Beaumont and Fletcher on the Restoration Stage* (1926).

See, also, *Beaumont and Fletcher: A Critical Study* (1956) by W. W. Appleton, and C. Leech, *The John Fletcher Plays* (1962), a penetrating and original interpretation which appeared after *Jacobean Theatre* was first published.

VII

The Danger not the Death

The Art of John Fletcher

PHILIP EDWARDS

★

THE problem of authorship in the Beaumont and Fletcher plays is such a tangle that, in discussing them, it is very hard to be just to individual dramatists. Fletcher's share in the fifty-odd plays is by far the greatest, and he is the constant in the canon. Beaumont dropped out early, Massinger came in late, and many of the plays seem wholly Fletcher's. To talk of Fletcher's art is perhaps a rough way of solving the problem, but there is some justice in it, as well as convenience. It would be wrong to give a lion's share of the credit to Fletcher if we were chiefly concerned with those early successes, *Philaster*, *The Maid's Tragedy*, *A King and No King*. Beaumont is supposed to have written the greater part of these plays, and it could not be proved that his mind was not responsible for their general design. But, except for *A King and No King*, most of the plays I have chosen to discuss are later plays, chiefly tragicomedies, in which Beaumont can have had no part. I shall try to differentiate the colleagues when I think it possible, but, in general, by Fletcher's art I mean the art of Beaumont, Fletcher, and Massinger in association, which John Fletcher took a leading part in creating and sustaining.

All the members of the team were gentlemen; they fashioned their sophisticated, and in some ways highly original form of drama for an audience of gentlemen and would-be gentlemen; it was in great favour at court. The popularity of the plays was immense, and continued, after Fletcher's death in 1625, right to the closing of the theatres in 1642. It was a good twenty years after the Restoration before their stage-popularity began to decline. In the *Essay of Dramatic Poesy* (1668), Dryden remarked, 'Their plays are now the most pleasant and frequent entertainments of the stage; two of theirs being acted through the year for one of Shakespeare's or Jonson's.' Yet Fletcher's name is now never, as it was for 150 years, automatically bracketed with Shakespeare's. The plays have sunk very low indeed. Even the sympathetic reader finds them bizarre, perplexing and unattractive.[1] It would be better if there were a chance of seeing the plays, because they insist on the judgement of an audience rather than of a reader, but the overriding difficulty is the lack of a court of criticism in which they can be tried. They do not answer the legitimate expectations of readers accustomed to Marlowe, Shakespeare, and Webster. They do little to explain the human condition; their comment on contemporary society is trifling; their psychology and politics are often (not always) jejune; identification with the characters is a superhuman effort. They seem too consciously artificial and too proudly elaborate: more like opera than Ibsen.

The verse, too, is often a barrier. It is not figurative in the Jacobean manner. Where Shakespeare writes,

> Our natures do pursue,
> Like rats that ravin down their proper bane,
> A thirsty evil; and when we drink, we die,

Fletcher (or Beaumont) writes,

> Yet so
> I shall but languish for the want of that,
> The having which would kill me.

The reader is rarely invited to pause and reflect on the crystals of the verse. The detached line does not declare the nature of a character or a dilemma, the drift of a scene, the mood of a play. There is no virtue in short, quotable passages; probably no corpus of plays has fewer single lines which come back easily to mind. Not only this, but a whole speech which, in its context, has life and force, often becomes inert when detached and taken alone, or, if not inert, it quickens into a different kind of life, sententious perhaps, or too pretty. This is true even of the best:

> KING. Thou dost not mean this; 'tis impossible;
> Thou art too sweet and gentle.
> EVADNE. No, I am not:
> I am as foul as thou art, and can number

[1] The characteristic modern distaste may conveniently be seen in L. G. Salingar's chapter in *The Age of Shakespeare*, ed. Ford (1955), pp. 429-35.

As many such hells here. I was once fair,
Once I was lovely; not a blowing rose
More chastely sweet, till thou, thou, thou, foul canker,
(Stir not) didst poison me. I was a world of virtue,
Till your cursed court and you (Hell bless you for 't!)
With your temptations on temptations
Made me give up mine honour; for which, King,
I am come to kill thee.
(The Maid's Tragedy, V. ii. 60)

Fletcher was perfecting an art which is a long way below that of Shakespeare, but it seems much further below if we do not realize its difference from Shakespeare's. Fletcher's kinship with reality is strange to us, and we think it slighter than it is. With great skill, Fletcher and his associates imitated human life in their own singular fashion in order to interest, move, and delight a not unintelligent audience. The audience did not ask plays to be a succedaneum for religious experience; they looked elsewhere (those who were interested) for an insight into the mystery of things, and Fletcher did not, and probably could not, give them more than they asked. As for the verse, we have to remember its clarity and purity, and how much Dryden, not so far away, disliked a dramatic style which was 'pestered with figurative expressions'. The fact that small units of the verse have no detached power is a signal to us of how Fletcher organizes his effects. The indivisible unit of Fletcher's verse is the rhetorical organization of a whole scene, and it is the context which gives the verse its power. It would be better verse, no doubt, if it could be greatly admired when detached, but once again Fletcher has been satisfied with accomplishing his immediate ends. It does not by any means follow that once we know what Fletcher was trying to do, we immediately approve of his achievement, whether we are speaking of the verse or of the plays as a whole, but until we are fairly clear about what he was up to, we are not really free either to condemn or approve.

★ ★ ★

The special contribution of Fletcher is acknowledged to be in the art of tragicomedy. In a well-known passage in her *Jacobean Drama*, Una Ellis-Fermor spoke of a 'middle mood' between comedy and tragedy, the creation of which was the main achievement of Beaumont and Fletcher—'an imagined world neither tragic nor comic which yet, taking something from each, resulted in something different again from either'. The mood of this middle world 'could be introduced into any play, irrespective of formal distinctions between tragedy, tragicomedy and comedy'. Some injustice may be done by this generalization to Fletcher's important achievements in light-hearted comedy; but such comedies present no challenge to criticism: if we are talking about what is different and difficult in Fletcher, and if we remember that the middle mood is a very wide mood, then the generalization serves. Fletcher himself spoke of the distinguishing feature of tragicomedy as 'bringing some near to death' in the epistle before *The Faithful Shepherdess*: 'A tragi-comedy is not so called in respect of mirth and killing, but in respect it wants deaths, which is enough to make it no tragedy, yet brings some near it, which is enough to make it no comedy.' This third kind of play had been defended by Guarini in his apologia for tragicomedy. In an important passage, quoted by E. Waith (p. 48), he explains how tragicomedy takes from tragedy 'great persons but not great actions; . . . the danger, not the death' (*le persone grandi e non l'azione*; . . . *il pericolo, non la morte*).

Even in tragedy, Fletcher tends to dissolve great actions and issues into the stuff of tragicomedy. There is only one play, *The Maid's Tragedy*, in which there is the grain of true tragedy, and that may be to Beaumont's credit. It is a great pity that the most used anthology of Fletcher, the Mermaid edition, should give such prominence to those poor tragedies, *Bonduca*, *Valentinian*, *Thierry and Theodoret*, and omit so much of what Fletcher did so well. Fletcher automatically sees the heroic in terms of the 'comic ordering' which Guarini desires; it is this gift, or vice, which makes his partnership with Massinger generally unhappy. For Massinger, given a romantic plot, would always edge towards the possibility of tragic dilemma; in tragedy and tragicomedy each was pulling against the other. Fletcher's tragedies, Waith remarked, 'turn out to be either poor tragedy or tragicomedy plus death'; and the deaths are the feeblest parts of the plays. The death of Virolet in *The Double Marriage* (Fletcher and Massinger) is extremely silly and spoils an excellent play. It is clearly thought tragic to have the hero killed by his wife, whom he has been forced to divorce, although they still love each other. So he appears on the stage, improbably disguised as his worst enemy, and, taking him for this enemy, his wife nobly stabs him. Fletcher seems unable to make a character die for a good reason; he is much happier if the wound proves not to be fatal, happier still if it is 'the danger not the death'. The fortunate outcome of dangerous situations, and the repentance by evil men of their evil designs, are valued more in real life than in drama; if we are not prepared to have them in drama, there is little hope of liking Fletcher. In *The Island Princess*, the princess is trapped by her own rash promises into a betrothal with a stranger; in a fit of despair, like Beatrice in *The Changeling*, she conspires with an accomplice to have the unwanted man done away with. Fortunately, *this* De Flores is a man who may listen respectfully to the princess, but wouldn't dream of performing such villainy. So the princess is saved from herself. *A Wife for a Month* has several scenes of a half-yielding to persuasion or temptation. The good character listens to the bad; at times he pretends to be taken in, at times he really is taken in at first; in either case, what seems to the audience to be a successful temptation, eventually fails. The scenes are most effective. In this kind of play we want the danger to be avoided, we want the good characters to be firm and to see through the tyrant. If Othello suddenly saw through Iago, or if we realized (before any deaths) that he had seen through him all the time, then Shakespeare would be writing in the middle mood, as I understand it, and our great relief would be one of the audience-reactions on which tragicomedy depends. *Othello* with a happy ending would be a smaller play; but still a *possible* play, neither tragedy nor comedy.

The happy endings themselves are 'theatrical' (as they have to be). The necessary help or information arrives in the nick of time, and there is a good deal of ripping off of disguises. Yet these endings are usually well prepared for. If Fletcher, in turning things to good and removing the danger, fails to follow out the logic of character, he does follow a possible logic of the action. The best example is *A King and No King*, which I shall shortly discuss. In both *A Wife for a Month* and *The Island Princess*, the danger can be averted if an insurrection is successful in time; the insurrection in both plays has been sparked off by the villainy which is oppressing and imposing the danger on the protagonists.

* * *

The shaping elements in Fletcherian tragicomedy are not hard to isolate. They are mystification, debate and persuasion, prurience, improbable plots with elaborate complications, strong scenes. These elements are not defects or blemishes which prevent Fletcher from giving us more 'normal' plays, they are the necessary constituents of his art; if they are sins, the whole art is sinful. In describing these elements, we ask how each affects the structure of a play, its credibility, characterization, and the audience's response.

The basic mystification in Fletcher is the time-honoured one by which an obstacle to a marriage is removed when one (or both) of the partners turns out to be other than had been supposed. It may be a matter of disguise, or it may be that a character has never known his true identity. In *Beggars' Bush*, the rightful earl does not know his real inheritance and lives as a merchant abroad; his unknown father, disguised as a prince of the beggars, watches over him; his humble beloved does not know that she is really the daughter of a duke. In *A King and No King*, the king is a changeling, and the sister whom he loves is not his sister at all.

Fletcher's audience expected the mystification: they expected something to be hidden from them which would, when revealed, solve the entanglement of the plot. They had their eyes and ears open for hints that a character was not what he or she seemed. Who is this bold woman, whose coming is strange, and whose behaviour sorts ill with her low condition? There was a double pleasure in the mystery, ascending and descending; the pleasure of being kept out of the secret and the pleasure of being let into the secret. In one of the poems prefacing the first Folio, Cartwright writes to Fletcher of the pleasure of waiting:

> None can prevent the fancy, and see through
> At the first opening; all stand wond'ring how
> The thing will be, until it is; which thence
> With fresh delight still cheats, still takes the sense;
> The whole design, the shadows, the lights such
> That none can say he shews or hides too much.

The more important, descending pleasure is one we hardly recognize as a legitimate literary or theatrical response: it is the pleasure, both intellectual and emotional, of the delayed epiphany which explains all that has gone before and makes a unity and a harmony of it. Carew has a good image for this in his lines on Thomas May's *The Heir*:

> The whole plot doth alike itself disclose
> Through the five acts, as doth the lock that goes
> With letters, for till every one be known,
> The lock's as fast, as if you had found none.[2]

[2] Carew, *Poems*, ed. R. Dunlap (1949), p. 92.

The best justification of a play built on a carefully concealed and carefully exposed mystery is *A King and No King* (a collaboration between Fletcher and Beaumont). For all the audience can see, Arbaces the king moves forward under the impetus of his own desires, which his will and his strong moral sense can only brake and not halt, further and further into the maze of incest, and in the end is more firmly entangled when it appears that his sister, Panthea, has fallen also and is in love with him. It is both a dreadful and a puzzling entanglement. What the audience does not know—for all that part is only hints and carefully advertised mystery—is Gobrias' plot. What is concealed is that Gobrias, the Lord Protector, is Arbaces' father; it is his wish that Arbaces and his no-sister Panthea should fall in love, so that when the truth that Arbaces is no king comes out, as it must one day come out, Arbaces will not be disgraced but keep his position, now as consort to Panthea, the true-born queen. It is not only his wish that they should fall in love but it is, in some measure, also his contrivance. It is clear, knowing this, that Arbaces will have to suffer if he is to be saved; the truth of his low birth can be divulged only when (from Gobrias' point of view) the moment is ripe, when the two are confirmed in the love which must give them such distress, and when the capricious king will clutch at and accept news which he would in other circumstances spurn, since it is now his one means of escape from the maze. We reach a moment which is simultaneously the crisis for Arbaces and for Gobrias; the moment when there is nothing before Arbaces but the unthinkable is the moment when the truth can be revealed. When the situation is now at last made clear to the audience, not only are they immensely relieved that Arbaces is saved (being reasonable and well-intentioned people they wish him to be saved) but what was puzzling in the behaviour of the brother and sister is now explained. Arbaces and Panthea were not sinful creatures, yet they loved each other as though they were; the explanation of Panthea's 'immodesty' is that she was not Arbaces' sister and she experienced the normal attraction of woman to man. The necessity and the naturalness of the love are made clear by Gobrias' revelation. The surprise is far from being a low trick on the dramatists' part to make the play end happily and save themselves the unpleasantness of driving Arbaces and Panthea into the fire; it is a triumphant disentanglement which explains why everything in the play up to that point is as it is. Other things besides Arbaces' love are now made clear; the faults in his character which seemed strange flaws in his royalty seem less strange when we know that he never was royal.[3]

Once the secret of a play was known, the play was not finished. There must have been many, like Pepys later, who went to see the plays knowing the story perfectly—as perfectly as we know *The Importance of Being Earnest*. Their pleasure is different, more intellectual and less emotional; there would be a keen enjoyment of the dramatist's art and appreciation of the moves by which he prepared for his revelation; a relish for the skill with which the author has given a double level of meaning to the speeches of a disguised character, for example, one for the assumed situation and one for the real situation.

The effect of mystification and disguise on the structure of a play will already be clear. Much of the action of the play will be dictated by the need to keep the audience ignorant, yet to put such hints in their way as will make the revelation acceptable. Mysteries occasionally need cumbrous expositions: *Beggars' Bush* has perhaps the most indigestible exposition in Tudor and Stuart drama. As for credibility, it is clearly out of court. The suppositions which lead to the mysteries are absurd and fantastic, but no one is affronted. How the heroine was lost, or by what strawberry marks she is recognized, is a purely mechanical matter, to be got over as quickly as possible. What matters, so far as credibility is concerned, is the truth of the emotions given to the characters when they are in ignorance, and the truth of them when all is made clear, and the truth of the relations between these two sets of emotions. It is not easy to maintain this last truth, nor is Fletcher always successful. It may be necessary, in order to deceive the audience, to give a disguised character too much of the nature of the assumed character, and there may be some inconsistency with the 'real' character.

Mystification would not be effective in Fletcher if the audience were not prepared to admire the virtuosity of his art and be moved by it at the same time. The same may be said of the element of debate and persuasion. It is hardly too much to say that Fletcher's plays pivot upon a delight in argument, as keen in the author as in the audience; 'they cannot be good poets who are not accustomed to argue well'. First,

[3] Though I do not agree with some of the conclusions in A. Mizener's admirable discussion of 'The High Design of *A King and No King*', I am much in debt for many valuable suggestions made in the course of his article.

there is eloquence itself, the art of persuasion, when x sets out to change y's mind or recommend a course of behaviour to him. Every play has its set-piece of persuasion. *Thierry and Theodoret* opens explosively with Theodoret's efforts to shame his mother from her life of debauchery; Zenocia in *The Custom of the Country* pleads with her lover not to save her life by committing fornication with the she-tyrant; the mother in *The Bloody Brother* argues passionately for the reconciliation of her sons; the chaste Lucina in *Valentinian* is one of many who plead the case of honour against the lustful designs of a tyrant (she is less successful than most). It is a belief in eloquence as well as a delight in it that we are being shown, and this belief and delight have far-reaching effects on the kind of characters Fletcher provides in his plays. The characters must be fit to take part in plays dominated by argument; they must be creatures of reason as well as of passion, to be swayed or not to be swayed as they are good or less good, and as the course of action proposed is itself good or bad. A complexity of character is needed. Vice is often seen, not as a simple definition of character, but as an aberration in a not undignified being, for there must be reasonableness and honour to appeal to. Evadne in *The Maid's Tragedy* is a good example, a shameful creature, but Melantius' sister, and capable of tears and repentance in the face of her brother's great humiliating appeal to her. Antigonus in *The Humorous Lieutenant* is another. As a king and a father he has his virtues; lechery is his vice. He seeks to seduce his son's beloved. Here is her persuasion and his repentance:

ANTIGONUS.   You but fool still:
I know you love me.
CELIA.   As you are just and honest,
I know, I love and honour you; admire you.
ANTIGONUS. [*Aside.*] This works against me, fearfully against me.
CELIA. But, as you bring your power to persecute me,
Your traps to catch mine innocence, to rob me,
As you lay your lusts to overwhelm me,
Hell never hated good as I hate you, sir;
And I dare tell it to your face. What glory,
Now, after all your conquests got, your titles,
The ever-living memories raised to you,
Can my defeat be? my poor wreck, what triumph?
And when you crown your swelling cups to fortune,
What honourable tongue can sing my story?
Be, as your emblem is, a glorious lamp

Set on the top of all, to light all perfectly:
Be, as your office is, a god-like justice,
Into all shedding equally your virtues.
ANTIGONUS. [*Aside.*] She has drench'd me now; now I admire her goodness:
So young, so nobly strong, I never tasted.—
Can nothing in the power of kings persuade ye?
CELIA. No, nor that power command me.
ANTIGONUS. Say, I should force ye?
I have it in my will.
CELIA. Your will's a poor one;
And, though it be a king's will, a despised one;
Weaker than infants' legs, your will's in swaddling-clouts.
A thousand ways my will has found to check ye;
A thousand doors to 'scape ye: I dare die, sir;
As suddenly I dare die, as you can offer.
Nay, say ye had your will, say you had ravish'd me,
Perform'd your lust, what had you purchased by it?
What honour won? Do you know who dwells above, sir,
And what they have prepared for men turn'd devils?
Did you never hear their thunder? start and tremble,
Death sitting on your blood, when their fires visit us?
Will nothing wring you then, do you think? sit hard here?
And like a snake curl round about your conscience,
Biting and stinging? will you not roar too late then?
Then, when you shake in horror of this villainy,
Then will I rise a star in heaven, and scorn ye.
ANTIGONUS. [*Aside.*] Lust, how I hate thee now, and love this sweetness!—
Will you be my queen? can that price purchase you?
CELIA. Not all the world. I am a queen already,
Crown'd by his love I must not lose for fortune:
I can give none away, sell none away, sir,
Can lend no love, am not mine own exchequer;
For in another's heart my hope and peace lies.
ANTIGONUS. Your fair hands, lady! for yet I am not pure enough
To touch these lips. In that sweet peace ye spoke of,
Live now for ever, and I to serve your virtues!
CELIA. Why, now you shew a god: now I kneel to ye.

(IV. v. 38)

And why should he not be moved and altered? The repentance of villains is given credibility by a belief in the power of eloquence. Moreover, the complex villain, a mixture of good and bad, open to shame and the appeal of reason, who is required for plays of persuasion, is required too for the fortunate outcomes of tragicomedy. Many of the 'changes' of character leading towards the happy ending, which affect readers so adversely now, are, I think, quite acceptable, once one grants that passionate persuasion has its power, and that the characters are not fixed simply as good or bad.

A second type of disputation is the big scene of public debate. This is Massinger's forte rather than Fletcher's. It is Massinger who manages the extraordinary debate at the end of *The Queen of Corinth* in which two women who have been raped by the same man plead against each other for the fate of the criminal—one for his death, and the other that she should be allowed to marry him (but the harsher one has not been raped at all). Waith has shown how this and other such prickly perplexities in Fletcher were drawn from Seneca's *controversiae*—a fund of highly improbable situations designed to test the wits of rhetoricians in pleading causes. Fletcher took as much delight in the piquancy of Seneca's situations as Massinger took in the great court scenes which finally debated the issues (see, for example, *The Fatal Dowry* and *The Bondman*). There is a third type of debate to which critics have paid little or no attention. It arises out of the second type and is almost certainly influenced by the *controversiae*. During the course of a play, or part of a play, a person's conduct is exhibited dramatically in good and bad lights, in order to put the audience in the position of a jury and to ask them to pass a verdict of guilty or not guilty, honourable or dishonourable. The presentation of character and incident is dictated by the forensic structure. A very good example is *The Double Marriage*. Virolet is a conspirator whose wife Juliana undergoes torture on behalf of her husband. Virolet is allowed the chance of saving his wife and his colleagues by freeing the tyrant's friend who is held by a pirate. But in the attempt he falls into the same sea-prison himself. The pirate's daughter offers to free him and get him and the tyrant's friend ashore —if he will marry her. He consents. His motives are left extremely obscure. True to his word, he marries the pirate's daughter, and divorces his wife. As the lawyers go off, the pirate's daughter, Martia, speaks.

    MARTIA. Will you to bed, sir?
    VIROLET. As soon to Hell; to anything I hate most!

He fiercely refuses to keep company with her, once he has kept the letter of the bond between them. Now, and only now, is Virolet allowed to speak in his own defence and, by explaining his motives, confirm or refute the opinion which the audience-jury has had of him; he explains that he has done 'all for the best', accepted Martia's offer without taint of lasciviousness, in order to be able to bring back the tyrant's friend and so save his wife and his own friends from death, even at the price of ending his own marriage and happiness. The play is the best of the Massinger-Fletcher collaborations, and it is a great pity that it ends so lamely. But it is nearly always misunderstood because readers, failing to see that they are members of a jury asked to judge a man's honour from his actions alone, accuse the authors of wayward and feeble characterization. Again, a reader may, with ample justification, fail to be aware that Fletcher is here as everywhere throwing moral problems before him. Virolet's dilemma is so preposterous that, as a problem of choice, it is remote and unreal to us. It is possible that it was less remote to the young lawyers and aspirants to the law who frequented Blackfriars; they may have been able to strip the problem of its colourful fiction and see it in its essence as an exercise in choice between two evils.

From problems of morality we have to turn to the problem of immorality. Without a doubt, prurience is a strong element in Fletcher's plays. Yet it is fair to distinguish between his moral tone as a writer and his love of provocative scenes. His plays would yield a very fine anthology of persuasions to virtue and honesty of life; lasciviousness is always made to look hateful or, better still, contemptible: what better attitude could there be to lust than the amused scorn for the discomfitures of Cloe, in the play written in praise of chastity, *The Faithful Shepherdess*? There is no doubt which side Fletcher is on. I do not think we should be shocked because his chaste heroines, like Evanthe in *A Wife for a Month*, look forward to the marriage bed with keen anticipation. These heroines are fiercely and sincerely virtuous: they merely lack reticence and false modesty. The complaint that Fletcher is a prurient writer because in *A King and No King* the subject he is dealing with is *not really* incest is too absurd to answer.[4] Certainly, Fletcher (but more often his collaborators) can indulge in unusual licence, as in the male stews in *The Custom of the Country*, the rapes in *The Queen of Corinth*, the woman racked upon the stage in *The Double*

[4] See, for example, T. S. Eliot, *Selected Essays* (2nd ed., 1934), p. 196.

Marriage, the language of *Love's Cure* and most of *Thierry and Theodoret*. But ordinarily it is the case that Fletcher chooses a plot which will as frequently as possible allow a near but misty view of the more intimate relations between men and women, especially scenes of wedding-night frustrations; and he would not choose a plot which gives no room for sexual delinquency. His plays are sexy plays. *A Wife for a Month* is a classic example. The hero and heroine are allowed by the tyrant to be married for a month only; then they are to be put to death. The hero's eager looking-forward to his honeymoon is interrupted by the new savagery that he is not to go beyond kissing his bride; if he does, or if he tells her why he does not, *she* will die. All this is to lead to the *tour-de-force* of the bedroom scene, in which the distraught hero finally takes the way out of confessing impotence. The shaping spirit of the whole play up to this point is quite obviously the need to make this scene as provocative as possible. Prurience is a fact in Fletcher. He is a moral writer with highly immoral tendencies. It is up to the modern reader to decide whether he will be shocked by the sexiness or not.

It will be quite clear from what has already been said that Fletcher's plots are on a high plateau of improbability. The initial hypotheses are surprising enough, and the complications which follow outdo them in unexpectedness. The more complete the surprise, the greater the success. In such dramatic switchbacks, it will not be easy to create characters who can stay the course. The demands made upon a character in succeeding scenes are so contradictory that 'consistency of character' might seem to be an improper critical term to use in dealing with the plays. But Fletcher appears, to say the least, to have been interested in the problem of characterization which is posed by the kind of plays he writes. I have already tried to show that the belief that eloquence could change a man's behaviour often makes swift alterations credible. In addition, in his best plays, Fletcher takes great care to delineate characters whose temperaments will make sense of the ups-and-downs of the plot. *The Island Princess* is a series of contradictions, and this course of contradictions is allowed its measure of dramatic truth by the instability of the heroine, Quisara. She is noble, but she is impetuous; a little too romantic in her notions of honour, and fickle in her moods. She is the sort of person who will make a rash promise to marry the first man to perform a certain desperate task, who will plan the death of the stranger who performs the task, who will then repent her malice (before it is too late), who will fall out of love with her first love and fall in love with the stranger, who will put her new love to a wrong-headed test of his honour, and in the end learn the meaning of love when the stranger endures a greater and unexpected test. Each about-turn in the play shows us the consistency of inconsistency, and the power of the play is that, in the 'danger' and the happy release, Quisara is shown the example of steadfastness and the real meaning of honour.

It is the same with Arbaces in *A King and No King*. The flaws in his nobility, his vanity, self-importance, rashness, violence, changeability (all so carefully set out at the beginning of the play) make credible the stormy course of the plot. If this is granted, it will not perhaps be held against Fletcher that he starts with a plot that is a series of jolts and surprises, and then invents the characters to fit those plots. When he is interested in doing so, Fletcher achieves a plausibility for the plot in terms of character, and it may be that is all he or any dramatist need be asked to do. It is true, of course, that often his *dramatis personae* 'have no character at all', or only the stereotype of the noble lover or the lustful tyrant or the chaste woman or the loyal friend. It would be idle to pretend that Fletcher is interested in development of character (as opposed to simple change) or that motivation is not very often a matter of contrivance. Ricardo in *The Coxcomb* must fail his tryst if the plot is to go forward: the dramatist gets him drunk. In *Valentinian*, it is necessary that the king should have a ring from the husband of his quarry: he wins it from him at gaming. These perfunctory mechanical contrivances, quite irrelevant to the characters, show clearly enough how indifferent Fletcher could be to the links between the scenes. But it would be quite wrong to conclude that he is never interested in the flesh-and-blood of his characters; in half a dozen plays, he has exerted himself to marry action and character.

It is a small step now to the last and most important governing element in Fletcher's art. A play by Fletcher is primarily a series of strong scenes, a succession of situations, articulated, certainly, and making sense as a whole, yet very often giving the impression that the sum of the parts is greater than the whole. *Rollo, or the Bloody Brother* is a good example (the play is perhaps a revision by Massinger of an original by Fletcher). The first exhibit is a state of cold war between two brothers, kept alive by those whose interest it is to do so; next, there is a great set-piece of oratory in which the mother effects a reconciliation between her sons; Rollo is persuaded to break the truce; a banquet-scene follows in which Rollo's brother rightly fears poison; then a big scene in which Rollo brutally murders his brother in his mother's presence. These are the early scenes of the tragedy. It could possibly be argued that the reconciliation by the mother is part of a developing whole, a fragile patching which no one can believe permanent, a moment of suspension *leading* to the final rupture. But that is not the impression the play makes. The impression is distinctly episodic. We have a series of disjunctive scenes rather than a steady progress. The scene of reconciliation is a unit in itself, with a beginning, a middle, and an end; the audience relishes its wholeness, and asks what is the next part of this story to be dramatized. The *whole* play says little or nothing to us, but each individual scene has truth and force, and a recollection of the play by the audience is more likely to be of 'the scene in which . . .' rather than of 'the process by which . . .'

The worst plays in the Beaumont and Fletcher canon are those in which the desire to insert a scene of a particular kind overmasters the desire to keep the proper ordering of tragicomedy or tragicomic tragedy. There are seduction scenes in *The Knight of Malta* which are there only because of the pleasure in seduction scenes. The hero makes an awkward figure as seducer, and, of course, he concludes by saying he is only testing the virtue of his victim. Even in better plays, violence is done to probability (as it was not in *The Bloody Brother*) by insufficient care to relate the parts to a whole. In *The Humorous Lieutenant*, there is a very good scene indeed in which Celia upbraids her lover Demetrius for failing to believe in her fidelity and chastity. The arrogant and suspicious male is put out of countenance as Shaw wished Imogen to put Posthumus out of countenance. But the necessary condition for the big scene, Demetrius' mistrust, is quite incongruous and simply comic. Right in the middle of his plays (as always at the beginning) Fletcher's audience may be asked to assume something for the sake of argument: '*Suppose* Demetrius had been disillusioned in his mistress, then the consequences would be as follows.' The audience were apparently pleased enough with the consequences not to object to the improbable hypothesis. But it is very hard for us not to be disappointed.

The very fact of collaboration is, I think, an indication of Fletcher's tendency to think of a play as a collection of strong scenes, and his devotion to the situation for its own sake. In the later collaborations, it was Massinger who was generally asked to provide the exposition and the rounding off, while Fletcher chose to tie the characters up in their predicament, expose them to their 'danger'. There is obviously a tug-of-war going on, then, between the principle of architectural wholeness which is so necessary to the romantic type of tragicomedy (which is set forth in diagrammatic form, and in slow-motion tempo, in *The Faithful Shepherdess*), and an art which can sacrifice wholeness to the excitement of the part. The 'strong scene' method of composition is not in itself inimical to the proper 'comic ordering'; the better plays, like *The Island Princess*, prove that. The fierce logic of consequence required in true tragedy is really out of place in plays in which a predicament is something to be got out of, and tragicomedy can stand a good deal of that 'consequence' which is in fact a reversal of what has gone before. The difficulty with Fletcher is that he sometimes asks tragicomedy to take too much inconsequence; he does not always show the architectural power which we know he possesses.

The Fletcherian strong situation may often be chosen for its complexity and unexpectedness, but it is often a stock situation. Any reader of the plays remembers the chaste woman at the mercy of the desires of the man in authority, the two characters at odds atoned by a third (or by themselves), the two lovers suddenly baulked, the pathos of the deserted mistress. It is worth asking whether these repetitions are caused by an infertile fancy, or by audience demand, or by the challenge to ingenuity in ringing the changes in a known and liked situation. The more one reads Fletcher, the less one gets bored by his repetitions and the more one enters into the intellectual pleasure, which his audience surely had, of observing in what ways the treatment of a stock situation is different. In *The Loyal Subject*, there is yet another attempted seduction by a ruler. For the new twist in this scene (IV. iii), Fletcher takes two hints from earlier plays. One is from that famous scene in *A King and No King*, in which Arbaces sees the depth of his sin through the readiness and cheerfulness with which Bessus falls in with the suggestion that he act as procurer. The other is from Clorin's device in *The Faithful Shepherdess* (IV. v) to cure Thenot of his sentimental love by pretending to woo him wantonly. In the new play, Honora steps out of character to defend herself against the Duke and, as she argues the cause of chastity, she assumes a boldness though she has it not. The Duke, admiring her 'brave spirit', is unawares beginning to like what that brave spirit stands for. So that he is deeply shocked when Honora's boldness turns to forwardness and it looks as though she begins to woo him for that which he had himself sought. Wantonness becomes distasteful, and Honora's battle is won. A good deal of the pleasure in this scene must be the pleasure in the virtuosity and ingenuity shown in dealing with a familiar situation. As so often in Fletcher, it is the freshness of invention and the sparkle of the wit that count; Fletcher is the virtuoso and the spectators are the connoisseurs.

★ ★ ★

In Fletcher's art there is a quite extraordinary co-existence of an appeal to the emotions and to the mind. Here are these wild plots, these improbabilities which proudly call attention to themselves, these lubricious scenes continually leading the fancy towards the vision of sexual union—and here at the same time is an art demanding admiration for its skill in construction, its eloquence, its virtuosity. It was not a tired audience that applauded Fletcher: they had their wits about them. Of course, to provide plays asking for a mind alert to the intricacy of workmanship, and yet appealing to a desire for the new, the arresting, the improbable, the improper, may seem to denote decadence; and the word 'decadence' has been prominent in the criticism of Beaumont and Fletcher for many years. The accusation has been prompted in part by the refusal to allow that the Fletcherian is a legitimate *kind* of drama. Impatience with the form has led to short shrift with the significance. To alter a remark of Mizener's, it will be time to condemn the mood of Fletcher when his art is understood. Fletcher's imitation is controlled by the demands of 'comic ordering', of eloquence, of the moving power of the strong scene and the happy ending. It is an art which displays art and not conceals it. It is a form of drama which exists, and has a right to be recognized —and recognized as a legitimate form and not a perversion. If it is recognized, the question of decadence seems to dwindle in importance.

Yet there is still a temptation to condemn; a feeling of dissatisfaction, which takes form as an objection that Fletcher's plays are not enlivened with an intelligent or profound observation of men; that his audience goes its way no wiser than before. The feeling of dissatisfaction is partly warranted and partly unwarranted: it is a question of what one asks of drama. On the one hand, it is clear to everyone that Fletcher's plays are barren of the kind of comment which we find, or which we think is implied, in many other dramatists of his period. Even in what might seem to be the province of all dramatists, the discrimination among various types of conduct, he is much less keen than, say, Massinger, who was always concerned to differentiate the less obvious gradations of imperfection.[5] There is very little indeed to say about Fletcher's 'ideas'. There is a good deal about honour in the plays, but it is the honour of his age, the honour of Sir Kenelm Digby, an honour enfeebled by a long peace, too much analysis and too much nostalgia. In *Bonduca*, Caratach's absurd chivalry towards the enemy is comic, not heroic, and so is that of Demetrius in *The Humorous Lieutenant*, who feels himself impaired until he is able to show to the enemy a greater courtesy than they have shown him. Honour in Fletcher is a magnanimous virtue, tending towards peace and reconciliation; but it too often looks silly.

Fletcher is sometimes castigated for another of his 'ideas', the absolutism which he is supposed to have shared with Beaumont. Coleridge spoke of the pair as 'the most servile jure divino Royalists', 'high-flying, passive-obedience Tories.'[6] But here perhaps the playwright has been confused with the play. Some of Fletcher's characters are absolutists, and their non-resistance to the ruler is a dramatic issue in the plays in which they appear. In *The Maid's Tragedy*, Amintor's absolutism is the pivot of the action. His submissiveness to royalty makes him renounce Aspatia and take the royal gift of the royal whore; his continued submissiveness leads directly to the death of Evadne, whom he repudiates because she has violated the sacredness of kingship. The play tells us nothing about the views of its authors. Fletcher's kings are in general a corrupt lot, frequently conspired against and overthrown with gusto.

The big scenes in Fletcher cannot be made to yield insights, especially new insights, into the springs of human behaviour. In spite of the extravagance of his situations, Fletcher is concerned with a fairly

[5] The careful ranging of kinds of love and lust in *The Faithful Shepherdess* is traditional, and owes more to Book III of *The Faerie Queene* than to observation.
[6] *Coleridge on the Seventeenth Century*, ed. Roberta F. Brinkley (1955), pp. 655–6.

limited range of human types and a fairly limited number of emotions. He does not sub-divide vice and virtue very far. It is his art, not to deal with subtleties of behaviour, but to deal subtly with obvious types of behaviour.

On the one hand, then, it is true that it is useless to look for any arresting point of view in Fletcher's thaumaturgic art; there is nothing which resembles a controlling 'attitude to life'. But are the plays lacking in force as plays therefore? His art is a mode of imitation—the imitation of predicaments and their solution. Imitation cannot be meaningless: we either consent to it in being moved by it, or reject it because of its failure to move. We have to trust ourselves not to be moved by the meretricious. A few whole plays, and a great many individual scenes, have great dramatic merit. The seventeenth-century audience saw no difficulty in granting this merit; they were not deterred by the conventions of improbability, or by a lack of depth in the playwright's views. They responded to Ansemero's refusal to renounce Christianity (*Island Princess*), Celia's humiliations of both father and son (*Humorous Lieutenant*), or Arbaces' histrionics on first meeting Panthea, as they responded to scenes in other plays by other authors. Granting the hypothesis of the situation, they were moved by the conflict of wills, the perplexity of choice, the pity or the heroism, the anxiety or the triumph, or whatever it was they saw displayed. They acknowledged dramatic power. Fletcher may not portray what is grand and permanent in human nature, but he knew how to 'move admiration'. The last word might well be with Dryden, though he was speaking in quite another context: "Tis true, that to imitate well is a poet's work; but to affect the soul, and excite the passions, and above all to move admiration, which is the delight of serious plays, a bare imitation will not serve.'

Note

Biography: Thomas Middleton, 1580–1627
The son of a London bricklayer, he matriculated at Queen's College, Oxford, in 1598, but appears to have left without a degree. Before 1604, when a son was born, he married Maria, sister of the actor and musician, Thomas Marbeck. He lived at Newington in 1609, and was buried there.

Works. His *Wisdom of Solomon Paraphrased* was published in his seventeenth year, and was followed by some satires and *The Ghost of Lucrece* (1600), a poem. In 1602 he began writing plays in collaboration for Philip Henslowe, and then quickly established himself as a writer of comedies for boys' companies with *The Phoenix* (1602) and *The Family of Love, A Mad World, My Masters, Michaelmas Term, Your Five Gallants* and *A Trick to Catch the Old One* (all written between 1602 and 1606?). His company, the Children of Pauls, disbanded, and Middleton turned to writing in collaboration with Dekker and William Rowley. *A Chaste Maid in Cheapside* (1613) he wrote by himself for the Lady Elizabeth's company, and *The Changeling* (1622), a tragedy, with Rowley. Several plays were performed by the King's Men, including *The Witch* (1610?–16?) and *A Game at Chess* (1624) which fell foul of the censor for its political satire. It is not known if his finest play, *Women Beware Women* (1621?–27), was ever performed.

Beginning in 1613, he wrote many Lord Mayors' 'Pageants' and 'Entertainments' for the City of London, whose Chronologer he was from 1620 to his death.

Modern Editions. The standard edition is by A. H. Bullen (8 vols., 1885–6); all quotations in the following chapter are from this text. There is a two-volume selection of plays in the Mermaid Series (1887–90). *The Changeling* has been edited in the Revels Plays by N. C. Bawcutt (1959) and will be followed by *A Chaste Maid* and *Women Beware*.

Scholarship and Criticism. Two compendious studies of Middleton's plays and of problems of chronology and authorship are S. Schoenbaum, *Middleton's Tragedies* (1955) and R. H. Barker, *Thomas Middleton* (1958). There are stimulating essays by Una Ellis-Fermor in her *Jacobean Drama* (1936) and by T. S. Eliot, first published in *For Lancelot Andrewes* (1928).

VIII
Middleton's Experiments with Comedy and Judgement

R. B. PARKER

★

At the heart of Middleton's very personal comic style is a tension between skill in the presentation of manners and a desire to denounce immorality. The very brilliance of his manners comedy, with its ingenious intrigue, verbal wit, and vivid representation of contemporary London scenes and behaviour, is apt to obscure his concern with deprecation, especially in his two major comedies, *A Trick to Catch the Old One* and *A Chaste Maid in Cheapside*, where moral judgement is played down. Nevertheless, the concern is still there; and unless it is recognized, the distinctive nature of these comedies cannot be grasped, nor the extraordinary tensions which govern the satiric tragedy of *Women Beware Women*.

The struggle between satiric observation and determined moralizing is most clearly seen in an early play like *The Phoenix*, where Middleton fails to fuse the two elements. This play centres on a character called Phoenix, an irreproachable young prince who sets out, with his friend Fidelio, to discover incognito the viciousness of the kingdom he is to inherit. Phoenix's rather pompous moral tone is fixed from the start:

> ... indeed, a prince need not travel farther than his own kingdom, if he apply himself faithfully, worthy the glory of himself and expectation of others; and it would appear far nobler industry in him to reform those fashions that are already in his country, than to bring new ones in, which have neither true form nor fashion ... therefore I hold it a safe stern ... to look into the heart and bowels of this dukedom, and, in disguise, mark all abuses ready for reformation or punishment. (I. i. 90)

To which Fidelio replies, with an almost eighteenth-century complacency:

> Thou wonder of all princes, president, and glory,
> True Phoenix, made of an unusual strain!
> Who labours to reform is fit to reign.

The two friends rapidly discover that Fidelio's father-in-law, the Captain, is planning to sell his loyal wife, Castiza, in order to get back to piracy; and that the evil Lord Proditor is not only prepared to buy her, since he cannot seduce her, but is also plotting to assassinate the Duke, Phoenix's father, and blame the murder on the absent prince. By disguising himself as a scrivener, Fidelio manages to thwart the sale of his mother, and Phoenix, briefly unmasking, banishes the Captain with great severity:

> If past this evening's verge the dukedom hold thee,
> Thou art reserv'd for abject punishment.   (II. ii. 323)

Phoenix, in turn, disguises himself as an impoverished gentleman, and so worms his way into Proditor's confidence that the latter employs him to assassinate the Duke. Accordingly, Phoenix is able to denounce Proditor dramatically at the very moment when the murder is supposed to take place. Proditor, too, is permanently banished:

> So ugly are thy crimes,
> Thine eye cannot endure 'em:
> And that thy face may stand perpetually
> Turn'd so from ours, and thy abhorred self
> Neither to threaten wrack of state or credit,
> An everlasting banishment seize on thee!
>   (V. i. 194)

He goes out cursing.

There is nothing intentionally amusing about Proditor or the Captain. They are tragicomedy villains. And their unrelieved nastiness is matched by the incredible and equally humourless purity of Castiza, Fidelio, Fidelio's betrothed, and Phoenix himself. All of these pure characters—with the exception of Fidelio, who acts as 'feed' to Phoenix —have emphatic speeches on morality: Castiza defends 'credit', the value of a pure reputation; Fidelio's betrothed denounces incest; and Phoenix comments at length on the evils he discovers—for example:

> Reverend and honourable Matrimony,
> Mother of lawful sweets, unashamed mornings,
> Dangerless pleasures! thou that mak'st the bed
> Both pleasant and legitimately fruitful!
> Without thee,
> All the world were soiled bastardy.
> Thou art the only and the greatest form
> That put'st a difference between our desires
> And the disorder'd appetites of beasts,
> Making their mates those that stand next their lusts.
> Then,—
> With what base injury is thy goodness paid! . . .
> (II. ii. 164)

It is interesting to note the resemblance between this speech and Milton's famous 'Hail, wedded love, mysterious law' passage in *Paradise Lost* (IV, 750 ff.). Although he frequently satirizes Precisians, Middleton has puritan characteristics himself.

Such moralizing and black-or-white characterization clash oddly with the presentation of the rogues of the play. Falso, uncle to Fidelio's betrothed, casts a most unavuncular eye on his niece's person and inheritance, but the air of tender grievance with which he meets her resistance makes the villainy here more humorous than grim:

> A foolish, coy, bashful thing it is; she's afraid to lie with her own uncle: I'd do her no harm, i' faith. I keep myself a widower a' purpose, yet the foolish girl will not look into 't: she should have all, i' faith; she knows I have but a time, cannot hold long. (II. iii. 33)

Moreover, Falso uses his position as J.P. to encourage his servants in highway robbery and to protect them when they are caught; yet his memories of his own youth on the road are disarmingly lyrical:

> I remember now betimes in a morning, I would have peeped through the green boughs, and have had the party presently, and then to ride away finely in fear: 'twas e'en venery to me, i' faith, the pleasantest course of life! one would think every woodcock a constable, and every owl an officer. But those days are past with me; and, a' my troth, I think I am a greater thief now, and in no danger. I can take my ease, sit in my chair, look in your faces now, and rob you; . . .
> (III. i. 64)

Tangle—'one that has been muzzled in law like a bear, and led by the ring of his spectacles from office to office'—is another, slighter sketch in the same vein. He goes to law for the fun of it, paying his way by advising other litigants; at present he says he has nine-and-twenty suits in law, all not worth forty shillings:

> A stake pulled out of my hedge, there's one; I was well beaten, I remember, that's two; I took one a-bed with my wife against her will, that's three; I was called cuckold for my labour, that's four; I took another a-bed again, that's five; then one called me a wittol, that's six; he killed my dog for barking, seven; my maid-servant was knocked at that time, eight; my wife miscarried with a push, nine; *et sic de caeteris*. I have so vexed and beggared the whole parish with process, subpoenas, and such-like molestations, they are not able to spare so much ready money from a term, as would set up a new weather cock; the churchwardens are fain to go to law with the poor's money. (I. iv. 137)

According to Tangle, litigation has replaced sword and buckler as an exercise for gentlemen, and he and Falso have a curious, semi-symbolic joust with law terms.

Finally, there are Falso's daughter—the Jeweller's Wife—and her lover, the Knight: the one in search of 'pleasure', the other after 'revenue'. This comment on the relations between the aristocracy and middle-classes[1] is both humorous and realistic—consider the lovers debating the Knight's price:

> KNIGHT. It stands upon the frame of my reputation, I protest, lady.
> JEWELLER'S WIFE. Lady? that word is worth an hundred angels at all times, for it cost more; if I live till tomorrow night, my sweet Pleasure, thou shalt have them.
> KNIGHT. Could you not make 'em a hundred and fifty, think you?
> JEWELLER'S WIFE. I'll do my best endeavour to multiply, I assure you.
> KNIGHT. Could you not make 'em two hundred?
> JEWELLER'S WIFE. No, by my faith . . . (III. ii. 1)

The Knight eventually escapes arrest for debt in an excellently realistic scene where the disgruntled catchpolls, balked of a bribe, are momentarily 'blinded' by one of his friends. The others, however, are summoned to judgement by the omniscient Phoenix. Tangle, unhinged after losing several suits, is forcibly cured by Quieto, a 'humour' of repentant litigiousness, who bleeds him of law terms in a scene reminis-

[1] For the social implications of Middleton's comedy see L. C. Knights, *Drama and Society in the Age of Jonson* (1937).

cent of Crispinus' vomiting in Jonson's *The Poetaster*. This use of grotesquerie for criticism becomes one of Middleton's most characteristic devices in later plays. Falso and the Jeweller's Wife are, more orthodoxly, deprived of wealth and rank and placed on probation.

It seems incongruous, however, that these lively and humorous rogues should be brought to judgement by such a cardboard figure as Phoenix with his Haroun Al Rashid disguisings; and the comic tone is irremediably smashed by the harsh sentences imposed on Falso and the Jeweller's Wife, and by Phoenix's high moral tone towards the latter:

> Stand forth, thou one of those
> For whose close lusts the plague ne'er leaves the city.
> Thou worse than common! private, subtle harlot!
> Thou dost deceive three with one feigned lip,
> Thy husband, the world's eye, and the law's whip.
> Thy zeal is hot, for 'tis to lust and fraud,
> And dost not dread to make thy book thy bawd ...
> (V. i. 227)

Such incongruity is not limited to this particular play, moreover. The same uneasiness of tone and incredible retribution can be seen in all Middleton's early comedies, caused in each case by his difficulty in bringing immoral comic characters to severe condemnation. He diverts attention by making his final scenes theatrically striking: *The Family of Love* and *Michaelmas Term* end with court-room scenes, and *Your Five Gallants* with a masque in which the rogues unwittingly betray themselves to punishment; but in none of these plays is the *dénouement* an inevitable result of the previous action, and, with the exception of those in *The Family of Love*, the final judgements always demand from the audience too abrupt a switch from sardonic amusement to stern incrimination—rather like Hal's uncomfortable rejection of Falstaff at the end of *Henry IV*, but with less preparation, and less excuse. Having enjoyed the wiles of the rogues, it seems pompous, even hypocritical, for us to become suddenly indignant about them; yet without such indignation Middleton's punishments are too harsh and his indictments self-righteous.

The dichotomy of *The Phoenix* is an extreme case, however, and in his other early comedies we can watch Middleton trying to avoid this conflict by successively reducing their moral intensity. His first device for this is already visible in *The Phoenix*: the energy and lyrical delight in dishonesty shown by Falso and Tangle. This kind of humorous inflation makes Middleton's rogues inhabitants of a new dimension, where normal morals are not so much broken or revolted against as replaced by different values. The best example, before the major comedies, is Ephestian Quomodo, the dishonest draper of *Michaelmas Term*, whose hunger for the sort of gentility brought only by land makes him lyrical about his dupe's estates:

> O that sweet, neat, comely, proper, delicate, parcel of land! like a fine gentlewoman i' th' waist, not so great as pretty, pretty; the trees in summer whistling, the silver waters by the banks harmoniously gliding. (II. iii. 91)

His pleasure and the energy with which he pursues his dreams are so naïve and genuine that they disarm over-righteousness.

In *The Phoenix* this comic dimension is fragmentary and in conflict with the main perspective of the play, but hints of its extension to all society may already be seen in the defence of Furtivo, Falso's servant caught on the road:

> ... heaven forbid we should be all true men! Then how should your worship's next suit be made? not a tailor left in the land: of what stuff would you have it made? not a merchant left to deliver it: would your worship go in that suit still? You would ha' more thieves about you than those you have banished, and be glad to call the great ones home again, to destroy the little. (III. i. 168)

This becomes Middleton's second means of reducing moral tension. Furtivo's hint of a fully corrupt society is expanded in *Your Five Gallants*, most of which is concerned with the mutual cozenings of five criminals—a process neatly summed up by the cutpurse of the quintet who finds he has stolen the same piece of jewellery twice:

> Does my boy pick and I steal to enrich myself, to keep her, to maintain him? why, this is right the sequence of the world. A lord maintains her, she maintains a knight, he maintains a whore, she maintains a captain. So in like manner the pocket keeps my boy, he keeps me, I keep her, she keeps him; it runs like quicksilver from one to another. (III. ii. 100)

Good characters still exist in *Your Five Gallants*, however, and eventually arrange a judgement; but by the time of *A Mad World, My Masters* Middleton has eliminated the good people completely from his comic world, and with them the need for moral indignation or over-severe punishment.

Punishment is not completely abandoned in the later plays; but in a world without virtuous characters, the rogues have to be made to punish each other. Consequently, Middleton's plotting is made tighter because his various characters have to interact more. A typical early plot in Middleton is built up of several sets of characters of almost equal importance, all revolving around a central character, or situation, which ties them together: like a multi-ringed circus with a single ringmaster. The various sets have little relationship to each other apart from this link to a common centre; at most they have some family link which does not affect the action: in *The Phoenix*, for example, the fact that Castiza is Fidelio's mother, or Falso the father of the Jeweller's Wife, has no plot significance. The connections are gratuitous. In the later comedies this looseness of structure is abandoned and the several intrigues are linked laterally, as well as to a common centre, so that behaviour in one sub-plot directly affects the others.

This extra neatness of intrigue automatically reduces the solemnity of the punishments. As Bergson points out,[2] one of the roots of comedy is a hint of mechanicalness in human behaviour, the suspicion that man is not autonomous; so that the more consistently manipulated the intrigue appears, the funnier seem the characters. Their vice appears less serious because they are obviously not in control of their careers.

Yet we should be wary of accepting the relative immunity of these rogues as Middleton's final comment on his comic world. His first impulse was clearly to denounce vice, no matter how comic; and even in the more farcical experiments which precede his two major comedies there are such outcroppings of very serious comment as the Old Father's criticism of prostitution in *Michaelmas Term* or Penitent Brothel's repentance in *A Mad World, My Masters*. There is discomfort behind Middleton's solution, in fact: an uneasiness which becomes clearer in the curious Dampit scenes in *A Trick to Catch the Old One* and the outrageousness of situation in *A Chaste Maid in Cheapside*, and which finally develops into the dreadful world of *Women Beware Women*.

The plot of *A Trick to Catch the Old One* is a triumph of ironic construction, which can only be illustrated by summarizing the whole

[2] See H. Bergson, *Laughter: An Essay in the Meaning of the Comic*, trans. C. Brereton and F. Rothwell (1911).

thing. The hero is Theophilus Witgood, a young spendthrift country gentleman who has been forced to mortgage his estate to his uncle Pecunius Lucre, a London merchant. Witgood loves Joyce, niece of Walkadine Hoard, another usurer who hates Lucre because the latter once overreached him in a swindle. To recover some of his money from Lucre, Witgood persuades a courtesan who has been his mistress to pose as a rich country widow, and enlists the help of a friendly Host to pose as the 'widow's' servant. When Lucre hears of a projected match between his nephew and this 'widow', he welcomes Witgood, advances him £50, and promises, rather vaguely, to make him his heir. Similarly, Witgood's creditors, hearing of the 'widow's' wealth, cease dunning him and press him to accept further loans. Complications then arise because other suitors appear, amongst them none other than Walkadine Hoard, intent as much on injuring Lucre as on benefiting himself. Witgood sees a chance here to settle his loyal courtesan comfortably in life, and advises her to accept Hoard. Accordingly, she allows herself to be spirited away to Cole-harbour in an excellently contrived and fast-moving tavern scene (III. iii). Lucre, pursuing, is assured by the 'widow' that she will not favour his enemy Hoard, if Lucre will return Witgood's property. This Lucre reluctantly does. But Witgood is arrested by his creditors, irate that he should have lost the rich match. He then puts pressure on Hoard by claiming a precontract to the 'widow', and this, with the Courtesan's persuasions and his own delight in overreaching Lucre and appreciation of his wife's supposed estates, persuades Hoard to buy Witgood off by liquidating his debts. Witgood having secretly married Joyce in the meantime, the party assembles to celebrate Hoard's wedding when Hoard's brother, Onesiphorus, with his friends Limber and Kix, who caught sight of the Courtesan for a moment in the opening scene of the play, turn up and to Lucre's great delight identify the 'widow' as Witgood's ex-mistress. Hoard's complaints are strong-mindedly suppressed by the Courtesan, who promises to be a good wife, and the play ends with her and Witgood kneeling to renounce evil courses in the future.

Except for the coincidence of Onesiphorus Hoard and his friends, which anyway does not affect the situation but only increases the fun by disabusing Hoard, this plot is consistently built around character—the wit and desperation of Witgood and the mutual hatred and business sharpness of Hoard and Lucre: all three Middleton inflations, yet quite consistent and fundamentally credible. Except for the neutral characters of Joyce and Hoard's brother, who only appear for a moment, there is not a single honest person in the play. Yet retribution is kept to a minimum: Witgood and the Courtesan escape scot-free with much gain; Witgood's unpleasant creditors are paid and unpunished; and the disasters of Hoard and Lucre are presented solely in terms of out-manœuvring. The moral aspect of the situation is avoided. Only when the Courtesan justifies her desire to reform does a serious note sound. And the sardonic tone is immediately restored by the dubious knowledge of marital dishonesty revealed in the two 'recantations'.

This successful and consistent irony, moreover, lends the language a tension and significance which is typical of Middleton's mature dramatic style, where the meaning of a speech comes as much from the situation in which it is spoken as from what it says or what it conveys through image patterns. The subtlety of this characteristic is almost impossible to examine out of context, but to give an obvious and simple example, when Hoard inquires for the 'widow' at the tavern from which he is to spirit her away, the reply is:

DRAWER. He says none came in yet, sir, but one mistress Florence.
HOARD. What is that Florence? a widow?
DRAWER. Yes, a Dutch widow.
HOARD. How?
DRAWER. That's an English drab, sir: give your worship good morrow. *Exit.*
HOARD. A merry knave, i' faith! I shall remember a Dutch widow the longest day of my life. (III. iii. 12)

The initial irony of this is deepened when the phrase 'Dutch widow' actually occurs in Hoard's eventual disabusement.

Into this consistent, sardonic, and unmoral world are introduced three curiously inorganic and unpleasant scenes to do with a drunken, upstart lawyer and usurer called Dampit. His only connection with the main plot is that Witgood meets him once in the street and Hoard invites him to his wedding. The difference in tone is even more remarkable. Like Middleton's humorous rogues he has an inflated self-confidence and pride in his villainy, but in him the energy is incoherent and almost maniac:

Report it; Harry Dampit, a trampler of time, say, he would be up in a morning, and be here with his serge gown, dashed up to the hams in a cause; have his feet stink about Westminster Hall, and come home again; see the galleons, the galleasses, the great armadas of the law; then there be hoys and petty vessels, oars and scullers of the time; there be picklocks of the time too: then would I be here; I would trample up and down like a mule . . . (I. iv. 43)

The other two scenes depict his loss of reason and squalid death from drink, with a spectator commenting:

Note but the misery of this usuring slave: here he lies, like a noisome dunghill, full of the poison of his drunken blasphemies; and they to whom he bequeaths all, grudge him the very meat that feeds him, the very pillow that eases him. Here may a usurer behold his end: what profits it to be a slave in this world, and a devil i' th' next? (IV. v. 58)

Dampit's mercenariness is basically no different from Hoard's or Lucre's, but the virulence of the attack on him is remarkable. Unless there was some untraced personal satire involved, it provides a clue to a side of Middleton obscured by the neatness of the main plot: it appears to have been used as a safety-valve for disgust.

All the techniques and also the uneasiness of Middleton's comic world find their fullest expression in *A Chaste Maid in Cheapside*, generally considered his most original and characteristic comedy. Middleton wrote several comedies after *A Chaste Maid* but they all dilute the originality which he achieved in this play: most of them are collaborations where the influence of another writer, or writers, blurs his own comic vision; in *No Wit, No Help Like a Woman's* and *More Dissemblers Besides Women*, which he most probably wrote by himself, the edge of his irony is blunted by a romanticism adopted from Beaumont and Fletcher; while *A Game at Chess* is an Aristophanic political allegory unlike anything else by Middleton, closer to his city pageants and masques, in fact, than to his comedies proper. The only further development of Middleton's comic world after *A Chaste Maid* is to be found not in his comedies at all, but in the satiric tragedy of *Women Beware Women*.

A Chaste Maid centres on a love affair where the intrigue necessary for success is more important than the sentiments involved. Joyce Yellowhammer, daughter of a London goldsmith, is in love with a penniless gentleman called Touchwood Junior. The match is opposed by the girl's mercenary parents, who cynically intend her for the profligate Sir Walter Whorehound. They also engage her brother Tim, an idiot from Cambridge who wields clumsy syllogisms and insists on speaking Latin, to a Welsh 'gentlewoman' who is actually one of Sir Walter's discarded mistresses.

Sir Walter's recommendation is that he is heir to the rich Sir Oliver and Lady Kix, who have produced no children and argue about this loudly and indecently in public. In absurd contrast to the Kixes is Touchwood Senior, who has had to part from his wife because his extraordinary potency produces more children than he can support. Touchwood Senior agrees to help his brother's intrigue, and accordingly, after two unsuccessful elopements, arranges to disinherit Sir Walter by getting Lady Kix with child. This outrageous twist of situation is developed farcically. Touchwood Senior is unnecessarily gorged with aphrodisiacs by his brother and persuades Sir Oliver to drink a worthless medicine which he claims will increase his potency if he exercises while it is digesting. After some dancing about on the furniture, Sir Oliver is dispatched on a five hours' horse ride while Touchwood Senior, with many *doubles entendres*, proposes to 'physic' the compliant Lady Kix.

A third complication is the Allwit family, where Allwit cheerfully lets his wife be Sir Walter's mistress so long as he himself can live at Sir Walter's expense. Allwit's delight in this atrocious situation is an excellent—perhaps the culminating—example of Middleton's technique of immoral inflation. Besides many smaller speeches he has one great speech in the second scene, beginning:

> The founder's come in town: I'm like a man
> Finding a table furnish'd to his hand,
> As mine is still to me, prays for the founder,—
> Bless the right worshipful the good founder's life!
> I thank him, has maintain'd my house this ten years; . . .
> (I. ii. 11)

This speech, which is too long to quote fully as it deserves, ends with Allwit singing a gay refrain about 'dildos'. His fantastic inversion of values extends even to self-righteously circumventing Sir Walter's attempts to marry, so that the knight may not forsake Mrs. Allwit. In fact, whenever Allwit appears in the play there is fantastic distortion. In the celebrated scene of the christening of Mrs. Allwit's seventh bastard the realism of the gossips' behaviour becomes Skeltonically indecent in Allwit's asides, looking suspiciously at wetness beneath their stools; and the comedy of manners of the 'promoters' who picket

Allwit's house to watch for infringements of the new lent laws of 1613 is inflated to grotesqueness by his asides:

> The bawds will be so fat with what they earn,
> Their chins will hang like udders by Easter-eve,
> And, being stroak'd, will give the milk of witches.
>   (II. ii. 67)

This farcical note is intensified by the Country Girl, ex-mistress to Touchwood Senior, who palms off his bastard on the promoters by pretending it is meat—an absurdity reminiscent of practical jokes in the *commedia dell' arte*.

The *dénouement* is reached when Touchwood Junior and Sir Walter Whorehound have a scuffle, in which the knight is wounded. This brush with death arouses Sir Walter's conscience, and he is upbraiding the anxious Allwits for encouraging him in vice when, news arriving that his opponent has died and that Lady Kix is with child, the Allwits refuse Sir Walter asylum with a bland and impudent gall which is as horrible as it is amusing. Touchwood Junior and Joyce are merely shamming death, however, and when their funerals meet amid general lamentation, they declare themselves alive and are married on the spot. Touchwood Junior gets his girl; Touchwood Senior's future is assured by the grateful, self-congratulatory, and wholly unsuspecting Sir Oliver Kix; the Allwits agree to set up a bawdy house in the Strand; the Welsh woman marries Tim, whose mother cynically advises him to use his university logic to prove his wife honest; even Yellowhammer congratulates himself that one feast can be made to serve two weddings. Only Sir Walter is punished—by his wound, his conscience, and arrest for debt.

In *A Chaste Maid in Cheapside*, then, we get a culminatory illustration of the elements we have seen emerging in Middleton's previous comedies: a completely immoral society, preying on itself; an ingenious plot, kept briskly moving by ironic manipulation and inventiveness— though in this *A Trick to Catch the Old One* is perhaps superior; ordinary language charged with double meanings by the situation in which it is used; characters whose viciousness is so wholeheartedly energetic and self-conscious that they go beyond mere reporting; and a *dénouement* which allows most of the villains to evade punishment.

Middleton's uneasiness in this society is again apparent, however. Sir Walter Whorehound's criticism of Allwit is deadly serious:

> None knew the dear account my soul stood charg'd with
> So well as thou, yet, like hell's flattering angel,
> Wouldst never tell me on't, lett'st me go on,
> And join with death in sleep; that if I had not
> Wak'd now by chance, even by a stranger's pity,
> I had everlastingly slept out all hope
> Of grace and mercy.... (V. i. 26)
>
> ... still my adulterous guilt hovers aloft,
> And with her black wings beats down all my prayers
> Ere they be half-way up. What's he knows now
> How long I have to live? O, what comes then? (V. i. 75)

This is the strongest expression yet of the serious note of Penitent Brothel in *A Mad World*, the old father in *Michaelmas Term*, and the spectators of Dampit's death.

Moreover, there is an uneasiness in the very gusto of the scenes and the exaggeration of the characters. In their extreme devotion to immorality and their self-conscious explicitness, Middleton's monsters all along look back to the unnatural jauntiness of 'vices' in the morality plays. Their grotesqueness can be funny or horrible, and often there is a hint of both. In *A Chaste Maid* the grotesque exaggeration is pushed as far as it will go. The outrageous situations now have a shock-value which is very like the discomfort to be felt in Wycherley, and probably for the same reason: moral condemnation is sensed just below the surface, only hidden by the speed and vivacity. There is also criticism implicit in the ironic symmetry of the plot.[3] The energetic competitiveness of the intrigue in which dog eats dog and rogue bilks rogue need only be pushed a little further, made a matter of life and death, and the delicate net of plot and counter plot becomes a web of mutual destruction. And the more consistent the intrigue is, then the more inevitable will appear the destruction. Farce will then seem like savage predestination.

All that is needed for this gusto and intrigue to become destructive is for the idea of death, which intrudes into the comedies only briefly, to be maintained more consistently and returned to at the end of the play. At the end of *A Chaste Maid*, in fact, the idea of death is deliberately, almost impudently, played with in the mock funeral of Touchwood and Joyce, where the very unrealism of the device may be an indication of the same moral tension which made Middleton resort to

---

[3] This element in Middleton's technique is extensively treated by Schoenbaum and Barker.

similar devices in his early comedies. Here the reminder of death is twisted into a final assertion of exuberance, when Touchwood Senior takes up the lovers' burial shrouds and says:

> Here be your wedding-sheets you brought along with you;
> You may both go to bed when you please too.   (V. iv. 43)

Death gives place to the exultancy of marriage.

But the conceit is revealingly reversed at the beginning of *Women Beware Women*, where the young bridegroom, Leantio, says shudderingly:

> To have the toil and griefs of fourscore years
> Put up in a white sheet, tied with two knots;
> Methinks it should strike earthquakes in adulterers,
> When even the very sheets they commit sin in
> May prove, for ought they know, all their last garments.
> (I. i. 20)

The reversed use of the image is a measure of the difference in perspective between the two plays. Yet, except for this difference, the world of the tragedy is exactly the same as that of the mature comedies, and the two treatments throw valuable light on each other.

Women Beware Women[4] presents the familiar Middleton world of complete and humorous corruption: the witty immorality of Livia is an excellent example of his technique of comic inflation; but this world is now shown to be frighteningly vulnerable. We watch three young people corrupted by their own weaknesses and the pressure of a degenerate environment. In the main plot Bianca is immature, sexually aroused, and conscious that her birth entitles her to a higher social position than that provided by her husband; Leantio is vulgar, mercenary, cynical, and lustful: in the secondary plot Isabella's love for her uncle is a sexual attraction. Their weaknesses leave these characters at the mercy of their degenerate environment. Except for the Cardinal, all the other characters are either consciously wicked, or bestial, or stupidly cynical, mercenary, and proud of their worldly wisdom.

The values of this society are emphasized by the repetition of certain key images and ideas. Its greed and sensuality are expressed in images of gluttony—the appetite for food being used continually to illustrate

---

[4] 1621 is the usual dating of the play, though the only sure date we possess is that of the first edition in 1657. Bentley, judging from stylistic evidence, suggests that it should be put later, after *The Changeling*.

sexual appetite, either by direct comparison, metaphorically, or implicitly in *doubles entendres*. Lust is also expressed in images of rankness—an apparent splendour based on filth, which is in turn identified with disease, sometimes specifically with venereal disease as in Leantio's:

> When I behold a glorious dangerous strumpet,
> Sparkling in beauty and destruction too,
> Both at a twinkling, I do liken straight
> Her beautified body to a goodly temple
> That's built on vaults where carcasses lie rotting; . . .
> (III. i. 95)

Sometimes disease imagery is used less specifically to illustrate moral sickness, as in the speeches of the Cardinal; and contributing to this sense of hidden corruption are occasional references to poison. Poison, of course, is used by all except one of the characters who murder at the end.

A second theme is an omnipresent mercenariness which always expresses worth in terms of money or material possessions. Love is regarded as a marketable commodity: note, for instance, the terms in which Guardiano and Fabritio discuss Isabella's marriage, or the warnings of Sordido to the Ward about buying on trust. Money is an argument used by all the seducers of the play, and the essential vulgarity of Leantio is marked from the first by the material terms in which he describes his bride, so that it is little wonder that, after his wife's betrayal, he can listen to Livia's assurance that 'want's the key to whoredom', and cynically agree:

> Troth, then, I'll love enough, and take enough.
> (III. ii. 376)

The standards which society sets up to guide its members, moreover, are shown to be completely inadequate and easily perverted to serve the very vices they are designed to combat. Livia, in the familiar manner of Middleton's comic rogues, cheerfully equates 'bounty' and 'liberality' with licence, uses the claims of 'custom', 'courtesy', and 'pity' to entice Bianca and Isabella to ruin, and excuses her behaviour with a plea of 'affection'. 'Honour', too, is easily perverted: the Duke promises 'wealth and honour' in return for Bianca's chastity, and it is in the name of the family 'honour' that Hippolito leaves his niece's bed to murder his sister's lover. The social untrustworthiness may be illustrated by Middleton's unusual emphasis in this play on the word 'stranger'. It symbolizes the selfish isolation of all characters. Bianca is a stranger to Florence and the word 'stranger' is continually used to explain the apparent courtesy with which she is greeted (e.g. I. i. 112, II. ii. 288, II. ii. 435): a politeness, however, which merely lures to destruction. Bianca is exploited and destroyed by society and dies realizing her isolation:

> What make I here? these are all *strangers* to me,
> Not known but by their malice. . . .   (V. i. 248)

Conversely, Hippolito and Isabella are not strangers but relatives. Of their love Guardiano at first says:

> . . . there's no lust, but love in't,
> And that abundantly; when in *stranger* things
> There is no love at all but what lust brings.
> (I. ii. 71)

To ruin her niece Livia has deliberately to destroy this link and make the lovers seem strangers, so that Isabella can contract with her uncle in these terms:

> Pray, make your love no *stranger*, sir, that's all,—
> Though you be one yourself, and know not on't,
> And I have sworn you must not. *Aside.*
> (II. i. 226)

'Stranger' is thus simultaneously a symbol of isolation and exploitation and a misused social term, an obligation to courtesy which is perverted to treacherous ends. The only standard actually observed is a surface respectability summed up by Hippolito:

> Put case one must be vicious, . . .
> . . . there's a blind time made for 't,
> He might use only that,—'twere conscionable;
> Art, silence, closeness, subtlety, and darkness,
> Are fit for such a business; . . .   (IV. ii. 5)

This picture of complete corruption is manipulated with the identical irony of the comedies. Middleton uses the devices of coincidence and dramatic irony to wring the last drop of folly, meanness, and ridicule out of his situations. In the story by Malespini which Middleton borrowed for his main plot, Bianca Capello, a Venetian noblewoman, eloped with a commoner, Pietro Buonaventuri (i.e. Leantio), and was seduced at Florence by Francesco de Medici (the Duke), with the connivance of a Signora Mandragone (Livia); Pietro consoled himself with a rich widow, Cassandra Buongiani (Livia), and was assassinated by Roberto Ricci, the widow's nephew (Hippolito). In the secondary plot, borrowed from a French story by Meslier, Hypolite is helped to seduce his niece, Isabelle, by a nun (Livia). Thus Middleton combines his two sources so that Livia—identified with both Signora Mandragone and Cassandra Buongiani in the main plot and with the nun in the secondary plot—is forced to fall in love with the husband of the woman she has betrayed. Similarly, Hippolito—identified with both Hypolite and Roberto Ricci—has to murder Livia's lover while indulging an incestuous relationship which Livia has arranged. In anger at Leantio's death Livia betrays the incest she has fostered, and is thus made to set in motion a series of revenges which brings her own death.

The ridiculous side of the characters is also exploited by dramatic irony. Leantio, for instance, returning unaware of his wife's infidelity in III. i, is given a rapturous soliloquy of expectation which at the end of the scene he balances with an identically parallel speech of disillusion; he is made to cut a very undignified figure in the misery of this awakening, trying comically to bluster and being deflated, bullying his mother and being deceived. The scene of the play which justifiably is most celebrated is the scene in which Guardiano and the Duke seduce Bianca 'above' while Livia plays chess with the Widow below: Livia's *doubles entendres* in this scene help to minimize the glamour of the occasion quite as much as Guardiano's open mercenariness or the Duke's own cynical arguments. And at the end irony is given full rein in the masque, with its oblique commentary on the preceding action, and in the multiple intrigue by which characters merely encompass their own destruction. The better-natured but stupid characters, moreover, have to endure the humiliation of hearing their own worldly arguments twisted against them. The complacency of the stupid characters is so emphasized that there is a suspicion of comedy always present whenever the Widow, Fabritio, the Ward and Sordido, or even Guardiano appear. This comedy throws an ironic sidelight onto the self-deception of the cleverer characters and makes it impossible for the audience to entertain any grand, inflated, tragic feelings about human misfortune and misery.

The devices of coincidence and irony are thus exploited in ways which expose the stupidity and powerlessness of the characters and deprive them of the dignity of free will and self-determination. Middleton's creatures march blithely to destruction, betrayed by their own weaknesses to a pattern of retribution whose ironic consistency is quite beyond their control. There is no sense that they might avoid an ignominious fate: they are automata, 'moral idiots'. The result of this is that the spectator's sympathies are alienated and self-identification made impossible. As has been pointed out, an insistence on the automatism of man, physical or moral, is one of the techniques of comedy. *Women Beware Women* is a closed system which we see from the outside, and its consistency is in essence comic.

To this world of his comedies Middleton adds, however, a sense of doom. This is almost invariably expressed in religious terms. Its main expressions are, of course, the warnings of the Cardinal, who is a mouthpiece of denunciation rather than a character in the round. His first speaking appearance is in IV. i, where he upbraids the Duke for his adultery with Bianca, reminding him of the evanescence of life and the pains of hell which await sinners. He next appears in IV. iii, in an impassioned but vain attempt to stop the Duke marrying Bianca; and in the final scene it is he who sums up the play:

> Sin, what thou art, these ruins show too piteously.
> (V. i. 264)

A sense of religious doom is not wanting before the speeches of the Cardinal, however. Both Leantio and Hippolito have guilty consciences; Leantio sees Bianca's infidelity as his punishment for having stolen her away from her family; and Hippolito recognizes from the first that his love for his niece is:

> ... not a thing ordain'd, heaven has forbid it;
> And 'tis most meet that I should rather perish
> Than the decree divine receive least blemish.
> (I. ii. 156)

Yet, despite their realization, both drift helplessly into sin. The ideas of hell and damnation are also kept alive by casual references and, especially, by a terrible irony which lets the characters pay lip service to the standards they are transgressing. The Duke for instance, alarmed by the Cardinal's denunciation of adultery, determines to have Leantio murdered so that he may marry Bianca in church! Similarly, characters conceal their sin by blandly swearing to their innocence with the oath: 'May I want pity (or penitence) at my greatest need,' a shallowness which not only reveals the blindness of the characters but also reminds the audience of the standards which are being violated.

Middleton thus identifies his arbitrary pattern of retribution with the Christian ideas of sin and hell, and there seems to be no sense of incongruity as he modulates from his own ironic vision to the Cardinal's assurances of damnation. This eschatology is completely pessimistic, without any suggestion of the doctrine of redemption. It is the despairing determinism of Faustus' two texts, 'The wages of sin is death' and 'If we say we do not sin, we deceive ourselves . . .': a doctrine which rigorously denies both grace and free will.

Yet the Cardinal's speeches also serve to destroy the comic immunity of *Women Beware Women*. His warnings also presuppose a self-responsibility in the characters, which the ironic manipulation of plot has tacitly denied. His denunciations treat the sinners as such people are treated in the real world: with an emotional reaction of horror and indignation; so that if the audience fully identifies itself with these denunciations—as it is meant to do—it can no longer maintain the aloofness proper to comedy.[5] Seen through the Cardinal's eyes, the creatures of *Women Beware Women* are no longer lively puppets, but sinners whose dreadful position can arouse pity and terror. The whole perspective of the play is altered.

Thus the playwright is left with two alternative ways of treating his *dénouement*: he can either find some way to maintain and re-emphasize his satiric aloofness, or he can begin to treat his characters as responsible souls capable of arousing tragic emotion. There are elements of both these treatments in the *dénouement*; tragedy, however, keeps in a minor key, whereas the satire is savagely exaggerated.

The chief impression is one neither of pity nor terror, but of confusion. In R. C. Bald's phrase, 'action runs amok'. Not only do the characters murder each other with ironic consistency, they do so simultaneously with the most *recherchés* instruments. People die in hysterical

---

[5] See Bergson, p. 139: 'The comic . . . appeals to the intelligence pure and simple; laughter is incompatible with emotion. . . . Take a downright vice . . . you may make it ludicrous if, by some suitable contrivance, you arrange so that it leaves our emotions unaffected. Not that the vice *must* then be ludicrous, but it *may*, from that time forth, become so. *It must not arouse feelings*; that is the sole condition really necessary, though assuredly it is not sufficient.'

confusion all over the stage, from poisoned incense, a poisoned shower of gold, from poisoned arrows shot by suborned Cupids—Guardiano even disappears unexpectedly through a trapdoor; and all this is done so rapidly and in such cross currents of comment—remarks by the observers, excerpts from the masque, asides by the murderers, curses from the victims—that the only possible reaction from the audience is a horrified bewilderment allied to laughter. Such effect seems to have been intended by Middleton, at least in part, because he arranges that the inevitable confusion of the audience is shared, formulated, and thus confirmed, by the remarks of Fabritio and the Duke, onlookers at the masque who cannot understand what is happening. As each surprising death occurs, one of these two characters emphasizes it with a question or an exclamation of surprise, and the Duke sums up for both of them, and for the audience too:

> I've lost myself in this quite.
> (V. i. 183)

The effect of the confusion, then, seems to have been deliberately highlighted, and, when we analyse it, we find that it results largely from a speeding-up of previous satiric elements. In it the elements of coincidence, dramatic irony, manipulation, and helplessness are emphasized to the point of farce: the characters are never less in control of their destinies; they are manipulated with absurd consistency to their improbable deaths; and the giddy speed with which this is accomplished seems to emphasize their helplessness and the author's manipulation. The effect is so nearly absurd that it quite insulates the characters from emotional sympathy.

The end of *Women Beware Women* is, admittedly, not a success. Its failure, however, is not to be traced to an abandonment of the earlier spirit of the play, either from boredom or in appeal to the popular appetite for sensationalism, but rather to an over-intensification of the very elements which distinguish Middleton from his fellow dramatists. It is, in fact, a return to the grotesque humour into which Middleton retreats in his later comedies from this same problem of punishment. In the early comedies the difficulty of reconciling his immoral characters with a moral *dénouement* results in a split of tone and the use of such theatrical devices as *deus ex machina*, court scenes, or unmotivated masques—the staginess of *Women Beware Women*'s *dénouement* is a return to this tendency. Later the split is avoided by withdrawing the moral element in the comedies and concentrating on ingenious intrigue and fantastically inflated villains; but uneasiness with the seeming immunity of this world leads in *A Chaste Maid* or the Dampit scenes of *A Trick to Catch the Old One* to a kind of exaggeration which is in itself critical, in which disgust and condemnation are implicit. Here, in *Women Beware Women*, the same savage rejection lies in the final exaggeration. But the exaggeration is also a refusal to allow the characters the full humanity presupposed by the Cardinal's speeches, and therefore equally a retreat from the tragic implications of determinism. In each case the author dissociates himself from the fates of his characters; his exaggeration is a distancing device. Middleton's comic world thus has two polarities: a completely amoral vitalism and a more than Calvinistically determined scheme of retribution. He attempts to reconcile them in a strange mixture of realism, irony, and exaggeration, and from either extreme takes refuge in grotesquerie. Whether this problem was a philosophic one or an artistic one rising from technique it is impossible to say.

Note

Biography: John Webster, c. 1580–c. 1630
The first record is of his collaboration on a play for Philip Henslowe, in 1602, but he once wrote that he had been 'born free' of the Merchant Tailors' Company of London. It is possible that he studied at the Middle Temple.

Works. The White Devil (1612), The Duchess of Malfi (1614) and a tragicomedy, The Devil's Law Case (1616?) are the only extant plays which all scholars agree were his unaided work. The Guise (before 1623) is lost. His earlier collaboration was chiefly with Dekker (including work on Westward Ho, Northward Ho, and Sir Thomas Wyatt before 1607). Appius and Virginia he wrote with Heywood, or in close imitation of him in some scenes, either in 1603-4 or about 1630. In 1604, he wrote an Induction for Marston's Malcontent and in 1624 a mayoral pageant, Monuments of Honour. His later collaboration included work on Anything for a Quiet Life (1621) with Middleton, and on A Cure for a Cuckold (1624) with Rowley. He also wrote some characters in the Overbury Collection (1615) and some occasional verses.

Modern Editions. The Works were edited by F. L. Lucas (4 vols., 1927); for the earlier collaboration with Dekker, F. T. Bowers' edition of Dekker must be consulted (vols. i and ii; 1953-5). The White Devil and The Duchess of Malfi are edited for the Revels Plays by J. R. Brown (1960 and 1965). In the following chapter all quotations are from Lucas's edition.

Scholarship and Criticism. C. Leech's John Webster: a Critical Study (1951) is the only up-to-date and comprehensive book on Webster. Rupert Brooke's Webster and the Elizabethan Drama (1916) was influential and is still stimulating. T. Bogard has studied Webster's use of the examples of Marston and Chapman in The Tragic Satire of John Webster (1955), and G. Boklund has traced The Sources of 'The White Devil' (1957) and provided a wider study, The Duchess of Malfi: sources, themes, characters (1962).

J. Smith and I. Jack have divergent essays in Scrutiny (1939 and 1949), and H. T. Price a keen examination of the imagery of The White Devil in P.M.L.A. (1955); Muriel Bradbrook has two notes on illuminating details of The Duchess in Modern Language Review (1947).

Muriel Bradbrook's Themes and Conventions of Elizabethan Tragedy (1935), Una Ellis-Fermor's Jacobean Drama (1936) and I. Ribner's Jacobean Tragedy (1962) have important chapters on Webster.

IX

'The White Devil' and 'The Duchess of Malfi'

J. R. MULRYNE

★

AFTER Shakespeare's plays, Webster's tragedies, *The White Devil* and *The Duchess of Malfi*, are more often produced today than the work of any other Jacobean dramatist. In some ways this continued popularity is difficult to explain, for, while *The Duchess of Malfi* might possibly command unthinking and even sentimental esteem, *The White Devil* challenges and disturbs far more than it flatters. We can adjust ourselves readily enough to so narrow and intense an insight as emerges from Tourneur's plays for example, because we can stand against it and see it objectively. But Webster succeeds in coming so close to our sympathy, by his evident delight in the figures and the world he creates, that we are forced to come to terms with the experience he offers us. It may be, however, that *The White Devil* has remained popular at the expense of disregard for an important part of what it has to communicate, and some emphasis on the neglected part is required. As for *The Duchess of Malfi*, the need is not for a new approach, but for distinguishing what that tragedy has to offer us as dramatic poetry.

It is usual to speak of *The White Devil* as a play evoking an emotional response that is deep and full and ill-defined. Much may be said in support of this view. The effect seems to be achieved largely through the iteration of broadly evocative words—devil, hell, blood, lightning, storm, whirlwind, fury, thunder, death—in a setting that moves between furtive midnight situations and the splendour of Princes' courts, the pageantry of a Papal election, or the formal dignity of a court of law. Wide use is also made of religious terminology, and such socio-religious concepts as 'charity' and 'justice' are frequently employed as broad emotional counters. Animals associated with violence—wolf, lion, pole-cat—are constantly named, while adjectives such as 'black', 'dark', 'horrid' are used for their emotive potency. And it is true that we often carry away with us from reading or seeing the tragedy some few vivid emotional impressions—of Vittoria's magnificent self-assertion in the face of all odds, of Isabella's meek devotion, of the deep and courageous agnosticism that enfolds the last act of the play. But to be content with these observations is to do scant justice to an alert, agile, and restless intelligence that deeply qualifies the experience the tragedy offers us.

If we examine Webster's metaphoric use of language we will discover, as Eliot has remarked, that it affords close comparisons with that of the metaphysical poets. Brachiano's words to Vittoria, whom he believes fickle, are a good example:

>   Thy loose thoughts
>   Scatter like quicke-silver.
>   (IV. ii. 101)

Here a very considerable imaginative energy is at work compelling a new fact, making available a new experience, out of two previously separate facts. But the language is rarely under such pressure as this. Much more characteristic is the use of illustrative analogy:

> CAMILLO. The Duke your maister visits me—I thanke him,
> And I perceave how like an earnest bowler
> Hee very passionatelie leanes that way,
> He should have his boule runne.
> FLAMINEO. I hope you do not thinke—
> CAMILLO. That noble men boule bootie? Faith his cheeke
> Hath a most excellent Bias, it would faine
> Jumpe with my mistris.   (I. ii. 61)

These lines indicate a mind that is alert, observant, witty, an intellect that is notably agile. Even more characteristic is a certain cerebral ingenuity, a reaching out for comparisons to areas of experience not at all obviously related, and by their very unrelatedness and their (often) 'unpoetic' associations bringing to the image a bizarre effect. So Lodovico comments on Zanche:

> Marke her I prethee, shee simpers like the suddes
> A Collier hath bene washt in.   (V. iii. 248)

Here the ingenuity is arguably legitimate; it subserves a definite poetic purpose. On other occasions it evokes only amused surprise:

> Come, come my Lord, untie your foulded thoughts,
> And let them dangle loose as a bride's haire. (IV. i. 1)

It is the bizarre note that is dominant here. We are astonished and amused at the feat performed in seeing the two subjects as at all related, rather than made more keenly aware of the situation upon which comment is being offered. This is the vice to which an intellect such as Webster's, as discovered in this play, is peculiarly subject.

The play's versification gives us some further insight into Webster's sensibility, or rather into that dramatic arrest of it that is *The White Devil*. The blank verse line can attain a freedom from the constraint of metrical domination that places it far from the characteristic verse of Marlowe or even of Chapman, and recalls Donne's handling of metrical cadence. The rhythms of the speaking voice, vigorous, disorderly and at times breathlessly animated, override the metric pattern, and verse slides easily into prose, often the hurried prose of a Flamineo. The sense conveyed is one of unordered activity. Together with that restless intellect, it epitomizes an important part of the experience offered by *The White Devil*.

If we examine the play in more specific terms, we shall discover how the type of mind we have been speaking of affected its construction, its moral outlook and emotional tone. Given the events of his tragedy, Webster could so have handled them as to confirm the values of the traditional Revenge play, involving an appeal to our sense of pity and of outraged humanity at the murders committed. This would have allowed a simple moral viewpoint from which to order our attitude to his characters. But he has the murders of Camillo and Isabella enacted in dumb show, distancing the events from our sympathy; any incipient pity we may feel for Isabella, a response already unlikely in the weird midnight setting, is immediately deflated by Brachiano's absurdly businesslike comment:

> Excellent, then shee's dead.
> (II. ii. 24)

Camillo's death is also effectively insulated from our pity. The Conjurer's introductory words come close to burlesque:

> Strike louder musicke from this charmed ground,
> To yeeld, as fits the act, a Tragicke sound. (II. ii. 36)

And again Brachiano's comment is laconic:

> 'Twas quaintly done . . .
> (II. ii. 38)

The same amused repudiation of pity is made explicit on the appearance of Isabella's ghost. Francisco begins by disbelieving its actuality, a response common enough, but goes on:

> remove this object—
> Out of my braine with't! what have I to do
> With tombes, or death-beds, funerals, or teares,
> That have to meditate upon revenge? (*Exit Ghost*
> So now 'tis ended, like an old wives story.
> (IV. i. 116)

And it is not only the simple values of the traditional Revenge play that Webster repudiates as unsuited to vindication in his tragedy. His sensibility demanded the creation of a world in which no set of values is shown as the 'right' one, no attitude as intrinsically better than any other; a world of, in the most literal sense, moral and emotional anarchy.

The first act of the play establishes this immediately and powerfully. The ceremonious opening of the second scene is a brief moment of security (when the accepted values of a polite and ordered society seem to be operant) between the disorder of scene one—Lodovico's headlong bitterness in collision with the equivocal politic 'good sense' of Antonelli and Gasparo—and the more involved disorder of scene two. The whispers of Brachiano and Flamineo very quickly mine that opening security. If its values were replaced by Brachiano's illicit infatuation, its depth suggested by that

> Quite lost, Flamineo

we could probably make the substitution with some composure. But Flamineo's cynicism cuts clean across Brachiano's idealizing of love, making it impossible for us to accord it our full esteem. And after the logical and theatrical complexity of the gulling of Camillo, the 'set piece' with which the scene ends is a fine dramatic embodiment of the anarchy the play deals in. Even the pair, Vittoria and Brachiano, at the centre of the stage are far from being in accord. Brachiano's infatuation is as deep and inarticulate as at the scene's opening, but it is met, not by answering passion, but by Vittoria's pert and self-possessed replies:

> Sir in the way of pittie
> I wish your hart-hole.

and

> Sure Sir a loathed crueltie in Ladyes
> Is as to Doctors many funeralls:
> It takes away their credit.[1]
> (I. ii. 198)

Vittoria is given to self-advancement, not passion. And this central disaccord undergoes comment from two very different sources, Flamineo on one side of the stage, and Cornelia on the other. Flamineo lecherously interprets what passes, his words like a snigger:

> BRACHIANO. I will but change
> My Jewell for your Jewell. FLAMINEO. Excellent,
> His Jewell for her Jewell, well put in Duke.
> BRACHIANO. Nay let me see you weare it. VITTORIA. Here sir?
> BRACHIANO. Nay lower, you shall weare my Jewell lower.
> FLAMINEO. That's better, she must weare his Jewell lower.
> (I. ii. 213)

And Cornelia's denunciation further complicates this chaos of attitudes. Her words, though in themselves mere cliché, are given immense weight by the *coup de théâtre* as she steps forward among the unsuspecting group:

> BRACHIANO. Be Dukedome, health, wife, children, friends and all.
> CORNELIA. Woe to light hearts!—they still forerun our fall!
> (l. 258)

---

[1] The witty inversion to which 'credit' is here subject is a minor example of that witty playing with established concepts that occurs throughout the tragedy.

The rhyme gives the force of an irresistible conclusion. Zanche flees before it and Vittoria acknowledges it by her almost abject pleading: 'Dearest mother heare me. . . .'

Cornelia's view has its moment of triumph as she brings before the others' minds the presence they are, as she asserts, wronging, that of Isabella. Their words tail off into the frayed ends of speech. But in a few lines Cornelia's attitude is itself completely overthrown by Flamineo's inversion of all accepted moral standards and normal human feelings:

> I would the common'st Courtezan in Rome,
> Had bene my mother rather then thy selfe . . .
> Lycurgus wondred much, men would provide
> Good stalions for their Mares, and yet would suffer
> Their faire wives to be barren—   (I. ii. 328)

Cornelia in her turn can only flee before its inverted integrity, crying, 'Misery of miseries!'

In reading or seeing the first act we will have been aware not only of the moral chaos it embodies, but also of a current of humour that is never far from the surface. Certainly Brachiano's tense appetite or Lodovico's bitterness or Cornelia's moral fervour are serious and compelling enough. But the introduction into scene two of the elaborate gulling of Camillo, springing from the same sort of delight in complicated deceit that informs many Jacobean comedies of intrigue[2] (and becomes both more refined and less vigorous in the following century), is the first appearance of a humour that is never absent for more than a few lines. It is the product of a restless intelligence that rarely ceases to mock every serious value, every impressive situation or striking pose, every 'affirmation' that the tragedy has to offer us. We have sensed its presence already in the handling of the Revenge Play convention and it constantly modifies our response, even to that most memorable of scenes, the trial of Vittoria. Here too, for all its pageantry, and for all Monticelso's careful preparations, the same irrepressible humour is only just under the surface. It appears overtly both before and after the arraignment, in Flamineo's mock trial with the Lawyer,

[2] The two catalogues of knaves in the play—the Conjurer's and Monticelso's—also remind us forcibly of the world of Jonson's or Middleton's City Comedies.

and in his feigned madness. Both to some extent burlesque the judicial proceedings (as does the Lawyer's pompous jargon) and both impress upon us what we already know, that Vittoria is guilty of incontinence. But this is what it is the court's business to decide. And so we watch the passionate self-assertion of Vittoria, Brachiano's magnificent gestures and the thwarted anger of Francisco with something of amused detachment in our response. The amusement reaches its peak after sentence has been passed and Vittoria utters her absurd cry:

> A rape, a rape! MONTICELSO. How? VITTORIA. Yes you have ravisht justice,
> Forc't her to do your pleasure. (III. ii. 285)

We are not only amused but incredulous. We feel something of the same amused detachment in the quarrel scene between Brachiano and Vittoria. We are aware that all the passionate speeches, accusation and counter-accusation, Vittoria's repentance and Brachiano's, their return to their accustomed wickedness, are built upon the shifting sands of Francisco's deceit. And much the same may be said of the gulling of Lodovico in Act IV. We cannot respond with anything like complete seriousness to his change of heart from villainy to honesty, and back to villainy, for we are unsure of Monticelso's sincerity and we know certainly of Francisco's knavery. An elusive but unmistakable current of humour is made to play about almost every scene and incident; it sets at a distance the anarchy the play embodies and yet in some ways intensifies it, for it is utterly corrosive of any value that would seem about to stem the tide of anarchy and give us a resting place for our sympathy.

One character, Flamineo, comes close to being simply an embodiment of this temper. No situation, no character, and no value remains invulnerable to the exercise of his eloquent, cynical wit. His comments forced us to modify our response to the meeting between Vittoria and Brachiano in I. ii; he performs the same function in the House of Convertites scene and before the arraignment. Even the 'grave Leiger Ambassadors', otherwise wholly serious figures, undergo the searching and distorting glance of his mockery; no gravity could sustain the maliciously precise imagery of:

> He carries his face in's ruffe, as I have seene a serving-man carry glasses in a cipres hat-band, monstrous steddy for feare of breaking—

He lookes like the claw of a blacke-bird, first salted and then broyled in a candle. (III. i. 76)

Thus the Spanish Ambassador is epitomized, as Camillo and Vittoria had been before him. But the most astonishing piece of mockery on which Flamineo engages—the most astonishing on which a tragic dramatist could *have* him engage—is when in Act V he pretends to the experience of dying, a mockery of the last reality. He is persuaded of the treachery of Vittoria and Zanche as soon as they discharge the pistols, but is nevertheless allowed to indulge in an orgy of imagined suffering; it is appropriately grotesque:

> O I smell soote,
> Most stinking soote, the chimneis a-fire,
> My liver's purboil'd like scotch holly-bread;
> There's a plumber laying pipes in my guts, it scalds.

Immediately after the imagined torture he rises and remarks:

> O cunning Devils! now I have tri'd your love,
> And doubled all your reaches. I am not wounded:
>   (*Flamineo riseth.*
> The pistols held no bullets: 'twas a plot . . .
>   (V. vi. 142 ff.)

Up till this point the audience believes with Vittoria that Flamineo is mortally wounded. Its expectations are abruptly deflated—as they were in the dumb-show scene. In the midst of an act of death and confrontations of death the incident is not far removed from burlesque. Upon reflection it will become clear how fantastic was the impulse that drove Webster to write it. The darkness of the last act is shot with a ray of mockery, and a strand of bizarre amusement penetrates our response to the contemplation of death offered there.

One characteristic of Flamineo's wit deserves emphasis. Consider his excited delight in Doctor Julio:

> O thou cursed antipathy to nature—looke, his eye's bloud-shed like a needle a Chirurgeon stitcheth a wound with—let me embrace thee toad, & love thee O thou abhominable lothsome gargarisme, that will fetch up lungs, lights, heart, and liver by scruples. (II. i. 303)

The word that immediately springs to mind is 'grotesque'. We use it, not only because the language employed links areas of thought and sensation in most unusual relationships, but because the attitudes represented lie very close to the extremity of our experience. The grotesque invites our laughter and as soon quenches it in a sense of baffled surprise. The laughter of Flamineo cannot therefore play the role that laughter most often plays in drama, the role of a normative agent. Such a function would be inappropriate to the world of this play, where no norm is proposed. Flamineo's wit is, indeed, peculiarly sterile (the use of 'abhominable' in the passage quoted is suggestive). It has the effect much more of making us uneasy, of unsettling our response, than of adjusting it.

Flamineo has more than once been described as simply a mouthpiece for Webster, and with reason. For the same delight that went into creating him—there is no mistaking the superabundant vitality of his language—and into his amused mockery of others shows itself again in the dramatist's handling of several situations in the play. We have mentioned already the scenes in which Lodovico, Brachiano, and Vittoria repent and turn again to wrongdoing, their virtuous (and Lodovico's vicious) sentiments made equally hollow by being based upon nothing firmer than Francisco's deceit. Something of the same delight emerges from the play's use of hypocrisy. One thinks of such incidents as the extraordinary dialogue at the opening of Act IV when the 'innocent' Francisco develops his high-minded platitudes, while Monticelso takes upon himself to urge on him the Machiavellian course of action he fully intends. And there is that other scene (V. vi) of extended hypocrisy as Flamineo, and then Vittoria and Zanche, pretend to a selfless loyalty to the memory of Brachiano. (Flamineo is even allowed to reverse his attitude completely and explicitly within thirty lines—see lines 3 and 32–3.) But the most surprising hypocrisy in the play concerns the meek and, one would have expected, entirely undeceitful Isabella. She accepts with resignation Brachiano's angry repudiation of their marriage (II. i. 195–206) but, fearing that the separation might bring about war between her brother and her husband, she acts on Francisco's return as if *she* had reproached Brachiano, rather than he her. Lines 255–65 are a precise parody, complete with comic exaggeration, of the earlier lines, with Isabella taking over Brachiano's words and he hers. The absurd nature of the situation is pressed home on us by Isabella's virtuosity in cursing Vittoria:

> To dig the strumpets eyes out, let her lye
> Some twenty monethes a-dying, to cut off
> Her nose and lippes, pull out her rotten teeth, ...

Francisco's comment adds the final touch of humour:

> Now by my birth you are a foolish, mad,
> And jealous woman.   (II. i. 248–67)

No more unapt description of Isabella could easily be imagined; all her words are an outrageous parody of her true feelings. A similar mocking delight in the brittleness of attitude emerges, in particularly excited terms, from III. iii, where Flamineo and Lodovico deliberately *agree* to adopt an attitude of 'genteel melancholy', and then Lodovico drops his assumed guise for its opposite as soon as he hears of his pardon. None of these incidents is employed principally to forward the plot, or to give insight into character—the usual functions of hypocrisy on the Jacobean stage. They are simply further strands in the texture of mockery that Webster weaves about the events of his tragedy.

Another aspect of that mockery concerns itself with single words and concepts. We are often quite uncertain how much weight to give to words that represent familiar values. In the Trial scene, for example, the words 'charity' or 'uncharity', 'justice' and 'injustice' are bandied about from side to side without ever taking real roots in meaning. The insecurity behind such words is a necessary corollary of the world of moral chaos Webster discovers to us. But insecurity gives way at times to something much closer to mockery. In Act V, for example, Zanche reveals that Brachiano, just murdered by Lodovico and Francisco, had been responsible for Isabella's death. Lodovico is delighted that their deed has been 'justified'. But Francisco regards his delight as mere sentimental naïveté:

> Tush for Justice!
> What harmes it Justice?
>   (V. iii. 277)

The concept has been so drained of meaning that the absurd question seems to make sense. The meaning of 'charity' undergoes an even more evident mockery. Lodovico and Gasparo, surprised by the returning company at their work of devilish hatred mouthing curses over the dying Brachiano, cover their dismay with:

> for charitie,
> For Christian charitie, avoid the chamber.
>   (V. iii. 173)

No more complete distortion of a word's meaning is possible. The impulse that led Webster to choose that particular form of words at that particular moment is comparable for its fantastic humour to the incident of Flamineo's counterfeiting of death.

There is one moment at which Webster appears to break through the texture of dramatic illusion, in order to concentrate all the separate beams of this mockery. It occurs during Francisco's soliloquy in IV. i. Banishing the figure of Isabella's ghost from his mind, he turns to the job in hand:

> Come, to this waighty businesse.
> My Tragedy must have some idle mirth in't,
> Else it will never passe. I am in love,
> In love with Corombona; . . .   (l. 122)

Here the dramatist is offering an unambiguous comment upon the whole revenge narrative with which his play purports to deal. 'Idle mirth' and the lilting cadence of 'I am in love | In love with Corombona' establish the ironic tone of 'waighty' in the first line. This is the extreme point to which mockery can go; it extends to reflecting on the seriousness of writing the drama itself.

Webster's restless, mocking intelligence is a presence that is continually modifying the great and passionate events his narrative offered him. There is indeed a constant tension in this play between an impulse that creates, and one that criticizes, making the experience it communicates a more complex one than has generally been allowed. The success it enjoys is precarious. It takes a delight in thwarting our readiest impulses—those most viable in the theatre—and deflating the values we have always accepted; one can sympathize with the bewilderment of that first audience so unceremoniously handled in the Preface to the play. And yet, though precarious and disturbing, a full response to *The White Devil* is a rewarding experience. For the tragedy succeeds in embodying within the dramatic form, even if hazardously, a sensibility composed of such apparently incompatible impulses. It is a success

Webster was never able to repeat, and we may look in vain among Jacobean plays for a tragedy that both disturbs and exalts in quite the same fashion.

* * *

In the above discussion we have done no more than mention that act which many have found the most impressive in the play. Act V is largely an examination of the attitudes forced on individuals by the one inescapable fact in the play's chaotic world, the fact of death. But even here Webster refuses to draw us clear of mockery. We have referred already to Flamineo's preposterous charade of dying; we may add his 'interview' with Brachiano's ghost, its tone poised nicely between mockery, aggressiveness, and fear. And there are the astonishing Flamineo–Zanche and Francisco–Zanche 'love' episodes to distort, and in the distortion to parody, any sympathetic impressions of romantic love we may still cherish. All possible ironies are also drawn out of the disguise assumed by the avengers, and Webster deliberately strengthens them by giving Flamineo several speeches—his only sincerely complimentary speeches in the whole play—to descant on the impostors' prowess or virtue. Most striking of all is the incident of the feigned Capuchins at Brachiano's deathbed, when the Church's stately Latin *formulae* are read, only to be burlesqued by a similarly antiphonal chant, but now of savage glee, as Lodovico and Gasparo exult over the dying man.

It is against such a background that the various reactions to death must be seen. To isolate from its context the self-assertion of Vittoria or Flamineo, for instance, and to advance it as representative of the play's way of seeing death, is to damage severely the complex nature of this act. Self-assertion is as much the momentary product of the chaotic and deceit-ridden circumstances of Webster's world as master over them. T. S. Eliot's phrase 'cheering oneself up'[3] as descriptive of the Stoic defiance of death is only inappropriate here in that it suggests a reaction far too leisurely and deliberate to describe adequately Vittoria's and Zanche's courage, a courage forced out of despair. Behind Vittoria's brave words:

> Yes I shall wellcome death
> As Princes doe some great Embassadors;
> Ile meete thy weapon halfe way.   (V. vi. 220)

[3] *Selected Essays* (1932), p. 131.

we cannot forget her hurried desperation when Flamineo first threatened her, nor his grotesque counterfeiting of death, and all the ironies of that play with the pistols. Yet sanctioned by some of Webster's most deeply felt poetry, there is undoubtedly a sense of clearer air here, of freedom from all the deceit and the hypocrisy, if only for a moment. Webster rarely comes so close to offering us an unconditional affirmative.

Flamineo's death is rather more characteristic of what we have come to recognize as the dominant tone of this play. It would be surprising if the equivocal humour we associate with him did not qualify to some extent that proud invitation:

> Search my wound deeper: tent it with the steele
> That made it.   (V. vi. 239)

One should hesitate to attribute to 'bad workmanship' the mere garrulity of his two last speeches, compared with Vittoria's concise last words. And the note of mockery, of an irony that offers comment upon the virtuous commonplaces on his lips, should at least be suspected in: ''Tis well yet there's some goodnesse in my death' (V. vi. 269). Throughout he has been simply a voice, eloquent, witty, mocking, and it is therefore supremely fitting that he should convey his experience of death in these terms:

> I have caught
> An everlasting could. I have lost my voice
> Most irrecoverably.   (V. vi. 270)

Whereas Vittoria, and to some extent Flamineo, rose for a moment at death above the insecurities of their world, Brachiano's madness is a mental disorder that can but echo the disordered world of which he has formed part. His delusions play about those two aims, the satisfaction of lust and monetary gain, which have driven men to activity in it, and the humorous overtones of madness (to a Jacobean audience) have the effect of burlesque: it sees and does not see, confounds 'Deepe Sence with follie' (V. iii. 74). Cornelia's madness is of a different kind, evidence of a retreat from the disordered universe before her. She is utterly uncomprehending when one of her sons kills the other:[4] 'Why here's

---

[4] This in itself is the most poignant illustration of the inability of conventional values (in this case the duelling code) to cope with the self-regarding energy of almost all the characters in the play.

no body shall get any thing by his death' (V. ii. 30). She had at least expected the motive of personal gain to lie behind action in Brachiano's court. Flamineo had not even that motive, and so her bewilderment overturns her brain. Her (for the most part) exquisite dirge 'Call for the Robin-Red-brest and the wren, . . .' suggests one way of escaping disorder; but it is escape and not confrontation or solution.

The play ends with Giovanni. We have seen him three times before:[5] in II. i when his precocious chivalry almost succeeded in reconciling Brachiano to Isabella; after the arraignment when he announced his mother's death to Francisco; and in V. iv when as newly created Duke he banished Flamineo from his presence. On all three occasions he is represented as a sympathetic figure, escaping the deceit and mockery of his world. He could well have been used in the last scene, therefore, to enforce a sense of a new order appearing, after the disorder of 'these bad times'. Certainly an intention of this kind can be drawn out of his words, but the emphasis upon it is slight. What is most striking about his last speech of conventional moralizing is its perfunctoriness:

> Remove the bodies—see my honoured Lord,
> What use you ought make of their punishment.
> Let guilty men remember their blacke deedes
> Do leane on crutches, made of slender reedes.
> (V. vi. 300)

The very lack of emphasis on the idea of a new order, and the near-nonchalance of that word 'use', suggest that Webster did not wish to enforce any sense of a coming health. His imaginative perception of disorder was too keen to bear so easy a compromise.

★ ★ ★

The Duchess of Malfi is a less challenging play than *The White Devil*, if on its own terms more satisfying and complete. Much of the earlier play's tense exuberance has gone, replaced by a more leisurely manner, and a dramatic style that achieves its effects in many scenes by a very close approach to naturalism. This ease of statement is made possible by the acceptance of an easily identifiable social and moral viewpoint, with reference to which each of the characters may be judged. The social norm operates principally in terms of a well-run state, where reward

[5] Apart from appearing as an actor in the first dumb-show, and a momentary appearance in V. iii.

follows upon desert, and the moral norm appears chiefly in terms of constancy in sexual relations and openness in other dealings. Throughout the play we are never left in doubt as to our evaluation of any action; the steadiness of tone Bosola can assume in Act IV is evidence of this:

> The Office of Justice is perverted quite
> When one Thiefe hangs another.   (IV. ii. 329)

or in the last Act:

> when thou kill'dst thy sister,
> Thou tookst from Justice her most equall ballance,
> And left her naught but her sword.   (V. v. 52)

Francisco's 'Tush for Justice' would be quite out of place here. When death comes, each character dies acknowledging the ill he has done. He acknowledges, that is, a principle above and beyond himself, in contrast to Flamineo's 'Noe, at my selfe I will begin and end' (V. vi. 258).

It is at the Duchess's own death that we have most firmly impressed upon us the sense of man as a small frail creature, very far from commanding his universe—a sense entirely alien to the purely human-directed and human-centred activity of *The White Devil*:

BOSOLA. Thou art a box of worme-seede, at best, but a salvatory of greene mummey: what's this flesh? a little cruded milke, phantasticall puffe-paste: our bodies are weaker then those paper prisons boyes use to keepe flies in: more contemptible: since ours is to preserve earth-wormes: didst thou ever see a Larke in a cage? such is the soule in the body: this world is like her little turfe of grasse, and the Heaven ore our heades, like her looking glasse, onely gives us a miserable knowledge of the small compasse of our prison. (IV. ii. 123)

Some lines later the Duchess is strangled:

> Pull, and pull strongly, for your able strength,
> Must pull downe heaven upon me:
> Yet stay, heaven gates are not so highly arch'd
> As Princes pallaces—they that enter there
> Must go upon their knees.   (IV. ii. 237)

It is not emotionally unacceptable that she should die with explicit Christian humility, the attitude at the opposite pole from stoic self-assertion. In this play the courage that is born of despair gives way to a meek yet resolute acceptance of death. Man is by no means made despicable in his dying, but he is securely 'placed' here in relation to his environment, and to a Fate that is never defined but is always a powerfully felt presence.[6] The whole temper of the play lends itself far less easily to posturing or to grandiose statement than did that of *The White Devil*. It is the product of a sensibility that is more chastened, more aware of suffering, less tense and excited than that which governed the earlier play.

The tragedy's peculiar tone is indeed deeply influenced by the quiet, uninsistent rhythms of conversation—in the betrothal scene, or the scene in the Cardinal's lodgings at Rome, or again the bedchamber scene in Act III, or the desultory jesting of part of the first scene, or that other scene of aimless jest about Count Malatesta (III. iii). One often senses in fact a self-critical intelligence behind the words on the page, checking any tendency to false rhetoric, deflating over-emphatic statement or posturing. In its simplest manifestation this takes the form of an enquiring comment upon one character's words by another. During the first scene, for example, after Antonio has over-praised the Duchess at length and in good set terms, Delio remarks:

>   Fye Antonio,
> You play the wire-drawer with her commendations.
>   (l. 210)

The same watchfulness is evident in this short exchange:

> FERDINAND. He that can compasse me, and know my drifts,
> May say he hath put a girdle 'bout the world,
> And sounded all her quick-sands.
> BOSOLA. I doe not
> Thinke so.
> FERDINAND. What doe you thinke then, pray?
> BOSOLA. That you
> Are your owne Chronicle too much: and grosly
> Flatter your selfe.   (III. i. 104)

This command of tone is at work throughout; its effect is to bring events closer to our sympathy than those of almost any other Jacobean play.

There are at least two occasions on which this self-critical intelligence

[6] See Bradbrook for a most suggestive comment upon the manner in which Webster handles this 'Fate'.

is used with a sensitivity that makes for dramatic genius. Bosola in dying takes over the role of moral interpreter, summing up for us the play's lessons with calm detachment:

> Fare you well—
> It may be paine: but no harme to me to die,
> In so good a quarrell: Oh this gloomy world,
> In what a shadow, or deepe pit of darknesse,
> Doth (womanish, and fearefull) mankind live!
> Let worthy mindes nere stagger in distrust
> To suffer death, or shame, for what is just—
> Mine is another voyage.   (V. v. 122)

Those last four words, simple, direct, and immediately evocative of this particular human predicament, coming upon the rhymed and sententious couplet, are an outstanding dramatic realization. Even more impressive is one of the Duchess's last speeches:

> What would it pleasure me, to have my throate cut
> With diamonds? or to be smothered
> With Cassia? or to be shot to death, with pearles?
> I know death hath ten thousand severall doores
> For men, to take their Exits: and 'tis found
> They go on such strange geometricall hinges,
> You may open them both wayes: any way, (for heaven sake)
> So I were out of your whispering.   (IV. ii. 222)

Here the sudden drop from an exalted, generalized contemplation of death, to a sense of the particulars of the actual situation (the executioners' whispering) is evidence of a supreme dramatic awareness. And few dramatists are so securely in control of their tone that they can allow an emotion that is close to petulance to impinge upon such a solemn moment as the death of their play's central character. That Webster could and did do so shows how much of his concern in this play is directed towards an adequate portrayal of a tragic human experience.

There are occasions, however, when we are made extremely uncomfortable by faults of taste, by the absence of that same self-critical intelligence. At times a withdrawal from speech rhythms to a more stylized kind of utterance is successful, as in the consistently non-naturalistic Echo scene (V. iii). More often, in scenes that aim at complete naturalism, we are treated to a kind of solemn parading of commonplace or proverbial sayings and allusions, that retreats from conversation and in so doing damages the suppleness of the dramatic movement. In the bedchamber scene (III. ii), for example, the frank physicality and bantering tone of the first thirty lines are precisely right; the Duchess's later, 'I pre-thee When were we so merry?' is an apt reflection on them. But when Cariola is invited to say when she will marry, and she replies she never will, Antonio launches out into a series of classical allusions:

> O fie upon this single life: forgoe it:
> We read how Daphne, for her peevish flight
> Became a fruitlesse Bay-tree: Sirinx turn'd
> To the pale empty Reede: Anaxarete . . .
> (l. 31)

Webster's sense of dramatic propriety checks at this, and he has Cariola reply: 'This is a vaine Poetry.' Had this been allowed to stand, we could have accepted her comment as to some extent compensating for the awkwardness of the previous lines. But Webster has her immediately begin an unnatural and stiff discussion of the Judgement of Paris. The thread of the conversation has been lost, and Antonio's next question, contrived to allow a clever answer, is remarkable for the flaccidity of the verse:

> I doe wonder why hard-favour'd Ladies
> For the most part, keepe worse-favour'd waieting women,
> To attend them, and cannot endure faire-ones.   (l. 53)

All the supple give-and-take of the earlier lines is overlaid by a perverse determination to introduce a clever *exemplum*. There follows the, again, supremely apt speech of the Duchess, punctuated, as G. Rylands suggests, by the sweep of her hand as she brushes her hair. When Ferdinand enters, the rhythms of the scene immediately tauten, and Ferdinand's threatening and the Duchess's pleading note are finely caught. But again Webster is unable to resist the temptation to recite a fable:

> Upon a time Reputation, Love, and Death,
> Would travell ore the world: . . .   (l. 145)

The rhythms of this speech are entirely unconvincing in this dramatic context. This is in fact the bane of Webster's writing, that damaged *The White Devil* as well as this play. His commonplace book was always at his elbow, and while in borrowing from it he almost always immensely improved, he is nevertheless too often willing to interrupt the fluency of a scene by the introduction of commonplace *exempla*, far removed from the tenor of ordinary conversation. It is not that these are in themselves improper to drama, but that, given the overall movement of most scenes in this play, their introduction is unavoidably damaging.

A general tendency to relax the dramatic movement for the insertion of material that does not support the forwarding of the central dramatic interest is responsible for the agreed failure of the play's fifth Act; the point is not that the Duchess is dead, and therefore interest ceases, but that the deaths of Antonio, Ferdinand, and the Cardinal follow in too leisurely a fashion. Ferdinand's madness, terrible though it is, suffers greatly from being extended, and from being involved in the pantomime-action with the Doctor. The Marquis of Pescara scene (V. i) is almost childishly naïve; certainly it is connected with one of the play's main moral concerns, the desert-reward theme, but it is here dramatically unnecessary. And the Julia–Bosola intrigue in scene ii invites impatience only; it is almost without dramatic tension of any kind. Some of the same complaints could be directed against other parts of the play—against the unnecessary extension of the scene following Antonio's mock banishment, for example. The tragedy easily survives all these faults only by virtue of the superb control of tone and atmosphere elsewhere.

This discussion of the mode in which the dramatic writing is conducted—and sometimes fails—is relevant to an understanding of the play's central situation—the Duchess's relationship with Antonio—and the way it is challenged. Clearly enough Webster's concern is not primarily with a merely physical discovery of the relationship by Bosola or Ferdinand, but with a far more insidious penetration of its security.

Two scenes image for us that security: the betrothal scene and the scene in the Duchess's bedchamber. In both, and more particularly in the latter, is expressed the happiness and light of an undeceitful relationship. But they are never more than islands of light in surrounding darkness. For the world in which they are set is entirely alien to the values they represent, and upon which they are nourished. Instead of the recognition and reward of merit (Bosola emphasizes this aspect of the relationship when the Duchess tells him of her marriage) we have the Cardinal's and Ferdinand's malpractices. In place of the frank speaking, with its sense of a healthy human relationship, we find the aimless and insipid jesting of part of the opening scene or of the 'Count Malatesta' scene (III. iii), giving an impression of a world that is restless, insecure, watchful. More particularly, instead of a genuine selfless love, the world outside the Duchess's circle offers various distortions of the love-relationship. Bosola, for example, immediately he discovers that the Duchess is with child, directs at the Old Woman a series of jests that reduce love to the level of lust; Ferdinand's extravagant detestation when he hears of his sister's pregnancy exaggerates and distorts the physical aspect of the relationship. And the apparently 'irrelevant' scene in the Cardinal's lodgings, when both he and Delio (an unlikely character to employ) play with Julia's affections, indicates something of the purely physical and deceit-ridden 'love' this world entertains.

When the Duchess chooses to defy her brothers' world her choice inescapably involves an element of deceit or at best evasion. We of course fully sympathize with her decision to reject the over-fluent and over-insistent exhortations of the Cardinal and Ferdinand against re-marriage. But she is forced to tell them a deliberate lie, and from that moment on her relationship with the world beyond her own small circle is one of uneasy watchfulness. The lovers' contact with that world becomes more and more furtive and uncertain, aptly symbolized in prospect by a remark of the Duchess to Cariola:

> wish me good speed
> For I am going into a wildernesse,
> Where I shall find nor path, nor friendly clewe
> To be my guide. (I. i. 403)

The threat offered to their relationship by Ferdinand or Bosola is of a deliberately unspecific nature. It is imaged throughout in terms of a restless and malignant quiet, and it is this insidious and ill-defined pressure that tests their spirit and brings them both to death. It at once reveals its character in the night scene that follows upon the birth of the Duchess's first child. The setting, and the short sharp phrases in which Bosola and Antonio converse, are powerfully evocative of a sense of nervous insecurity, commingled with a vague foreboding as drops of blood blot out Antonio's name, and Bosola reads out the stars' unfavourable predictions. On each occasion that the threat is renewed it preserves the same tone of malignant quiet. When Ferdinand visits Amalfi to spy on his sister, he comes to her out of the darkness of the night and in a moment of ominous stillness, as she sits brushing her hair in false assurance that she is among friends. The indirectness of the threat is preserved by having him refuse to hear Antonio's name, though the Duchess would gladly disperse the almost claustrophobic uncertainty by mentioning it. When eventually he does hear it, Webster's near-immaculate feeling for atmosphere has the announcement made amidst the aimless jesting at Count Malatesta's expense. Again the emphasis is upon an evil stillness:

> PESCARA. The Lord Ferdinand laughes.
> DELIO. Like a deadly Cannon,
> That lightens ere it smoakes.
> PESCARA. These are your true pangues of death,
> The pangues of life, that strugle with great states-men—
> DELIO. In such a deformed silence, witches whisper
> Their charmes.   (III. iii. 65)

The last long series of challenges that bring the Duchess close to insanity, but fail to break her spirit, are equally stealthy and insidious. The noise of madmen at their gibbering dance brings relief only to her oppressed brain:

> nothing but noyce, and folly
> Can keepe me in my right wits, whereas reason
> And silence, make me starke mad.   (IV. ii. 6)

It is the other, unnervingly quiet kind of challenge that disturbs her. Ferdinand approaches his sister in darkness, and leaves her grasping a dead man's hand. He shows her a waxwork of her supposedly dead husband and children. Bosola, posing first as tomb-maker and then as bell-man, makes final trial of her spirit with all the paraphernalia of death. The shadowy theatricality of the waxwork show, of Bosola's pose as tomb-maker and bell-man, of the coffin and executioners on the stage, preserves the stealthy unreality that has been characteristic of the trials the Duchess has undergone.[7] It is a powerful sense of an oppressive stillness that finds no relief, so constantly felt and so impossible to recount in detail, that has enfolded her tragic progress from the youthful laughter of the bedchamber scene to a death at which

> her infelicitie
> Seem'd to have yeeres too many.
>   (IV. ii. 282)

---

[7] Antonio's experience is of the same order; the Echo scene and the scene of his death are possessed by the same stealthy uncertainty.

When she is dead, our sense of the unnerving stillness of her experience, its veiled and insidious threat, is given moral force in a consciousness of utter futility and waste. For Ferdinand does not know *why* he had Bosola murder her:

> I bad thee, when I was distracted of my wits,
> Goe kill my dearest friend, and thou hast don't.
> For let me but examine well the cause;
> What was the meanenes of her match to me?
> Onely I must confesse, I had a hope
> (Had she continu'd widow) to have gain'd
> An infinite masse of Treasure by her death:
> And that was the mayne cause.   (IV. ii. 298)

That reference to the 'infinite masse of Treasure' has been taken by critics to be indicative of a fault in Webster's construction of the play. Ferdinand's motive, they say, should have been made clearer from the outset. But the opposite is the case. From the beginning Webster has deliberately refused him a clearly defined motive; when he set Bosola to spy on his sister in the opening scene, his instructions were:

>   I give you that
> To live i'th Court, here: and observe the Duchesse,
> To note all the particulars of her haviour:
> What suitors doe sollicite her for marriage
> And whom she best affects: she's a yong widowe,
> I would not have her marry againe.
> BOSOLA. No, Sir?
> FERDINAND. Do not you ask the reason: but be satisfied,
> I say I would not.   (I. i. 268)

Any third-rate dramatist could have invented a reason to put in Ferdinand's mouth. Webster saw that to do so would be to damage irreparably the nature of the experience he wished to communicate. It is the very absence of a real motive in the oppressors that helps to make the Duchess's tragedy so unnerving. And Webster's mastery of the theatre, his control of tone and atmosphere, have so created the Duchess's experience of oppression that it corresponds to the malignant aimlessness of the threat.

One complexity has been suggested in Ferdinand's relationship with his sister: that he feels for her an incestuous passion. While it could easily be over-emphasized, the suggestion is far from ridiculous. In the remorseful speech quoted above, after the fumbling talk of 'An infinite masse of Treasure' Ferdinand speaks with far greater decision of what had obviously moved him more deeply: 'her Marriage—That drew a streame of gall quite through my heart.' And earlier speeches have been informed with the same sense of personal distress: after the most general moralizing exhortation we have the direct involvement of:

>Thou art undone:
>And thou hast taine that massiy sheete of lead
>That hid thy husbands bones, and foulded it
>About my heart.   (III. ii. 130)

There is a sense of an extremely close relationship defiled in:

>I could kill her now,
>In you, or in my selfe, for I do thinke
>It is some sinne in us, Heaven doth revenge
>By her.   (II. v. 82)

and in:

>Damne her, that body of hers,
>While that my blood ran pure in't, was more worth
>Then that which thou wouldst comfort, (call'd a soule).
>   (IV. i. 146)

Our instinctive protest at the suggestion is occasioned not so much by the cast of mind it proposes in Ferdinand, but by the rigid nature of the formulation. It implies far too readily the desire to consummate the passion. For this idea Webster gives no authority. We want rather a term which suggests Ferdinand's deep involvement with the image of the Duchess, in the realm of physique, as well as of character. Some sort of 'involvement' must be posited to account for the outburst of II. v in all its extravagance and its over-emphatic physicality. Ferdinand is of course unaware of the nature of his own emotions; it is tempting to suggest that this basic emotional imbalance is behind all his intense frustrated cruelty to his sister—but this is perhaps over-ingenious. Yet the naturalism of the play, its subtle insight into turns of mind, the fluctuations of speech and varying of rhythm give us some grounds for supposing that Webster may have intended a complexity of this kind.

We have noted already the preservation of an overall tone that gives a coherence of mood to the play, a coherence broken only by occasional faults of taste. But it is in smaller compass, on the level of single lines or speeches that Webster's dramatic and poetic genius vindicates itself most surely. And it is when the pressure on the verse is greatest, when it seeks to echo abnormal states of mind and emotion that we can most easily appreciate its artistry. There is, for example, that finely dramatic scene in which Bosola seeks to discover whether the Duchess is with child. One speech in particular embodies superbly the breathless impatience of the pregnant woman:

> DUCHESS. I thinke she did: come hether, mend my ruffe—
> Here, when? thou art such a tedious Lady; and
> Thy breath smells of Lymmon pils, would thou hadst done—
> Shall I sound [i.e., swoon] under thy fingers? I am so troubled
> With the mother. (II. i. 115)

The metrical pattern of the verse almost collapses under the short phrases and interjections, while the d's, t's, and s's give the actress ample opportunity for expressing impatience in her voice. What is perhaps the finest piece of dramatic writing in the play conveys a mood much more complex. The Duchess, believing Antonio and her children dead, has reached a state of emotional exhaustion touched with insanity. The repetition of 'I am not mad' in her speech, with its faint disturbance of metre and its note of thwarted insistence, is superbly evocative of a mind precariously balanced. And, as Muriel Bradbrook has pointed out, the image of the oar conveys exactly a sorrow that is almost a physical burden:

> I'll tell thee a miracle—
> I am not mad yet, to my cause of sorrow.
> Th' heaven ore my head, seemes made of molten brasse,
> The earth of flaming sulphure, yet I am not mad:
> I am acquainted with sad misery,
> As the tan'd galley-slave is with his Oare,
> Necessity makes me suffer constantly,
> And custome makes it easie. (IV. ii. 25)

And even when Webster seeks to follow his characters over the borderline between the normal and the insane his touch is unfaltering. There are few lines in drama as starkly terrifying as that put into Ferdinand's mouth as he wanders crazed over the darkened stage:

> Strangling is a very quiet death.
> (V. iv. 38)

Almost all Ferdinand's speeches in the last act share this same immediately felt quality, particularly those spoken in the confusion that reigns at the Cardinal's death. But, like the other examples quoted, they lose much by being divorced from their context—an indication of their stature as *dramatic* poetry.

Something of the same ability to enter into, to realize, the thoughts and emotions of the characters was present at moments in *The White Devil*, particularly in Act V, but it was not sustained there with anything like the persistence of, for example, the scene of the Duchess's dying in this play. For the earlier tragedy was much more a creature of the will and the intellect than this more humane, more humble, more elegiac play. *The Duchess of Malfi* challenges and exalts and disturbs us much less than its predecessor, but it carries with it a much greater emotional depth and coherence.

Note

Biography: George Chapman, 1559?–1634
He was born at Hitchin, Herts., son of a tenant-farmer or small landowner; on his mother's side related to the minor diplomatic and military family of Grimeston. He may have studied at Oxford, but by 1585 was in the household of Sir Ralph Sadler of Hitchin (1507–87), diplomat and soldier. He spent some years abroad, serving as a soldier in the Netherlands (1586?–1592?). The death of his patron, Prince Henry (1612), brought poverty, and after 1616 he published little. He took most pride in his Homer translations—'the work that I was born to do'.

Works. The Shadow of Night (1594), his first poem, and *De Guiana* (1596) reveal a connection with Ralegh's circle of writers and scientists, which may have included Marlowe (d. 1593), to whose poem, *Hero and Leander*, Chapman wrote a continuation in 1598. His other notable poems include *Ovid's Banquet of Sence* (1595), *The Tears of Peace* (1609), and verses prefixed to his translations. The first instalment of Homer, *Achilles Shield* (1598), was dedicated to Ralegh's rival, the Earl of Essex; but the chief patron of the project of translating all Homer was Henry, Prince of Wales. This task was completed in 1615–16.
Chapman first wrote plays for Henslowe's company, the Admiral's Men (1595?–1599); but the later plays (to 1613?) were mostly for boys' companies. In 1605 he collaborated with Jonson and Marston in writing *Eastward Ho* (1605), and with Jonson suffered imprisonment for references to the Scots in this play. (His *Invective against Ben Jonson* (1624?) shows that this early association did not last.) About seven of his comedies survive, including *Monsieur d'Olive* (1604) and *The Widow's Tears* (before 1609). Tragedies certainly to be attributed to him are: *The Tragedy of Bussy d'Ambois* (1604?; revised 1610?), *The Conspiracy and Tragedy of Charles Duke of Byron* (1608), *The Revenge of Bussy d'Ambois* (1610?), *Caesar and Pompey* (1612?), and *The Tragedy of Chabot* (1612?). He also wrote masques (Jonson said that 'next himself only Fletcher and Chapman could make a masque').

Modern Editions. T. M. Parrott edited *The Tragedies* (1910) and *The Comedies* (1914); all references in the following chapter are to these texts. Selected plays (including four tragedies) are available in the Mermaid Series (1895). *Bussy d'Ambois* is edited for the Revels Plays by N. Brooke (1964), for the Regents Renaissance Series by R. J. Lordi (1964) and for the New Mermaids by M. Evans (1965). Most of the verse is to be found in *Poems*, ed. P. B. Bartlett (1941) and *Chapman's Homer*, ed. A. Nicoll (2 vols., 1957).

Scholarship and Criticism. Chapman's plays and ideas are well treated in E. M. Waith, *The Herculean Hero* (1962), E. Muir, 'The Royal Man', *Essays on Literature and Society* (1949), J. Jacquot, *George Chapman* (Paris, 1951), and E. Rees, *The Tragedies of George Chapman* (1954).

X
Chapman's Tragedies

PETER URE

★

> 'Tis greatest now, and to destruction
> Nearest; There's no pause at perfection:
> Greatnesse a period hath, but no station.
> (Donne, *The Progresse of the Soule*)

AT the beginning of *The Tragedy of Bussy d'Ambois* the soldier Bussy, reduced by poverty and unemployment to retired walks and solitary meditations, comes alone upon the stage and speaks about the contrariness of a world where Honour goes with its legs in the air and Reward turns its back on its pursuer. It is a world where men flourish and come to be called 'great' by building themselves up into colossi; inside, though, they are full of rubbish. Lear, when he saw man stripped of his lendings, called him a poor, bare, forked animal; for Bussy unaccommodated man is the most tenuous, evanescent thing that can be: Pindar's dream of a shadow, Petrarch's torch carried in the wind, Jeremy Taylor's Man 'for which you cannot have a word can signify a verier nothing . . . forgotten like the dream of a distracted person'. Bussy's moral resembles Taylor's, too; no matter how elaborately a man dresses up, Time will preach his funeral sermon; he must resign himself to unaccommodation. He is like a tall ship sailing the high seas, 'ribb'd with brass', 'topt with all titles', but when the voyage draws to an end the great ship is dependent upon the pilot. This pilot is Virtue, and ends the soliloquy:

> We must to Virtue for her guide resort,
> Or we shall shipwrack in the safest port.

There can be little doubt, because of the character of the metaphor with which it is described, that this Virtue is not power, *virtù*, the Achillean 'High birth, vigour of bone, desert in service' (as Ulysses describes it in Shakespeare's play), but moral virtue, spiced with humility and self-knowledge; for the richly adventuring and brass-ribbed ship is guided by

> A poor, staid fisherman, that never pass'd
> His country's sight.

Only this man knows the dangerous reaches where *virtù* may be wrecked for want of Virtue.

The speech seems to have, then, a clear and unexceptionable moral. It is less easy to determine its relation to its speaker and his subsequent actions. It may sound like making difficulties, in a play, to doubt whether what a character says does not also tell us what he is, either directly or by its ironic contrast with his other deeds and words. But this is a genuine and recurring problem in all Chapman's tragedies. If we are to read this speech simply as an index of Bussy's state of mind when his story begins then most of that story is, by the standard of the as yet unfallen Bussy, an increasingly rapid process of moral declination and self-betrayal. 'Who is not poor, is monstrous', Bussy says in the third line; but by the end of the scene he has accepted a thousand crowns from Monsieur, King Henry III's brother, well knowing that this gift, which is conveyed to him out of Monsieur's ambitious desire to gather about him a party of bold but obedient spirits for a possible design upon the crown, entails dressing himself in the 'enchanted glass' of the court—a glass which reflects no amiable images, only demonic ones, sights that will make a man's eyes 'as hollow as his mistress' heart'. The very money itself is planted in blood, for when Monsieur's steward brings it to him Bussy answers his patronizing impertinence with a blow in the face. By the end of the Act he is responding in the same way on the stage of the court itself. The courtiers who mock him for his self-confidence and his new clothes become the victims of a vengeance during which Bussy's anger assumes the aspect of some terrible natural phenomenon, smashing men as though they were trees in a storm (II. ii. 77–104). All this, conducted in the open day of court, is only a prelude to a darker and more labyrinthine business. Bussy's adulterous love-affair with Tamyra, wife of Count Montsurry, is involved from the first in deceit and darkness and emerges into horror. The noble politician who so unthinkingly introduced him to greatness and now finds him too fiery to handle sees his chance to destroy him. Bussy himself loses control of his destiny, blinded by the juggling fiend whom he summons to his aid and in whom he trusts as rashly as Macbeth. If we wish to measure how far he has fallen from the grace of his first speech we need only look at another speech at the end of the fourth Act where he stakes everything on the game of politic murder and on the terrible image of the smiler with the knife:

> I'll bind his arm with silk, and rub his flesh,
> To make the vein swell, that his soul may gush
> Into some kennel where it longs to lie,
> And policy shall be flank'd with policy.

But outflanking the politicians is not within Bussy's competence; his 'cannibal valour' (Monsieur's phrase) resembles the tree-uprooting tempest, not the politic lightning that should melt 'the very marrow, and not taint the skin'. Poor and distorted instruments—a cowardly and jealous husband, a mistress tortured to yield her secret, a corrupted maid of honour—effect the end of the great Bussy, shot to death by gunmen from behind the arras. And when he dies his eyes are fixed upon a futurity which has nothing in common with the haven-heaven of the 'poor fisherman'. Man, he confirms in his dying moments, is indeed 'a dream but of a shade', but the Bussy of the first Act, who was to 'rise in court by virtue', blazed like a 'pointed comet' in Act II, and became by turns 'eagle' and 'snake' in the main business of the play, is now a 'falling star', quenched and silent.

If we read Bussy's story in this way, as one of moral declination, the feeling that a 'great' man has been wasted is substantially qualified by the reflection that he threw himself away upon objects that Virtue would have despised. He exemplifies the Achillean 'wrath', 'Predominant Perturbation . . . the Bodie's fervour and fashion of outward Fortitude' (*Homer*, II. 4), and he is shown to us only that he may be shunned, in accordance with Chapman's other famous principle that 'material instruction, elegant and sententious excitation to virtue, and deflection from her contrary [are] the soul, limbs, and limits of an autentical tragedy' (Parrott, p. 77). This is a reading which agrees with what we may presume to have been Chapman's general intention as a dramatist. It has the immense convenience of reducing a play which at first sight seems to have burst rather raggedly out of the cerements of moralized drama to its compass and to coherence again.

But with many readers of *The Tragedy of Bussy d'Ambois* the suspicion will persist that this coherence is indeed gained at the cost of a reduction —a reduction of the size, the 'feel', the splendours of the play and its hero. Most commentators certainly, while showing a bewilderment that may be generated by a measure of incoherence in the play, have implied that there is more in it than a firmly regulated moral assisted by an ironic showing-forth of the hero's defects. It was Edwin Muir who summed up most exactly the general direction of criticism: 'Chapman', he wrote, 'is not interested in human nature, or in practical morality, or in evil, but in the man of excessive virtue or spirit or pride', and again: 'His judgements of conduct are sometimes strange and almost incomprehensible . . . We do not come to know Bussy or Byron morally, as we know Macbeth and Hamlet, for the action has no real effect on them, since they live in a different world from the other characters, and are a law unto themselves' (pp. 20, 22–3). And there are other reasons, besides this sense of something strange and incomprehensible, for supposing that there is more in the play than meets the eye of the moralist and ironist.

What, for example, is the moralist to make of the poetic and elegiac excitement that Bussy's death calls forth? 'Chapman', answers Rees, 'is . . . following the convention that a tragic hero must die nobly and is here attempting to gain a little more sympathy for his protagonist than some of the spectators are likely to have at this point' (p. 47). But what if Chapman—as some spectators at least will be ready to testify— succeeds in his attempt? succeeds all too well for the reader to be able to keep his moral wits about him? Although sympathy with the protagonist is not the exact phrase one would have selected to describe the feelings generated by this remarkable scene, subtly sustained and majestically evocative as any Elizabethan play can show, we are at least in our amazement quite proof against the dry detachment from it all that might, had not Chapman so triumphantly drawn us in, preserve the proper distance between the moralist and the object of his reproof. We readily call objects sublime, Kant remarked, 'because they raise the energies of the soul above their accustomed height'; the title cannot easily be refused to this scene. The price we—and Chapman, too—pay for this amazement is some loss of coherence, some sense of the strange and the incomprehensible in Bussy's fate which disables us for too tidy and detached a condemnation of him. If we wish to describe what Chapman is doing here Muir's account seems truer to experience than that of Rees: 'We can feel', Muir writes, Chapman's 'impatience to arrive at those places where the souls of his heroes can expand to their full range, places on the frontier-line between life and death, time and eternity, where all terms seem to become absolute' (p. 22).

Throughout the play there are many places where Chapman fails to reprove and seems to admire. One way out of the incoherence that this causes is to suppose that such passages must be read ironically; that the spectator is required to measure what appears to be intended to arouse our admiration and amazement at Bussy, our sense that he lives 'in a different world from the other characters', by the altogether more base and commonplace actualities of Bussy's story as those have been set out, for example, in the first paragraphs of this essay. There are two objections to this view, which may be stated in the order of their increasing gravity. First, these summations of Bussy's character and status in the catalogue of men, made by other speakers from time to time in the course of the piece, invariably enlarge and elevate him. In the second scene, where Bussy, brawling with the Guise over a comparatively trivial matter of court-behaviour, conducts himself like the proverbial bad-tempered schoolboy, Monsieur turns aside to comment thus:

> His great heart will not down, 'tis like the sea,
> That partly by his own internal heat,
> Partly the stars' daily and nightly motion,
> Their heat and light, and partly of the place
> The divers frames, but chiefly by the moon,
> Bristled with surges, never will be won,
> (No, not when th' hearts of all those powers are burst)
> To make retreat into his settled home,
> Till he be crown'd with his own quiet foam.
>   (I. ii. 157)

If this is irony, it is of a singularly barren kind which hurts no one but itself; for we do not, in order to diminish a figure, gaze at it through a pair of binoculars. The spectator can see for himself how Bussy is behaving, and Monsieur's attempt to assist his vision must either be accepted at its face-value as a genuine attempt to enlarge the dimensions of what he sees or it must be dismissed as simply wrong: 'Your instrument is telling lies: we can judge that by our own unaided sight.' The speech then becomes exclusively a ground for inferences about Monsieur, not about Bussy at all. A major difficulty in interpreting Chapman's plays derives from a continual uncertainty about whether the things said by the lesser characters about the protagonist, in speeches which, as in this play, are remarkable for length, force, and elaboration of metaphor, are meant to be evidence about the speakers' own characters as well. But it is pretty certain that they are rarely if ever *exclusively* directed to that end, that they do give us information about the hero that must be taken into account. So it is that Monsieur later on in the play, when Bussy's fate is almost decided, offers us his binoculars again. The passage in which he does so may conveniently be used to advance the second of the graver objections to the attempt to reduce the play to coherence by the discovery of ironies.

At this point the jaws of the trap devised by Monsieur, Montsurry, and the Guise are just about to snap shut on Bussy. Tamyra, tortured on the rack by her frantic husband, has been forced to write a message to Bussy summoning him to her chamber by the secret passage. The Friar, the go-between of the adulterous pair, has died of shock at the brutalities inflicted on Tamyra, and Montsurry has disguised himself in the Friar's robe in order to act as the bearer of her message. Meanwhile Monsieur and the Guise are waiting near the secret passage for the arrival of Bussy. Monsieur is now about to witness the triumph of his scheme; as far as he is concerned, Bussy is already a dead man. It is at this crisis that he turns aside to moralize on his victim's fate, assuming a role and a tone which suit oddly with that of a politician waiting with his band of gunmen to eliminate a rival. Blake's words in *The Book of Thel* might be adapted to his purposes, for his argument is that 'without a use this shining man lived'. Nature, he says, in creating men like Bussy, works at random:

> here will be one
> Young, learned, valiant, virtuous, and full mann'd;
> One on whom Nature spent so rich a hand
> That with an ominous eye she wept to see
> So much consum'd her virtuous treasury.
> Yet as the winds sing through a hollow tree
> And (since it lets them pass through) let it stand;
> But a tree solid (since it gives no way
> To their wild rage) they rend up by the root:
> So this whole man
> (That will not wind with every crooked way,
> Trod by the servile world) shall reel and fall
> Before the frantic puffs of blind-born chance,

> That pipes through empty men, and makes them dance.
> Not so the sea raves on the Libyan sands,
> Tumbling her billows in each others' neck;
> Not so the surges of the Euxine sea
> (Near to the frosty pole, where free Boötes
> From those dark deep waves turns his radiant team)
> Swell, being enrag'd, even from their inmost drop,
> As Fortune swings about the restless state
> Of virtue, now thrown into all men's hate.
> (V. ii. 32)

There is of course a contrast between the baser actuality of Bussy's self-exposure to Fortune's storms by his commitment to an adulterous affair and how Monsieur sees his situation in this passage. But it is not one which diminishes Bussy, but gives us a nobler prospect of his ruin, linking him by means of those natural images, the falling tree and the turbulent ocean, with a region where reproof becomes irrelevant and the poet can at last indulge his secret and irrational love-affair with his hero, whom he values because he is astonishing, wasteful, and altogether unlike ordinary men. Tragedy is, as Yeats remarked, a drowner of dykes. The objection to reading such a passage as this as irony derives from the critic's sense of diction, rhythm, and metaphor, and he can only in the last resort turn round on the ironist and beg him to unstop his ears. This is not a comfortable thing to be obliged to do, for it makes it apparent that Chapman in this play is working with two substances: stirring the waters to make a foamy spectacle, but mixing the mud with the foam. The mud is all that part of the play which is a story of moral declination; left to itself it could sink to the bottom and be seen clear.

We shall also have to ask, in connection with Monsieur's speech and with others which enlarge our view of Bussy, *who*, in the fullest sense, is speaking them. The tone and substance of these characterizations of the hero do not accord well with the speakers' role in the muddy part of the story; they seem to draw upon a stock of evidence which is nowhere directly yielded by that story itself. It is not simply that King Henry is deceived about Bussy and out of his own weakness glorifies him (III. ii. 90–107), but that there is in Bussy, imperfectly conveyed to the audience by the story alone, some spring of being which touches off a response that does violence to the decorum of Henry's character.

So also when Bussy speaks about himself, after the duel-scene (II. i. 194–204), in the scene where he proffers himself as the king's 'eagle' (III. ii), and in the death-scene (V. iv), his speeches have a rightness and power, savage or elegiac, which strains the contextual link with story and person. They no more sound like boasting, for example, or hypocrisy, than Monsieur sounds like an ironist. The inner truth of their gesture is unaffected by its ostensible source in the character, because the ultimate source lies beyond that in Chapman's own response to the idea of the Achillean man, labouring in 'wrath':

> the strong
> Iron-hearted man-slaying Achilles
> Who would not live long.

We may have suspected, indeed, from the first lines of the play, from the soliloquy with which we began, that not every word in it would proceed from a perfectly coherent moral scheme and from fully objectified characters. For that speech contains two metaphors in implicit and troubling opposition to one another. Both describe great men, the first using the Plutarchian metaphor of the colossi:

> [They] differ not from those colossic statues,
> Which, with heroic forms without o'er-spread,
> Within are nought but mortar, flint, and lead;

The second is that of the ship and its captain:

> great seamen, using all their wealth
> And skills in Neptune's deep invisible paths,
> In tall ships richly built and ribb'd with brass,
> To put a girdle round about the world.

The 'great seaman' is a figure from the heroic age of Elizabethan adventure, active, vigilant, and wealthy; but he is as much a metaphor for the suspect 'greatness' as the neo-Stoic one of the straddling giant filled with rubbish. The play itself beats out these converging paths so that this dichotomy is never resolved, and we cannot feel at the end of it that we have simply been shown how empty and rubbishy-hearted is the Achillean man. It is, rather, suggested that death itself is an artificer and completes the work of those 'unskilful statuaries' who build colossi: the wounded Bussy props himself on his sword, determined to die on his feet like Vespasian, and cries:

> Here like a Roman statue I will stand
> Till death hath made me marble.
> (V. iv. 97)

And so Bussy is transformed into what Yeats called an 'uncommitted energy'.[1]

It would be wrong to exaggerate the degree of incoherence introduced into the play's structure by this double vision of its hero. Bussy has been, and is always likely to be, a rallying-point for critics because of the problematical manner of his presentation. But it would be untrue to theatrical experience of *Bussy d'Ambois* to accept all the implications of T. M. Parrott's view that 'the true theme [is] ... not the hero's passion for Tamyra, for the amour is plainly enough only an incident in Bussy's career' (p. 546). To agree with this would be to increase the risk, which has already been incurred, of abstracting Bussy too much from his context and turning the play into an anthology of poems about him. The intrigue takes up more than three Acts and is worked out with great coherence. One moral theme, for example (that Fortune is the natural victor over the man who exposes himself to her black storms), is neatly and theatrically enforced by an accident placed in its very centre (III. ii. 210): Monsieur, who is already actively casting around for the means to Bussy's destruction, happens to hear from the waiting-maid Pero, in the midst of some casual raillery, that she has seen Tamyra and Bussy together—for the prince a tonic discovery, for Bussy a deadly mischance. Tamyra, the only woman of any stature or importance in all Chapman's tragedies, except the Queen in *Chabot*, makes as vivid a demand for our attention in the theatre as the hero himself. But both Tamyra and her story strengthen the feeling that Chapman was as much absorbed in the fascination of 'greatness' as with working out a moral paradigm. This adulterous union is marked by a great display of crooked audacity on the part of both lovers, and this element received further emphasis in Chapman's revision of his play. But it is also marked by conduct on the part of the wronged husband Montsurry (his torture of his wife) which puts him beyond the range

[1] *A Vision* (1925), p. 188; the whole passage is relevant.

of a sympathy which wholly includes Tamyra and her brave resistance to his breach of 'manhood, noblesse, and religion' (V. i. 127). This is 'her other excellence' which sets off her offence. By it, as by much in the lovers' response to their danger (III. i), we are given the sense that their coming together is a dark but deep compulsion far removed from the ordinary life of the shallow or beastly courtiers who surround them. These elements in the intrigue—deceit and exaltation, strong currents of exceptional life, enemies whose viciousness ennobles their victims— aptly correspond in their mixed nature to a view of the hero which constantly shifts its perspective. We remember Chapman's interest in those Renaissance toys of canvas or pleated paper:

> a cozening picture, which one way
> Shows like a crow, another like a swan.

By this judgement, the amour, so far from being an incident in Bussy's career, does more than put the ironist's view of the play out of court; it helps us to discern the lineaments of a puzzling hero and by that much increases the coherence of his tragedy.

It was of course against Chapman's principles as a moralist, which are plainly stated in his poems and elsewhere, to excite in us anything approaching admiration or suspense of judgement towards the man of wrath or the body's fervour. But it is not wholly surprising that he did so in this play. The very bitter satirical passages in his poems, the pugnacity of his comments on the commentators on Homer, the invective against Ben Jonson, and his general habit of dissenting from a 'manless' age and allotting himself an exceptional role in it, are some evidence about his own temperament. Chapman would not be the first naturally 'wrathful' man whose encomia of calm and attempts to draw the lines of moral conduct derived their rigour from his knowledge of proneness to disorder within. The evidence suggests that in *Bussy d'Ambois* something not perfectly within the moralist's control came up from below the threshold of his mind, and that it was this that transformed a moral spectacle into a piece of tragic theatre.

★   ★   ★

This was not an event which Chapman permitted to occur again, to his satisfaction perhaps, but to our loss certainly, for none of his other tragedies equals *Bussy d'Ambois* in merit. This is not to assert that the more clearly defined moral structure of the later plays precludes a fiery apprehension of his heroes' natures, whether they are transgressors and men of wrath as Byron is or exemplars of calm and of the 'mind's constant and unconquered Empire' as Clermont (in *The Revenge of Bussy d'Ambois*) and Chabot are. What *Bussy d'Ambois* lacked was an unquestioned source of moral authority, of 'over-ruling Wisdom', able to measure 'greatness' and answer to its own name; but Chapman sets such an authority in each of his other plays: Clermont, Cato (in *Caesar and Pompey*), Chabot, and King Henry IV of France in the two-part play called *The Conspiracy and the Tragedy of Charles Duke of Byron*.

In the Byron plays Chapman adheres to the main lines of his source, which is to be found in his cousin Edward Grimeston's *General Inventory of the History of France*. The ground of the plays is the character of Byron as sketched by Grimeston, 'adventurous in war, ambitious beyond all measure':

> This Marshall had goodly parts, communicable to fewe, his Valour was admirable, and happy in all his Incounters; of an invincible Courage, infatigable and never tired with any toyle, continuing ordinarily fifteen dayes together on Horsebacke. He was not inclined to Voluptuousnesse, nor much to the love of Women, sober ynough, the which began to quench that furious humour, as Intemperancy & greatnesse increased, or that Rest did moderate his boyling passions. He was extremely Vaine-glorious, yea sometime, he would refuse his meate, and content himselfe with little to feede his Fantasie with Glory and Vanity . . . The excesse of his Ambition made him to brave it without judgement. He became so presumptuous, as he thought that the King, nor *France* could not subsist without him. He was become ill-tounged, speaking ill of all the Princes, threatning the Parliaments, and the Officers of Justice, some with death, and to dispossesse others of their Places.[2]

In Chapman's play this man has no source of inner authority, but builds himself up into a colossus by generating from thoughts of his past valour and services to France a series of fantastic images of his own splendour, so that he constantly ranges himself with the classical heroes, with Alexander who triumphed over Fortune, Hercules who adventured into Hell, Curtius who saved Rome, Orpheus who intoxicated his judges with his music. ('He flattred himself in his Vanity', writes

[2] *A General Inventory* . . . (1607), pp. 992–3.

Grimeston, 'and pleased himselfe as Pigmalion did in his Image, and Narcissus in his shadowe . . .') On this airy projection of his own worth he relies, so that in *The Conspiracy* certain enemies of the King of France find it easy to blind him by flattery and gradually ripen him for the mischief of treason. The play ends with his act of submission to the King, but by the beginning of *The Tragedy* he has revolted from his allegiance again. This time the King takes decisive measures. Byron, who remains oblivious to the fact that a monstrous crime will cancel a mighty merit (*Tragedy*, V. ii. 276), is trapped, brought to trial, and executed.

Byron is, therefore, like Bussy, a victim, but not of a Montsurry or a Monsieur, but of the King. Henry IV is the standard-bearer of moral authority in these plays, their true Alexander, owing his power to Virtue (under God) and not to Fortune. In *The Conspiracy*, although he is angry when Byron arrogates to himself all the glory for victory at the battle of Fountaine Françoise some years before (II. ii. 93-241), he at first tempers the wind against him (II. ii. 25-56), solemnly warns Byron against his sycophantic friends (III. ii. 244-72), and even, as a curative measure, sends him on an embassy to the court of Queen Elizabeth, which Chapman pardonably represents (IV. i) as a way of correcting Byron's false image of the state by exposing him to a true one. But when in *The Tragedy* these mercies prove ineffectual, Chapman is careful to show, by means of Henry's prayer over the newly-born Dauphin (I. i. 109-49), his resolve if possible to pardon Byron (I. iii. 29-38, a passage very close to Grimeston), the Masque of Cupid, an emblem of discord resolved, which is performed at court (II. i) and by other appeals to Byron through his ministers D'Escures and Janin (III. i), that what is at stake is the peace of an ordered and fruitful kingdom. This is the plenitude and forbearance by which we judge Byron's resolve to imitate Jehovah, and from the Chaos made by his intended revolution to 'sit brooding up another world', to ruin his country in order to re-advance it (I. ii. 30-5):

> If they bring me out, they shall see I'll hatch
> Like to the blackthorn, that puts forth his leaf,
> Not with the golden fawnings of the sun,
> But sharpest showers of hail, and blackest frosts.
> (III. i. 126)

It is after this issue has been thoroughly exposed that the King finally sends the spy La Fin, whom Byron trusts, to bring him back to court. Even after he has Byron in his power Henry still hesitates, consults his ministers, prays that his judgement in the matter may be guided by God (IV. ii). The final resolve to bring Byron to trial is taken against the advice of the ministers, who recommend summary execution. But Chapman had read in Grimeston about this aspect of the affair. The discriminations made by Grimeston are of fundamental importance to that aspect of the play that has earned it the title of Chapman's 'political testament':

> Many thought it was to shorten the course of Justice in so apparent a crime, and begin with the execution, dealing with the Duke of *Biron* as *Alexander* did with *Parmenio*, for Princes are Masters of the Lawes, they have one form of justice for great men, and another for those whose quality requires not so great respect. In these accidents there is no difference whether bloud be drawn before or after dinner, Necessity teacheth the disorder, and the Profit doth recompence the example, so as the Estate be preserved by the death of him that is prevented. But the king will none of that. He proceeds with more Courage and Generosity: these Examples of Execution had been blamed in his predecessors, he will have his subjects and all the World to know, that he hath power and authority sufficient to roote out by the forme of Justice, not the Authors of such a Conspiracie, for they be devils, but the Complices and the instruments how terrible soever. He will have the Solemnities and lawfull Ceremonies observed, and that they be judged by the rigour of the Lawes. (cf. *Tragedy*, IV. ii. 29–47)[3]

To Henry's insistence on the sanctions embodied in outward human institutions such as the law, with its manifest working, there are cross-references in Byron's contempt of them. The king resists the persuasions of his minister; but Byron in *The Conspiracy* owed his first fall to the analogous arguments advanced by La Fin and by the Spanish agent Picoté, who urges that

> simple loyalty,
> Faith, love, sincerity, are but words no things,
> Merely devised for form,   (I. ii. 116)

and retails a bit of international-conference gossip to support his point.

[3] *Op. cit.*, p. 968.

Later, La Fin takes up the theme: for other laws than that of friendship (which La Fin has an obvious motive for excepting at this juncture),

> He is a fool that keeps them with more care
> Than they keep him, safe, rich, and popular.
> (II. i. 138)

Love, reputation, loyalty are 'mere politic terms' which dissolve 'the free-born powers of royal man' (III. i. 31). Solicitations of this kind, combined with the sense of injured merit and vain-glory blazing with the oil of flattery, convince Byron that he owes nothing to any authority outside himself. As he boasts to Henry:

> men in themselves entire
> March safe with naked feet on coals of fire:
> I build not outward, nor depend on props,
> Nor choose my consort by the common ear,
> Nor by the moonshine in the grace of kings.
> (III. ii. 227)

With all its radical suspicion of kings and outward forms this was a doctrine which in another context (that of Clermont d'Ambois, for example) Chapman held very dear. That is why, here and elsewhere, Byron expresses it with such rich and cogent metaphor. Chapman's imagination and poetic power is fired by the idea itself; the eloquence with which this endows Byron, perhaps somewhat adventitiously, is the chief means for astonishing us with him, for maintaining always the sight of his active, imperious presence alive before the mind's eye. His eloquence is due also to Chapman's response to martial valour and the Achillean *virtù*, the body's fervour, of which his hero is an undoubted exemplar, and which, as we have seen in the case of Bussy, released Chapman's tongue to speak of wonders. But, in the Byron plays, the dramatist has so firmly grounded his moral scheme and embodied it so successfully in the continued contrast between the righteous Henry and the errant Byron that we are not likely to misunderstand where true order lies. For Byron is a wildfire without a centre; the context shows that his is a perversion of the sacred doctrine. His turbulence had its first rise in outward-going pride with its claims for excessive recognition of its worth by other men. Very early in his story, before he has yielded to the conspirators, he shows his awareness of the direction in which he may be going. It is a dangerous and a dreadful thing, he says,

> To trust our blood in others' veins, and hang
> 'Twixt heaven and earth in vapours of their breaths;
> To leave a sure pace on continuate earth,
> And force a gate in jumps from tower to tower.

Such men forsake

> all the sure force in themselves
> To seek without them that which is not theirs
> (*Conspiracy*, I. ii. 137 ff.)

And later he is troubled because he has 'cast himself into the arms of others' (III. iii. 33-4). At first dependent upon the nourishment which he greedily draws from the outward flatteries of La Fin and the conspirators, he is in the end even more critically dependent upon the king and his judges. The paradox of his fall is that his theory of self-sufficiency, which helped him to cut loose from the 'natural clime' of his society and to try to become a 'lonely dragon' like Shakespeare's Coriolanus, blinds him to the extent to which he has in reality given hostages to that society and put himself wholly in its power.

If Chapman, faced with the political world of the Byron plays, asked 'Where is the source of moral authority?', he answered 'in the just king', but at the same time hinted that in other circumstances the answer might be 'in the just man'. This is the answer given in *The Revenge of Bussy d'Ambois*, a play which explores, as do all Chapman's remaining tragedies, what happens when political power and moral authority are not coincident (as they are in the Byron plays) but at odds. We are back in the France of Henry III, where the central personage is now Bussy's brother Clermont. His friendship with the Guise, the suspicion it arouses in Henry (whipped on by the politic Baligny, a counterpart of La Fin), the eventual fall of the Guise and Clermont's consequent suicide are one main part of the story, dominating the first four Acts. The other is revenge for the murder of Bussy, which Tamyra and Bussy's sister Charlotte (a new character) urge Clermont to execute upon Montsurry. The delay classically demanded by the revenge-plot is caused partly by the cowardice of Montsurry, hardly at all by the revenger's reluctance, and very considerably by the inartificial fact that

Clermont and his author are too occupied in other matters. But Bussy's Ghost rises in the fifth Act to tell Clermont that God demands Montsurry's punishment, and Clermont at last persuades his terrified victim to fight and die.

Commentators have explained that Chapman was contriving a variation on the mode that he inherited from Kyd, Shakespeare, and Marston, and there can be no appeal from their verdict that his contrivance was a failure.[4] Clermont is the perfect 'Senecal man', an exemplar of calm and inward peace; burdening him with the revenger's bloody duty led Chapman into awkwardnesses which he could not surmount, although they are not so essentially disabling that they could not have been turned to positive advantages if the attempt had been made. Although there is some theatrical liveliness in the play (in the scenes with Montsurry and in the long series showing Clermont's arrest), its interest is chiefly historical: it is the most complete and whole-hearted of a number of attempts by previous dramatists to show us the Stoic Wise Man in a world of Neronian equivocation. Clermont endlessly manipulates the contrast between inward authority in the 'full' man and the outward blaze and glory of the 'empty' man, the rubbish-choked colossus. He himself, being inwardly solid with virtue and soul, needs no other authority but himself by which to live, and he may even choose his own time to die. Although he is fierily valorous his 'inward guards' are his real surety against the storms of Fortune. After he has—somewhat casually, it is true—renounced revenge (III. ii. 109–16), it is incongruous that this inner-directed man should in the end have to obey the external authority of the Ghost. The Ghost claims to proceed from God, of course, but we suspect that his appearance is really determined by the needs of the revenge-play mode. If so, the chosen genre has here curiously disrupted the moral scheme of the work of art.

Of Chapman's last two plays, there are several reasons why *Caesar and Pompey* could have been the most interesting. It is Chapman's only attempt to write a play about those characters of ancient history whose world had long fed his imagination through the writings of the Stoic moralists Plutarch and Epictetus; in devising the character of Pompey he tried to show a man educating himself to 'live with little' after the Stoic precept, so that a change has to be wrought in him before our

---

[4] See especially F. T. Bowers, *Elizabethan Revenge Tragedy* (ed. 1959), pp. 144–9, and J. W. Wieler, pp. 179–212.

eyes as Pompey endeavours to move from 'wrath' to peace; and the play is also a fresh venture because it is equally concerned with two other men as well: the Byron plays had an antagonist and a protagonist, *The Revenge of Bussy* a master and a disciple, but *Caesar and Pompey* develops both these kinds of relationship: Caesar is Pompey's mighty enemy, and Pompey is the pupil and ally of Cato. Yet despite all this, it seems the dullest of his tragedies. Its historical hurly-burly never achieves full form or meaning; it is ill-related to the three major characters and allows them little room and not much life. This is by no means an opinion which all the commentators, or even a majority of them, have shared. J. Jacquot, for example, discerned epic fullness and grandeur in the play, and Parrott has praised it for putting into Pompey's mouth 'words that we can only interpret as the poet's own utterances on the deepest mysteries of life and death'. But it will probably be agreed that, whatever its merits, Chapman's only Roman play is a branch that takes us away from the main body of his work. Therefore it seems more profitable here to spend time upon *The Tragedy of Chabot Admiral of France*.

This play was probably revised by Shirley after Chapman's death, but there is not much doubt that its design and essential virtues are Chapman's, however much they have been cropped and conventionalized by the younger dramatist. Its hero is closely related to Clermont, but this time Chapman has gone within his protagonist rather than set him up as our mentor. Chabot is a spotlessly honest judge whom a jealous chancellor persuades King Francis I to investigate, on the assumption, shared by both king and minister, that there is always *something* of which a man must needs be ashamed. Nothing is found, but Chabot's judges are bullied into delivering an adverse verdict. The easy conscience of king and court is startled into reappraisal when Chabot refuses the pardon that is then offered to him. But the damage has been done; the pain and poison of mistrust and 'unkindness' kill Chabot. He is like the healthy victim of an exploratory operation who dies under the knife because of the surgeon's careless over-confidence.

There is an excellent account of this play by Miss K. M. Burton,[5] in which she points out that in it 'a debate has a direct effect on the course of the action; it does not merely demonstrate the position which this or that character has taken up'. Two features especially deserve attention

[5] *Essays in Criticism* (1952), pp. 408–9.

as contributing to the impression of tight and dramatic organization throughout: there is the character of Montmorency the High Constable, at first hunting with the pack and then withdrawing; he acts as the visible pivot to a structure which shifts over a large space of ground, much as Pompey was intended but failed to do in *Caesar and Pompey*. Secondly, there is the moment where Chabot refuses his pardon (IV. i. 235)—'You cannot pardon me, sir'—an effect not so much of surprise as of peripeteia. After that nothing can be the same again for anybody. This is an unusual effect for Chapman, whose plays normally develop rather ponderously, the ground for action well prepared before the armoured vehicle rolls forward. Above all, the play is interesting because its major theme and that which controls its metaphors is an inner violence, a wrong done to the soul. Chabot's inner nature is delicate as a needle, trembling in its tender posture upon the sundial (I. i. 49 ff.), and his death is consistent with this temper. The play depicts a tragic assault upon and invasion of a man's inward authority, created by the envy and innovating spirit of power. In stretching his exemplar of calm upon this rack, Chapman recognizes the human weakness which is the subject of tragedy, a recognition obscured by didactic pressures in *The Revenge of Bussy*.

The relative merits of Chapman's different tragedies have been sufficiently indicated by the proportions of this chapter, and the effect as of a long *decrescendo* cannot be overcome. The body of his work separates itself from the rest of Jacobean tragedy. If there is a relationship to be discerned it is with the Roman tragedies of Jonson and Samuel Daniel, who share his interest in 'greatness' and its bearing on political order, and with the academic French Senecan work of Fulke Greville, who adds the interest in the consonance between the inward and the outward man, how one betrays the other, and how both struggle against enemies in society and demons in the soul. Also, the forms chosen by these neo-classic writers have something to tell us about Chapman's. What distinguishes Chapman and what made it possible for him to write his masterpiece in tragedy is a fiery and imaginative response to 'greatness' and its role among men. The story of his work is in part the story of how this response generated an antithetical rigour, binding some of his work with frost, but permitting some of it to rise to the level of elegy. So that if in some respects Chapman is second cousin to the mild, sad, and too well-mannered Daniel he still remains in others the heir of Marlowe.

The structure of his plays is not specially adventurous, making competent use of the three-fold division of the neo-classic theorists (protasis, epitasis, and catastrophe, terms of which the learned Jonson was fond). The natural unit of his composition and the one with which he operates most eloquently is the long speech, highly charged with metaphor, and often a complete 'poem' in itself. But it does Chapman violence to detach these from their contexts, for they are often carefully wrought into the dramatic fabric. His fondness for literary allusions, resembling that of such poets as Pope or T. S. Eliot, for borrowing chunks of matter from Epictetus, Plutarch, Ficino, and his other favourite sources of wisdom, has been much studied. Sometimes these remain far-fetched and inert, but often, as in the references to Seneca's *Hercules Oetaeus* in the last scene of *Bussy d'Ambois*, they nourish and deepen their contexts.[6] His speeches are not empty, repetitive, and formal, after the manner of the weaker neo-Senecans, but frequently make some genuine discrimination concerning the business of the play and the varying states of mind; they enforce or qualify a sequence, and do not run round in circles like the lamentations of Videna (in *Gorboduc*). One of the difficulties of grasping the whole of a Chapman play on first experience of it comes from our being told so much. His stories are initially rather simple and familiar, and the underplot is largely absent from them. With very many Jacobean tragedies from Fletcher to Ford and nearly all neo-classic comedies the bare bones of the tale itself can form a pleasingly ingenious network of scaffolding. But Chapman has at least this in common with Henry James: it would be useless to extrapolate his stories without the moral and characterological ado that is organized about them.

The final impression left by these tragedies might be that they are the work of a man who grew to be one of nature's academicians, resisting his age more than he explored it; and it is true that Chapman, although unusually learned, did not resemble Donne or Bacon in being unusually intelligent as well. This impression would need a good deal of correction from his other works, and on other grounds could not be accounted a wholly truthful one. For Chapman, by devising a drama that is controlled by an idea of heroic worth held up to us for our wonder, was exploring a new way in tragedy. The basis is beginning to shift, though only slightly, from the Shakespearian emphasis on personality towards a new stress on heroic ideals; the design is affected

[6] I owe this point to B. A. Harris.

by the concern with those moments or periods of intense emotion, such as the death of Bussy, the trial and death of Byron, or the contemplative *furor* of Clermont, by which it is not the man, as a coherent human being, who is brought nearest to us so much as the emotion itself—that passion which Yeats praised as the subject of all art and which 'can only be contemplated when separated by itself, purified of all but itself, and aroused into perfect intensity by opposition with some other passion, or it may be with the law'. It is this 'emptying' of the drama, as Yeats called it, of human character and its replacement by heroic energies which helps to differentiate the plays of such workers in the heroic mode as Fletcher and his successor Dryden from those of Shakespeare. Dryden was to declare that in a heroic play all things ought to be 'as far above the ordinary proportion of the stage, as that is beyond the common words and actions of human life'. His contemporary Thomas Rymer, in his notorious attack on Shakespeare in 1692, chose as his main target *Othello*, that supreme masterpiece of characterization in which the dramatist leads us to meditate not upon the passions of love and jealousy but upon the man and woman who love and suffer. For Rymer, this was to confuse Poetry, which is led by Philosophy, and is general and abstracted, with History 'which only records things higlety, piglety, right or wrong as they happen . . . history and fact in particular cases . . . are no warrant or direction for a Poet'. Chapman, although faintly and far-off, anticipates both the magnification of life with which Dryden amazes us, and the neo-classical critic's advocacy of Philosophy as a guide. In portraying Byron and Bussy and Clermont he seems on occasion not as much concerned with the particular case as with manœuvring his heroes into situations where they become almost catalytic exemplars of heroic vigour or virtue. 'What can remain with the Audience', Rymer asked indignantly about *Othello*, 'to carry home from that sort of Poetry, for their use and edification?' Chapman could have sustained such an inquisition with some confidence. He participates in however slight a degree in the movement which thirty years after his death was to flood the stages of England and France with God-defying Maximins and Rival Queens. The movement is important still. Although no one nowadays is on Rymer's side, perhaps his legatee is all that cultivated European distrust of Shakespeare's undignified concern with the particular case which has found expression, for example, in T. S. Eliot's plays, or in his remark that he had never seen 'a cogent refutation of Thomas Rymer's objections'. Rymer would have found most of Chapman as monstrous and unnatural as Shakespeare himself, but he might have had a kind word for his soldierly soldiers and his kingly kings, and for the dignity with which they are exalted in death. Chapman was, after all, contriving something more Philosophical than History when he measured 'greatness' by refining Stoic precepts from the turmoil of the court of France.

Index

[*This index excludes the information, systematically arranged for reference purposes, given in the notes before each chapter.*]

Ahab, Captain, 119
Aldus, P. J., 31 n.6
Alleyn, Edward, 43
Anne (wife of James I), 73
Antigone, 20
Aubrey, John, 43
Auden, W. H., 154 n.3

Bacon, Sir Francis, 59, 87, 93n. 9, 97, 109, 245
Bald, R. C., 197
Bale, John, *King John*, 103
Barker, R. H., 191 n.3
Beaumont, Francis, 159, 160, 161, 175, 188
  The Knight o, the Burning Pestle, 77
Bentley, G. E., 192 n.4
Bergson, H., 185 and n.2, 197 n.5
Blake, William, 152
  The Book of Thel, 232
Bowers, F. T., 91, 95, 242 n.4
Bradbrook, M. C., 65, 69, 73, 216 n.6, 224
Bradley, A. C., 11, 12, 24, 29, 33
Bredvold, L. I., 124 n.6
Brook, Peter, 1957 production of *The Tempest*, 134 n.1, 152
Bullough, G., (ed. of Greville), 86 n.1
Burbage, Richard, 43, 59
Burke, Edmund, 118
Burke, K., 37 n.10
Byrd, William, 94 n.11

Camden, William, 97
Canons, Church (1606 and 1640), 123
Carew, Thomas, 164
Cartwright, William, 164

Cassandra, 40
Cecil, William, 126 and n.10
Chapman, George, tragedies discussed, 227–46; 63
  Works:
    Bussy d'Ambois, 227–36, 237, 245–6
    Caesar and Pompey, 237, 242–3
    Chabot, 235, 237, 243–4
    Conspiracy and Tragedy of Charles, Duke of Byron, 237–41, 246
    Homer, 229
    Revenge of Bussy d'Ambois, 237, 240–5
Charles I, 125, 126
Charles II, 114 n.1, 129
Charlton, H. B., 92 and n.6
Chute, M., 114
Clemen, W. H., 18
Coleridge, S. T., 113, 119, 126 and n.9, 176
Creon, 20

Dallington, Sir Richard, 97
Daniel, Samuel, 97
  Vision of Twelve Goddesses, The, 47
  classical tragedies, 244
Day, John, *Law Tricks*, 101 n.19
Dekker, Thomas, comedies and domestic plays discussed, 63–73; 75–7, 78, 83
  Works:
    Honest Whore, The, 69–72, 109
    Magnificent Entertainment, 73
    Northward Ho, 72, 107
    Old Fortunatus, 76
    Patient Grissil, 69
    Roaring Girl, The, 69, 72
    Satiromastix, 43–5
    Shoemakers' Holiday, The, 64–9

Dekker, Thomas, Works: (*contd.*)
   Troia-Nova Triumphans, 73
   Westward Ho, 72, 107-8
Dell, E., 115 n.2
d'Este, family of, 95, 103
Digby, Sir Kenelm, 176
Dio, 88
Divine Comedy, 35
Don Quixote, 20
Donne, John, 113, 125-6, 131, 227, 245
Dorset, *Declaration of the County of Dorset* (1648), 115
Drummond, William, 45, 59
Dryden, John, 177, 246
   Absalom and Achitophel, 129-30
   Essay of Dramatic Poesy, 159, 161

Eastward Ho, see under Marston
Edmondes, Sir Clement, 97
Edward IV, 64, 68
Eliot, T. S., 75, 80, 170, 202, 212, 245, 246
   East Coker, 14
   The Waste Land, 17
Elizabethan Stage Society, *see under* Poel
Ellis-Fermor, Una, 104, 125; on Beaumont and Fletcher, 161
Epictetus, 242, 245

Feuillerat, A., 94 and n.12
Ficino, 245
Field, Nathan, 43
Fletcher, John, the art of Fletcher, 159-77 *passim*; 188, 245, 246
   Works:
     Beggars' Bush, 164, 166
     Bloody Brother, The, 167
     Bonduca, 162, 176
     Coxcomb, The, 172
     Custom of the Country, 167, 170
     Double Marriage, The, 162, 169, 170
     Faithful Shepherdess, The, 162, 170, 174, 176 n.5
     Humorous Lieutenant, The, 167, 173, 176, 177
     Island Princess, The, 163, 171, 174, 177
     King and No King, A, 159, 163-6, 170, 172, 174
     Knight of Malta, The, 173
     Love's Cure, 171
     Loyal Subject, The, 174
     Maid's Tragedy, The, 159, 160-2, 167, 176
     Philaster, 159
     Queen of Corinth, The, 169 170
     Rollo, or the Bloody Brother, 172, 173
     Thierry and Theodoret, 162, 167, 171
     Valentinian, 162, 167, 172
Florio, John, *Dictionary*, 103
Ford, John, 245

Gardner, Helen, 36 n.9
Gee, John, 44
Gesualdo, 94
Gielgud, Sir John, as Prospero, 134 n.1, 152
Gomersall, Robert, *Tragedy of Lodovic Sforza*, 93, 96
Gonzaga, family of, 95
Gooch, G. P., 123 n.5
Gorboduc, 245
Grafton, Richard, *Chronicle*, 93 n.9
Greek tragedy, chorus in, 20-1
Greene, Robert, *Selimus*, 93
Greville, Fulke, 86, 93, 114 n.1, 126 n.8, 128, 244: *Alaham*, 93
Grimeston, Edward, 237-9
Guarini, 162
   Pastor Fido, 100
Guicciardini, 95-8

Hall, Bp. Joseph, 122
Haroun Al Rashid, 183
Harris, B. A., 245 n.6
Haughton, William, *Englishman for my Money*, 92 n.5
Haydn, H., 96 n.17
Hayward, Sir John, 93 n.9
Heilman, R. B., 30
Henry, Prince, 73, 97
Henslowe, Philip, 69
Heywood, Thomas, plays discussed, 77-83; 63, 64, 67, 75, 77
   Works:
     Apology for Actors, 78
     Brazen Age, The, 81
     English Traveller, The, 64, 80
     Fair Maid of the West, The, 82
     Fortune by Land and Sea, 80

INDEX 251

Four Prentises, The, 64, 76, 79
Golden Age, The, 82
Iron Age, The (2nd part), 80, 81
Londini Status Pacatus, 79
Londons Ius Honorarium, 79
Love's Mistress, 82
Rape of Lucrece, 80
Woman Killed with Kindness, A, 64, 80
Hill, Christopher, 115 n.2
Hitchcock, Robert, 98
Hobbes, Thomas, 91, 94
Homily, Tenth (1547), 123

Importance of Being Earnest, The, 166
Ismene, 20
'Italofobia', 94 and n.13
Italy, as influence in Jacobean drama, 91–111
see also under Guicciardini, Machiavelli, Sforza, etc.

Jack, I., 104
Jacquot, J., 243
James I, 44, 73, 114 n.1, 123, 126
James, Henry, 245
Jocasta, 20
Jones, Inigo, 47–52, 134 n.1
Jones-Davies, M. T., 72
Jonson, Ben, 63, 64, 81, 82, 169, 206, 236; stagecraft discussed, 43–61; comedies, in relation to those of Dekker and Heywood, 73–8; comedies discussed, 85–7; Roman tragedies discussed, 113–31, 244
Works:
Alchemist, The, 46, 47, 56, 58, 59, 64, 114, 124, 127
Bartholomew Fair, 45, 52, 54, 57, 58, 59–60, 114
Catiline, 46, 52, 56–7, 113–31
Cynthia's Revels, 45, 127
Devil is an Ass, The, 45, 54, 56, 59, 60, 131
Discoveries, 45, 49, 59
Epicoene, or The Silent Woman, 56, 58, 59, 60, 119
'Epistle to Selden', 118
Every Man In His Humour, 46, 60
Every Man Out of His Humour, 47, 55, 85–7, 101

Magnetic Lady, The, 55
Mortimer His Fall, 46
New Inn, The, 43
Poetaster, The, 46, 54, 60
Sad Shepherd, The, 45, 51
Sejanus, 46, 53, 55, 57, 113–31
Staple of News, The, 55, 59, 60
Tale of a Tub, A, 50, 54
Volpone, 45, 54, 58, 59
Masques:
Blackness, 47, 50
Chloridia, 51
Haddington, 48, 49, 52
Hymenaei, 47, 48, 49, 50, 51
Oberon, 49, 51
Queens, 48, 52

Kant, 230
Kean, Charles, 1857 production of The Tempest, 133
Knights, L. C., 94 n.14, 182 n.1
Kyd, Thomas, 39, 45, 88, 90–1, 92 n.4, 242

Laski, H. J., 123 n.5
Leech, C., 41
Levin, H., 29 n.2
Lipsius, Justus, 95
Livy, 53
Lord Mayors' Shows, 73, 77, 78–9, 81
Lucas, F. L., 104
Lust's Dominion, 93
Lyly, John, 88, 93 n.8, 94

Machiavelli, 92, 96–8, 109
Malespini, 194
Malraux, A., 20
Marenzio, 94
Marlowe, Christopher, 160, 244; and Machiavelli, 92
Works:
Dr. Faustus, 46
Edward II, 92
Jew of Malta, The, 93
'Passionate Shepherd, The', 122
Tamburlaine, 45, 88
Marston, John, plays discussed, 85–111; 242
Works:
Antonio and Mellida, 85–92, 99–100, 106
Antonio's Revenge, 98
Dutch Courtesan, The, 109–11

INDEX

Marston, John, Works: (contd.)
    Eastward Ho, 108, 109
    Malcontent, The, 100–2, 106
    Parasitaster or the Fawn, 101 n.19, 103, 106
Marvell, Andrew, 121, 122, 125
Masques, staging of, 47, 52; in *The Tempest*, 151
    see also Jonson
Massinger, Philip, 63, 66, 159, 162, 169, 174, 176
    Works:
        A New Way to pay Old Debts, 66
        Bondman, The, 169
        Fatal Dowry, The, 169
        Great Duke of Milan, 96
    see also Fletcher, John
May, Thomas, *The Heir*, 164
Medici, family of, 95
Mermaid Theatre, London, 149
Meslier, 195
Meyer, E., 96 n.18
Middleton, Thomas, comedies discussed, 179–99; 69, 102, 106, 206
    Works:
        Changeling, The, 41, 163, 192 n.4
        Chaste Maid in Cheapside, A, 179, 185, 188–91, 199
        Family of Love, The, 183
        Game at Chess, A, 188
        Mad World, My Masters, A, 184, 185
        Michaelmas Term, 183–4, 185, 191
        More Dissemblers Besides Women, 188
        No Wit, No Help Like a Woman's, 188
        Phoenix, The, 101 n.19, 179–85
        Trick to Catch the Old One, A, 179, 185–8, 190, 199
        Women Beware Women, 106, 179, 185, 188, 191–9
        Your Five Gallants, 183, 184
Milton, John, 41, 181
    Comus, 152
Mirror for Magistrates, 93 n.9
Mizener, A., 166 n.3, 175
Mozart, 146
Muir, Edwin, 230

Nannini, Remigio, 97
Nicoll, A., 55
Northward Ho, *see under* Dekker

Oceanus, 20
Oedipus, 20
Old Vic, production of *The Tempest*, 144
Orsini, N., 97
Our Dumb Friends' League, 156
Overbury, Sir Thomas, *Characters*, 95

Pan, Peter, 156
Parrott, T. M., 229, 235, 243
Partridge, E. B., 119 n.4
Pavy, Salomon, 43
Peele, George, *The Battle of Alcazar*, 93
Pembroke, William, Earl of (1580–1630), 117
Pepys, Samuel, 166
Petrarch, 227
Petrarchanism, 121, 122
Phaedra, 20
Philander, *see* Vitruvius
Pindar, 227
Plautus, *Casina*, 59
Plutarch, 53, 234, 242, 245
Poel, William, 1897 production of *The Tempest*, 148–9
Pollux, Julius, *Onomasticon*, 48
Pope, Alexander, 114 n.1, 118, 122, 245
Pory, John, 48–9
Praz, Mario, 92 and n.4
Price, H. T., 31 n.5
Prometheus, 20

Racine, 34
Rare Triumphs of Love and Fortune, 92 n.5
Rees, E., 230
Robinson, Dick, 43
Rylands, G., 218
Rymer, Thomas, on *Othello*, 246

Sabbatini, Nicola, *Practica di Fabricar Scene &c.* (1638), 49
Salingar, L. G., 160 n.1
Schoenbaum, S., 191 n.3
Selden, John, 114, 118
Seneca (the Elder), 169
Seneca, 39; *Hercules Oetaeus*, 245
Serlio, Sebastiano, *Architettura* (1545), 47, 51
Servius, *see* Virgil
Sforza, family of, 95–6

INDEX

Shakespeare, William, tragic construction discussed, 11–41
Works:
  Antony and Cleopatra, 11, 13, 14, 16–17, 18, 20, 21, 23–4, 26–7, 29, 31, 34, 35, 36, 37, 38
  Comedy of Errors, 135
  Coriolanus, 12, 14, 20, 34, 35, 37, 241
  Hamlet, 11, 12, 13, 14, 15, 16, 18, 20–2, 27–8, 29, 30–1, 32–3, 34, 35, 38–40, 88, 102, 107, 139
  1 Henry IV, 15
  2 Henry IV, 183
  Julius Caesar, 12, 14, 16, 20, 35, 146
  King Lear, 11, 13, 16, 17, 20, 24–5, 26, 29, 32, 33–4, 35, 36, 38, 39, 40, 125, 227
  Macbeth, 13, 18, 20, 25–6, 29, 31, 34, 35, 36, 37, 38, 41
  Measure for Measure, 101 n.19, 143
  Midsummer Night's Dream, A, 12, 41, 77, 149
  Much Ado About Nothing, 15
  Othello, 11, 13, 14, 18–19, 20, 21, 22–3, 30, 32, 34, 35, 36, 134, 149; Rymer's attack, 246–7
  Phoenix and the Turtle, The, 19
  Richard II, 12, 28, 146
  Romeo and Juliet, 12, 13, 16, 20, 35, 38, 141
  Taming of the Shrew, The, 92
  Tempest, The, 29, 52; on the stage, 133–57; analysis of craftsmanship, 135–46; the verse and its speaking, 146–8; staging, costume and music, 148–52; characters and casting, 152–7
  Timon of Athens, 35, 38
  Titus Andronicus, 38, 88, 91, 93
  Troilus and Cressida, 40, 227
  Twelfth Night, 134
  Winter's Tale, The, 15, 29, 52
Sharpham, Edward, The Fleer, 101 n.19, 107
Shaw, George Bernard, 43, 60
Shirley, James, 243
Sidney, Sir Philip, Arcadia, 88
Simpson, Percy, 51
Smith, D. Nicol, 114 n.1
Spenser, Edmund, 94, 103, 105, 121, 176 n.5
Starkey, T., 105 n.25
Stoll, E. E., 102 n.21
Strafford, Earl of, 114 n.1
Suckling, Sir John, 122
Suetonius, 88
Swinburne, A., 113
Sylvester, William, 97

Tacitus, 53, 88, 95, 96–7, 124
Tarlton, Richard, 45
Tasso, 94
Taylor, Jeremy, 227
Three Ladies of London, 92 n.5
Tiberius, Jonson's treatment of his character, 95–7, 114 n.1, 122, 124, 131
Toffanin, G., 96 and n.18
Tom Jones, 35
Torretta, L., 94 n.13
Tourneur, Cyril, 95, 102, 103, 106, 201
  The Revenger's Tragedy, 101 and n.20, 102, 103
Virgil, Aeneid, 35; commentary by Servius, 48
Vitruvius, De Architectura (Philander's edition, 1544), 48, 50

Wagner, 146
Waith, E., 162, 169
Walley, H. R., 102 n.21
Watson, Thomas, 94 n.11
Webster, John, tragedies of White Devil and Duchess of Malfi discussed, 201–25; 72, 95, 102, 103–6, 131, 160
Works:
  Duchess of Malfi, The, 41, 131, 214–25
  White Devil, The, 41, 104–5, 201–14, 218, 225
Westminster School, 43, 44
Westward Ho, see under Dekker
Wieler, J. W., 241 n.4
Wilson, F. P., 21
Wilson, J. Dover, What Happens in 'Hamlet', 39 n.11
Wilson, Sir Thomas, 117
Wordsworth, William, 116
Yeats, W. B., 118, 233, 235 and n.1, 246
Yorkshire Tragedy, A, 64

Zanta, L., 95 n.15